The *Secrets* to Playing Piano By Ear

Version 1.0

Jermaine A. Griggs

Hear & Play Music Online!
http://www.HearandPlay.com

Foreword:

"The Secrets to Playing Piano *By Ear*!" Course

Music is one of the world's most popular pastimes, enjoyed by individuals all over the globe. Whether listening to recordings or attending live concerts, music has the ability to inspire and give pleasure to almost everyone.

For many students and professionals in the industry, playing a musical instrument is an even more enjoyable experience. BUT ... understanding how music is constructed; how scales and chords are formed; the relationship between major and minor keys; and how songs are created through melody, harmony, and chord progressions can enhance the musical experience even *further*.

Hear and Play's **"The Secrets to Playing Piano By Ear"** course is designed for students of any age, whether listener or performer, who want to learn how to play the piano by ear.

In this course, we will study:

•All major, minor, and minor melodic / harmonic scales

•All major, minor, and diminished / augmented chords

•The relationship between chords and scales

•The basic principles of sight reading

•How to integrate various chords into gospel / jazz music

•How to alter these chords to make them sound full

•Several Progressions such as "2-5-1" and the "1-4 turn-around"

•The Secret to recognizing chord changes in almost **any** songs

•How to play various hymns in all 12 keys

•Several chord patterns which can be used in most Gospel & Contemporary Jazz Music

USING THE SOUND LIBRARY (SL#)

You will notice numbers (ex – SL001) next to various diagrams. These are **audio** examples that you can access on the **BONUS CD!** Simply, insert the **Bonus CD** into your drive, go to the *Windows Start Menu -- Run* and type: D:\soundlibr.exe

You may also access our "**Piano Player Plus v1.0**" Software by typing: D:\pianoplay1.exe in the "Run" dialog box. Also, keep in mind that the **CD** must be in the drive to run these programs (unless you have copied them to your hard drive).

Determining Your Goals ...

Goals are important. *Your goals are the road maps that guide you and show you what is possible for your life.* If you plan on being successful in music, you must first identify your goals. Here is a quick assessment …

I will practice _____ hours a day

I will attempt to complete one lesson every:

___ day   ___ twice / week   ___ week   ___ month   ____ more than once / day

I will attempt to complete this course in _____ weeks

_____

Signature of Piano Student   **Date**

Table of Contents

LESSON 1: "Getting Started"   7

LESSON 2: "A Quick Lesson on Sight Reading"   16

LESSON 3: "A Quick Lesson on Rhythm"   25

LESSON 4: "Major Scales"   32

LESSON 5: "Intervals, Major Chords & Inversions"   50

LESSON 6: "Major Chord Progressions"   65

LESSON 7: "Modes and Minor Scales"   79

LESSON 8: "Minor and Diminished Chords"   91

LESSON 9: "Minor, Diminished & Major Chord Progressions"   105

LESSON 10: "Major, Minor & Dominant Seventh Chords"   131

Table of Contents (cont.)

LESSON 11: "Major, Minor & Dominant Seventh Chord Progressions"   147

LESSON 12: "Diminished Seventh, Major Sixth & Minor Sixth Chords"   166

LESSON 13: "Major Sixth, Minor Sixth and Diminished Chord Progressions"   182

LESSON 14: "Major & Minor Ninth Chords & Progressions"   193

LESSON 15: "Eleventh & Thirteenth Chord Progressions"   215

LESSON 16: "Altering Chords"   228

LESSON 17: "Harmonizing Melodies"   241

LESSON 18: "Techniques to Learning Songs by Ear"   255

LESSON 19: "More Hymns"   277

LESSON 20: "Improvising"   291

INTRODUCTION

"The Secrets to Playing Piano *By Ear*!" Course

Hello there!

I am Jermaine Griggs, the author of this course. Before we get started, I would just like to *congratulate you* on your decision to learn how to play piano by ear! You have made the first step by purchasing this course and if you stay committed, I promise you that you'll reap the benefits ... **very soon!**

In this course, I will try to present these *techniques* to you as clear as possible. As you will soon notice, the tone of this course is very *laid back.* That is, you're going to feel as though I am talking directly to you (this will be beneficial as it helps you to understand the information easier). With this in mind, I will not delay the course any longer ...

Again, congratulations and good luck with your *piano playing!*

Jermaine Griggs

President of Hear & Play Music, Online!

www.HearandPlay.com

www.PianoPlayerPlus.com

Lesson One

"Getting Started"

Before we can learn how to play scales, chords, and various progressions, it is vital that we learn the notes on the piano and how they relate to one another (I am assuming that you haven't learned this yet; if you have, simply skip this lesson of the course).

The best way to describe the notes on the piano is by comparing them to the notes of the alphabet. In fact, the notes of the piano actually borrow the first seven notes of the alphabet system (A – B – C – D – E – F – G). Each note differs in sound. Below, are all seven notes of the piano:

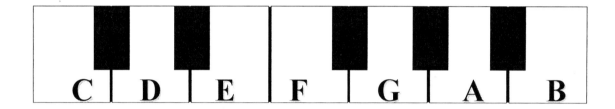

Here is a wider example of the notes of the piano:

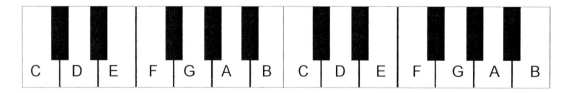

Notice that the same **seven** notes repeat themselves over and over again. That is, the notes sound the same but the pitches differ. For example, if you play a **C** and move to the right until you find the next **C,** you'll notice that if you play them simultaneously, both notes sound the same but one is higher than the other...

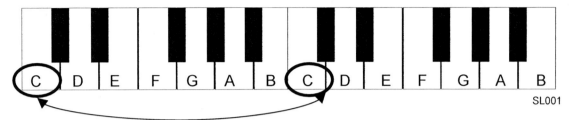
SL001

Both notes sound the same but the pitches are different

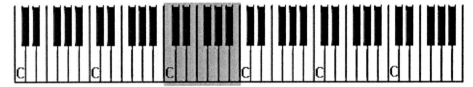

The notes above are said to be **one octave** (interval of an eighth) apart. You'll learn more about octaves in further lessons.

The note, **C** is to the piano what the letter "**A**" is to the alphabet. **Middle C** marks the center of the piano. As you'll notice, the **C Major Scale** is also the easiest and simplest scale of the twelve. It consists of all the white keys from any starting **C** to the next. The shaded notes below represent the C Major Scale (Cmaj, CM):

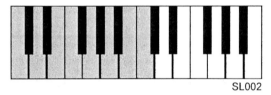
SL002

Later, you will learn all 12 of the major scales. I also recommend using the **"Piano Player Plus 1.0"** Software to test yourself on the different scales. With this program, you will be able to select random major scales while using your ear to depict which major scale it is. Very helpful!

Here is a useful tip if you are having trouble memorizing the notes of the piano ...

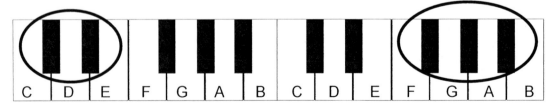

C is located directly to the *bottom-left* of the two-grouped **black** keys while F is located directly to the *bottom-left* of the three-grouped **black keys**.

EXERCISE 1.1

Match the following keys on the piano with its written note below: (not all notes will be used)

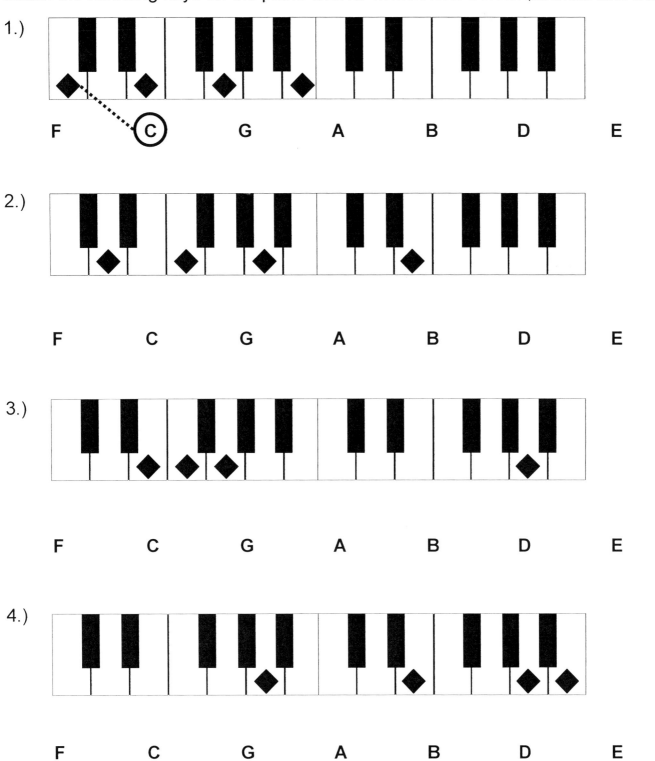

1.)

F   C   G   A   B   D   E

2.)

F   C   G   A   B   D   E

3.)

F   C   G   A   B   D   E

4.)

F   C   G   A   B   D   E

Answers are at the end of this section…

EXERCISE 1.2

1.How many letters of the alphabet are used on the piano?

_____

2. What is the complete name of the note which indicates the center of the piano?

_____

3. What is an easy way of remembering where "C" and "F" are located on the piano?

_____

4. How many major scales are there?

_____

5. What note comes after "G" on the piano?

_____

6. How many notes make up a major scale?

_____

7. Which scale is the easiest to play and why?

_____

Answers are at the end of this section...

What about the Black Keys?

Now that you've had some experience with the *white* keys of the piano, we will introduce the *black keys* …

If you've had any music experience or have been around musicians, you've definitely heard the words, "sharp" or "flat." These terms are the names given to the black keys of the piano.

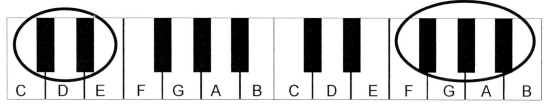

Actually, each black key has **two different names.** However, only one name can be used at a time. So then, the question is: "How do I know when to call a *black key a sharp or a flat?*"

The answer is very simple: *Sharp* is the name given to the black key directly to the **right** of a white key while *Flat* is the name given to the black key directly to the **left** of a white key.

Below is an example of "sharps" and "flats" …

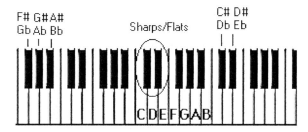

Notice the *black* key directly to the right of **C:** It can either be labeled as C sharp (because it is to the right of C) or D flat (because it is to the left of D).

To recap, if you are referring to the note directly to the right of **C**, you would use **C sharp** … but if you are referring to the note directly to the left of **D**, you would use **D flat.** (keep in mind that C sharp and D flat share the same key and sound exactly the same)

USING "#" and "*b*"

Sharps are notated with the symbol, #, while **Flats** are notated with the symbol, *b*

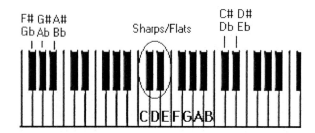

Notice that the *sharp* names for the three-grouped black keys above are: F#, G#, and A#. Why? Because one key is directly to the right of F, one is directly to the right of G and one is directly to the right of A. Contrary, the *flat* names for the three-grouped black keys are: G*b*, A*b*, and B*b*. This is because G*b* is directly to the left of G, A*b* is directly to the left of A, and B*b* is directly to the left of B.

Here is a chart to help you understand the flat / sharp relationship:

F#	Gb
G#	Ab
A#	Bb
C#	Db
D#	Eb

EXERCISE 1.3

Match the following keys on the piano to its written note below: (not all notes will be used)

1.)

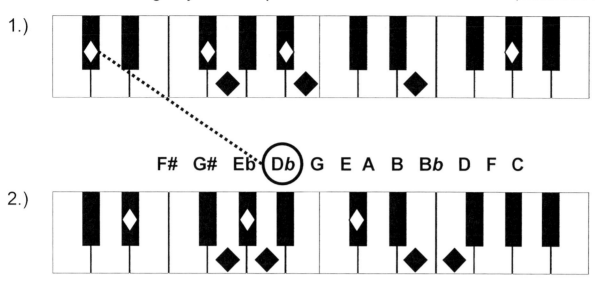

F#   G#   Eb   Db   G   E   A   B   Bb   D   F   C

2.)

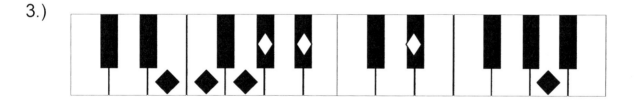

F#   G#   Eb   Db   G   E   A   B   Bb   D   F   C

3.)

F#   G#   Eb   Db   G   E   A   B   Bb   D   F   C

4.)

F#   G#   Eb   Db   G   E   A   B   Bb   D   F   C

EXERCISE 1.4

1. What are the two names given to the *black* keys of the piano?

_____

2. When are sharps used? When are flats used?

_____

3. How many different sharps are there? What are their names?

_____

4. Name <u>all</u> sharp / flat relationships below: (Ab = __ #) ... (Bb = __ #) ... (D# = __ *b*)

_____

5. How are sharps notated? How are flats notated?

_____

6. C# produces the same sound as what flat?

_____

7. The three-grouped black keys are what three flats?

_____

Answers are at the end of this section...

EXERCISE 1.1 – 1.4 ans.

1.1

1. C, E, G, B
2. D, F, A, E
3. E, F, G, A
4. A, E, A, B

1.2

1. Seven
2. Middle C
3. C is located directly to the left of the two-grouped black keys while F is located directly to the left of the three-grouped black keys.
4. Twelve
5. "A"
6. Eight
7. C Major because the scale consists of all the white keys from C to C (eight notes total)

1.3

1. Db, F#, G, Bb, B, E, G#
2. Eb, G, G#, A, Db, E, F
3. E, F, G, G#, Bb, Eb, A
4. E, F, A, B

1.4

1. Sharp / Flat
2. Sharps are directly to the right of a white key while Flats are directly to the left of a white key
3. There are 5 Sharps: C#, D#, F#, G#, A#
4. C# = Db, D# = Eb, F# = Gb, G# = Ab, A# = Bb
5. # , b
6. Db
7. Gb, Ab, Bb

TOTAL # CORRECT: _____

Lesson Two

"A Quick Lesson on Sight Reading"

Before we learn scales and chords, I thought it might be helpful to give you a head start on sight reading as I do encourage one to be knowledgeable in both reading notes and playing by ear. If you are already skilled in sight reading, simply skip this section of the course.

I. The Staff, Notes and Pitches

The Staff

Music **NOTES** are oval-shaped symbols that are placed on the lines and in the spaces. They represent musical sounds, called **PITCHES.**

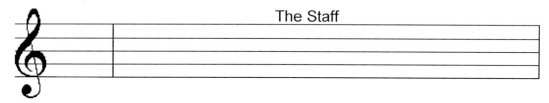

The lines of the staff are numbered from bottom to top.

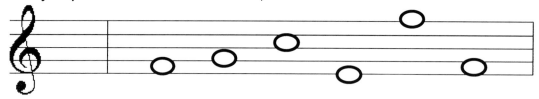

The spaces between the lines are also numbered from bottom to top.

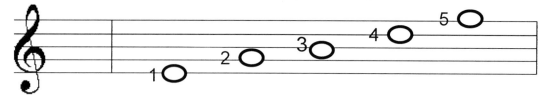

If the notes appear higher on the staff, they sound higher in pitch
If the notes appear lower on the staff, they sound lower in pitch (picture on next page)

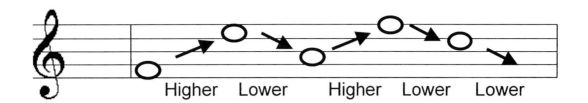

Higher   Lower   Higher   Lower   Lower

EXERCISE 2.1

Draw a staff by connecting the dots. Use a ruler or straight edge. Number the lines, then the spaces from low to high.

On the staff, mark an X in the following locations:

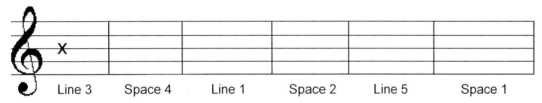

Line 3   Space 4   Line 1   Space 2   Line 5   Space 1

Write the notes like this ⬭ on the following lines and spaces:

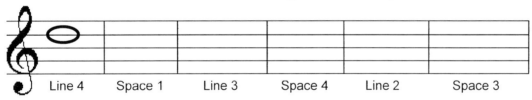

Line 4   Space 1   Line 3   Space 4   Line 2   Space 3

Indicate whether the 2ⁿᵈ note is higher or lower than the 1ˢᵗ note by using an H (higher) or L (lower):

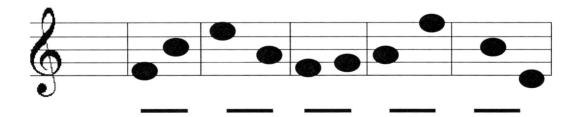

___   ___   ___   ___   ___

II. Treble Clef and Staff

As you learned earlier, music notes are named after the first seven letters of the alphabet, from A to G. By their position on the staff, they can represent the entire range of musical sound.

Clef Signs help to organize the staff so notes can easily be read.

The **TREBLE CLEF** is used for notes in the higher pitch ranges. The treble (or G) clef has evolved from a stylized letter G.

The following is an example of a treble staff:

LINE NOTES
In the treble staff, the names of the notes on the lines from bottom to top are *E, G, B, D, & F.*

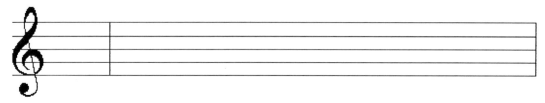

A helpful way to remember the notes on the lines from bottom to top is to memorize the following sentence: "Every Good Boy Does Fine"

SPACE NOTES
The names of the notes in the spaces from bottom to top spell **F A C E**

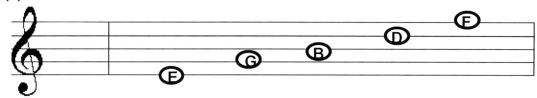

So Remember ... *Line* Notes Say **"Every Good Boy Does Fine"** and *Space* notes spell **F – A – C – E**

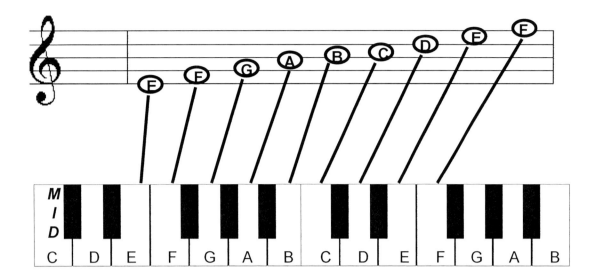

EXERCISE 2.2

Write the letter names of the following notes:

Draw the following notes on the staff:

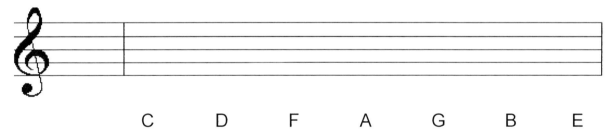

C   D   F   A   G   B   E

Indicate whether the following notes are on lines or spaces:

C = _____   G = _____

D = _____   A = _____

E = _____   B = _____

HearandPlay.com

III. Bass Clef and Staff

The **BASS CLEF** is used for notes in the lower pitch ranges. The bass (or F) clef has evolved from a stylized letter F: 𝄢

The following is an example of a bass staff:

LINE NOTES

In the bass staff, the names of the notes on the lines from bottom to top are **G, B, D, F & A.**

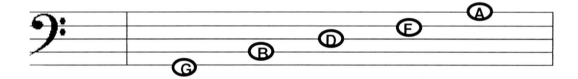

A helpful way to remember the notes on the lines from bottom to top is to memorize the following sentence: "**G**ood **B**oys **D**o **F**ine **A**lways"

SPACE NOTES

The names of the notes in the spaces from bottom to top are **A, C, E & G.**

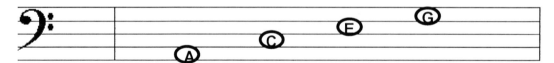

A helpful way to remember the notes on the spaces from bottom to top is to memorize the following sentence: "**A**ll **C**ows **E**at **G**rass"

ALL THE NOTES OF THE BASS STAFF:

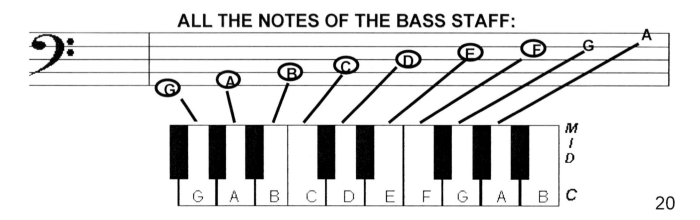

20

EXERCISE 2.3

Write the letter names of the following notes:

— — — — — —

Draw the following notes on the staff:

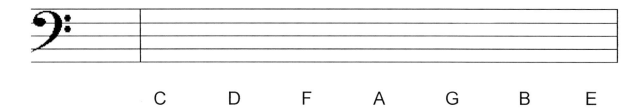

C   D   F   A   G   B   E

Indicate whether the following notes are on lines or spaces:

G = _____   A = _____

C = _____   E = _____

B = _____   D = _____

LEDGER LINES
Low and High Notes

•More than one ledger line may be added to extend the lower and upper ranges of the staff.

The next higher notes of the treble staff are **G, A, B & C.** The lower notes of the clef are **B, C & D.**

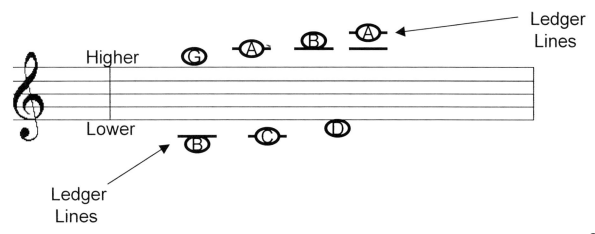

The lower notes of the bass staff are **F, E, D & C**

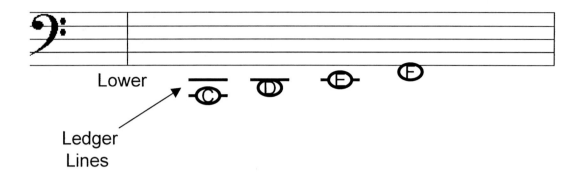

Lower

Ledger
Lines

EXERCISE 2.4

Practice drawing the low and high notes on the staffs below:

Name the following notes on the treble and bass staff:

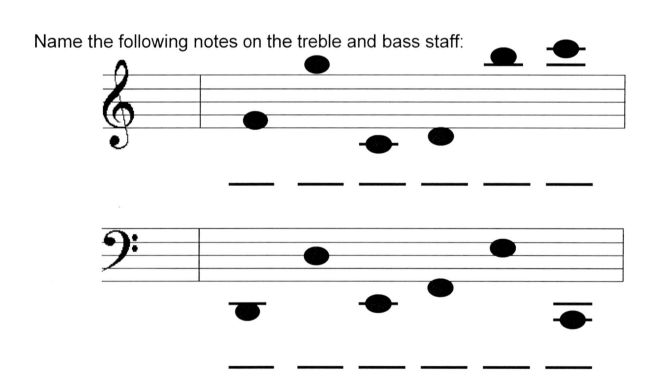

EXERCISE 2.5

1. How many lines are on a single staff? _____

2. How many spaces are on a single staff? _____

3. Is the 5th line at the bottom or top of the staff? _____

4. Which clef is also known as the G clef? _____

5. The note names of the lines in the treble clef from bottom to top are:

_____

6. The note names of the spaces in the treble clef from bottom to top are:

_____

7. The line through a middle C (below the staff) is called a _____.

8. Which clef is known as the F clef? _____

9. The note names of the lines in the bass clef from bottom to top are:

_____

10. The note names of the spaces in the bass clef from bottom to top are:

_____

Answers are at the end of this section...

EXERCISE 2.5 ans.

1. How many lines are on a single staff? Five

2. How many spaces are on a single staff? Four

3. Is the 5th line at the bottom or top of the staff? Top

4. Which clef is also known as the G clef? Treble Clef

5. The note names of the lines in the treble clef from bottom to top are:
E – G – B – D - F

6. The note names of the spaces in the treble clef from bottom to top are:
F – A – C – E

7. The line through a middle C (below the staff) is called a ledger line.

8. Which clef is known as the F clef? Bass Clef

9. The note names of the lines in the bass clef from bottom to top are:
G – B – D – F – A

10. The note names of the four spaces in the bass clef from bottom to top are:
A – C – E – G

TOTAL # CORRECT: _____ /10

Lesson Three

"A Quick Lesson on Rhythm"

At this point, you should be able to read notes on the **Grand Staff** (both staffs combined)

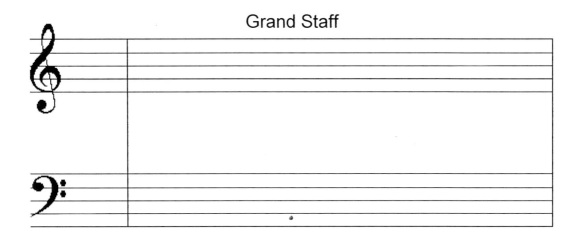

Grand Staff

Now that we know the *basics* of reading notes on the staff, we're going to move on to learning note values (which determine how long a note is held) and rhythms.

I. Note Values

While the placement of notes on the staff indicates the pitch, the duration of the note (how long the note is held) is determined by the note value.

DIFFERENT NOTES
In this lesson, you will explore **whole, half, quarter, eighth and sixteenth** notes.

WHOLE NOTES

A **WHOLE NOTE** is drawn as an open oval

SL003

HearandPlay.com

HALF NOTES

Two **HALF NOTES** equal the duration of one whole note and are drawn as open ovals with stems

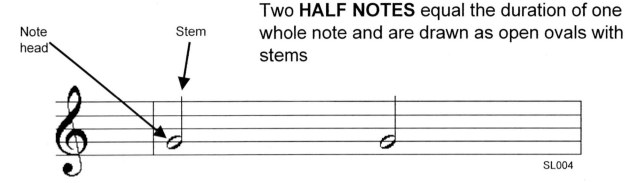

Note head

Stem

SL004

QUARTER NOTES

Four **QUARTER NOTES** equal the duration of one whole note and are drawn as filled ovals with stems

Filled Note head

Stem

SL005

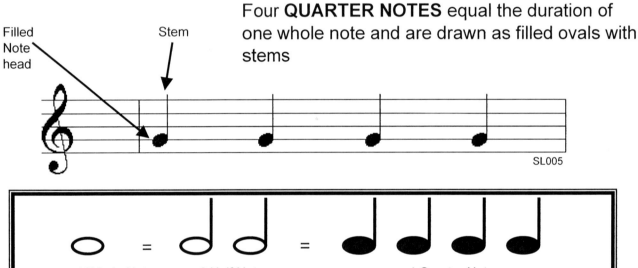

1 Whole Note   2 Half Notes   4 Quarter Notes

1 Half Note   2 Quarter Notes

TIME SIGNATURE AND NOTE VALUES

The **TIME SIGNATURE** appears at the beginning of the music after the clef sign. It contains two numbers, one above the other.

MEASURE

Bar line

Music is divided into equal parts by **BAR LINES**. The area between the two bar lines is called a *measure* or *bar*.

26

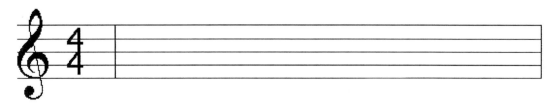

The upper number tells how many beats (or counts) are in each measure. The lower number indicates what type of note receives 1 beat. In this case, a quarter note (because there are 4 quarter notes in each measure).

A quarter note is equal to one count (or beat). Count (1, 2, 3, 4) and clap the rhythm evenly (once per beat).

SL005

1	2	3	4
Ta	ta	ta	ta

A half note is equal to two counts (or beats). Count and clap the rhythm evenly (holding your hands together for 2 beats). The beat numbers are written under the notes. Also, say "Ta – ah" (continuously) while clapping.

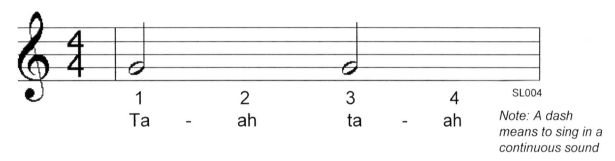

SL004

1	2	3	4
Ta	- ah	ta	- ah

Note: A dash means to sing in a continuous sound

A whole note is equal to four counts (or beats). Count and clap the rhythm evenly (holding your hands together for 4 beats). The beat numbers are written under the notes. Also, say "Ta – ah – ah – ah" (continuously) while clapping.

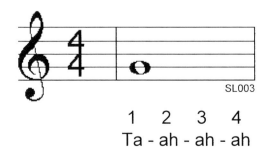

SL003

1 2 3 4
Ta - ah - ah - ah

EIGHT NOTES & SIXTEENTH NOTES

Two 8th notes equal 1 quarter note

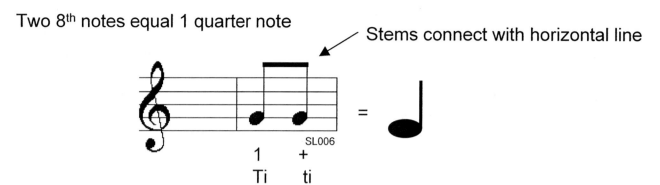

Stems connect with horizontal line

SL006

1   +
Ti   ti

Four 8th notes equal 1 half note

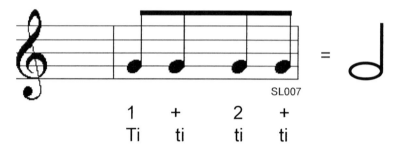

SL007

1   +   2   +
Ti   ti   ti   ti

Eight 8th notes equal 1 whole note

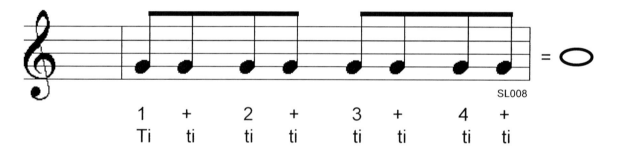

SL008

1   +   2   +   3   +   4   +
Ti   ti   ti   ti   ti   ti   ti   ti

SIXTEENTH NOTES

Sixteen notes have two stems instead of one. At times, they can easily be mistaken for eighth notes so watch of out for those stems!

4 sixteenth notes equal the duration of one quarter note:

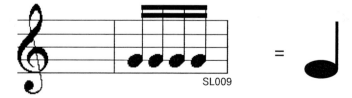

SL009

8 Sixteenth notes are equal to the duration of one half note:

16 sixteenth notes equal the duration of one whole note:

EXERCISES

There are several exercises available on the **"Piano Player Plus 1.0"** Software to test yourself on the different note values and durations. With this program, you will be able to build your ear skills by testing yourself on various rhythms. The software program will keep track of your progress.

SELF EVALUATION

1. On a scale of 1 – 5, how well do you understand all the notes of the piano

    1   2   3   4   5

2. On a scale of 1 – 5, how well do you understand all the notes of the treble clef

    1   2   3   4   5

3. On a scale of 1 – 5, how well do you understand all the notes of the bass clef

    1   2   3   4   5

4. On a scale of 1 – 5, how well do you understand whole, half, quarter, eighth, and sixteenth note values   1   2   3   4   5

5. On a scale of 1 – 5, how well do you understand the concept of ledger lines and why they are used   1   2   3   4   5

If your total score (#1 - #5) is less than **15,** we recommend that you repeat the sections that you are uncomfortable with.

Mini Lesson (3a)

"Half Steps & Whole Steps"

> A **Half Step** is from key to key
> With NO keys in between,
>
> A **Whole Step** always skips a key
> With ONE key in between.

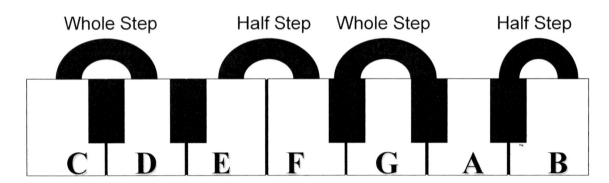

Whole Step   Half Step   Whole Step   Half Step

C D E F G A B

WHOLE STEPS & HALF STEPS

As you can see by the picture above, whole step intervals skip a key while half step intervals don't. For example, in the picture, C and D are **one** whole step apart because C# (also known as Db) is between them. E and F are **one** half step apart because there is **NO** keys in between them. F# (or Gb) and G# (or Ab) are **one** whole step apart because there is a note in between them (G). A# (or Bb) is a half step apart from B because there are no keys in between them.

Notes	D	E	F	G	A	B	C
C	1 W or 2 H	2 W or 4 H	2.5 W or 5 H	3.5 W or 7 H	4.5 W or 9 H	5.5 W or 11H	6 W or 12 H
D	6 W or 12 H	1W or 2H	1.5 W or 3 H	2.5 W or 5 H	3.5 W or 7 H	4.5 W or 9 H	5 W or 10 H
E	5 W or 10 H	6 W or 12 H	.5 W or 1 H	1.5 W or 3 H	2.5 W or 5 H	3.5 W or 7 H	4 W or 8 H
F	4.5 W or 9 H	5.5 W or 11H	6 W or 12 H	1 W or 2 H	2 W or 4 H	3 W or 6 H	3.5 W or 7 H
G	3.5 W or 7H	4.5 W or 9 H	5 W or 10 H	6 W or 12 H	1 W or 2 H	2 W or 4 H	2.5 W or 5 H
A	2.5 W or 5 H	3.5 W or 7 H	4 W or 8 H	5 W or 10 H	6 W or 12 H	1 W or 2 H	1.5 W or 3 H
B	1.5 W or 3 H	2.5 W or 5 H	3 W or 6 H	4 W or 8 H	5 W or 10 H	6 W or 12 H	.5 W or 1 H

W = Whole Step / H = Half Step

Note: These are the half step/ whole step relationships between each key. When a key is compared to itself, the chart is referring to the distance between the key and its octave. *Also, use the left column as the starting note.* Notes compared to the starting note will always be higher in pitch (to the right of the starting note on the piano).

30

Exercise 3a.1

Indicate whether the following intervals are WHOLE steps (W) or HALF steps (h):

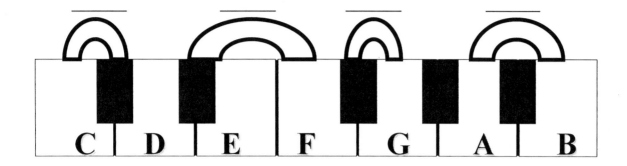

Indicate the number of whole steps in between the following keys:

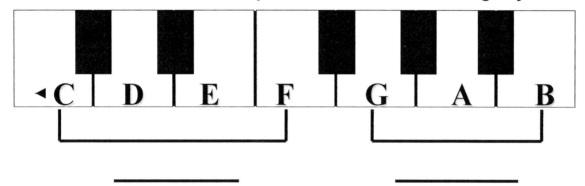

Draw the following intervals below:

a. five half steps from **D**

b. six half steps from **E**_b_

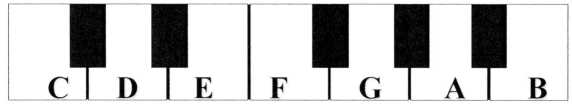

Lesson Four

"Major Scales"

Major Scales play a major role in the principles and techniques that you are going to learn through this course. For example, one of my favorite techniques is to take a one-fingered melody and replace it with full-sounding chords. However, in order to successfully master this technique (quickly and efficiently), you will have to know all **12 keys.** Keep in mind that this is not a matter of memorizing 12 different major scales, but understanding the theory in how major scales are created so that when necessary, you can quickly play any given scale.

We will be using a concept known as the "**Circle of Fifths"** to learn all 12 Major Scales.

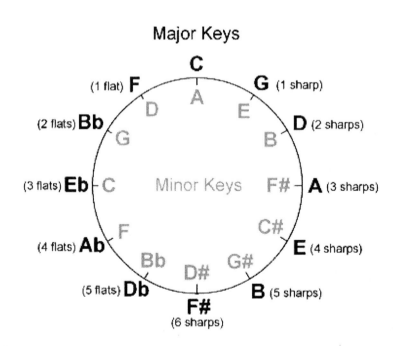

Prerequisites for this lesson: Must understand whole/half step intervals (Lesson 3A) and have basic sight reading skills

FINGERINGS FOR MAJOR SCALES

Correct fingering is very important. The following fingerings are for the left and right hand only when playing **major scales.**

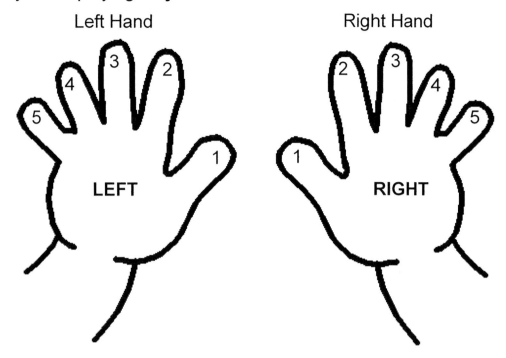

When playing a major scale, always put the **5** finger from your left hand on the first note of the scale (unless the scale uses the 2, 3 or 4 finger for the starting note). The same rule applies for the **1** finger with your right hand.

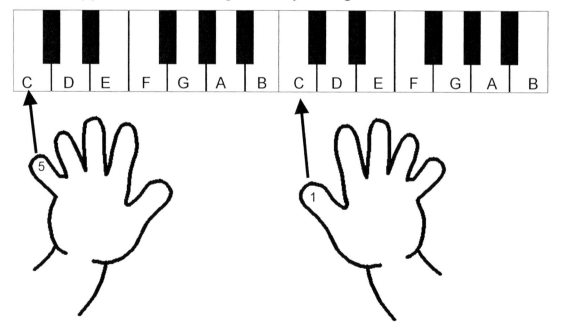

If you were playing a C major scale (with both hands) the above picture illustrates the correct position for each hand. That is, by starting with your **5** finger on your left hand and your **1** finger on your right hand. Keep in mind, however, that some scales start with the 2, 3, or 4 finger (refer to the chart on the next page).

RIGHT-HANDED SCALE FINGERINGS FOR MAJOR KEYS

MAJOR KEY (s)	FINGERING
C, D, E, G, A, B	1-2-3-1-2-3-4-5
F	1-2-3-4-1-2-3-4
B♭	2-1-2-3-1-2-3-4
E♭	2-1-2-3-4-1-2-3
A♭	2-3-1-2-3-1-2-3
D♭	2-3-1-2-3-4-1-2
G♭	2-3-4-1-2-3-1-2

LEFT-HANDED SCALE FINGERINGS FOR MAJOR KEYS

MAJOR KEY (s)	FINGERING
C, D, E, F, G, A	5-4-3-2-1-3-2-1
B♭, E♭, A♭, D♭	3-2-1-4-3-2-1-3
G♭	4-3-2-1-3-2-1-2
B	4-3-2-1-4-3-2-1

How to read the finger charts

Example #1: If you wanted to play an **F Major Scale** with your right hand, you would start with your **1** finger ending with your **4** finger.

Example #2: If you wanted to play a **B Major Scale** with your left hand, you would start with your **4** finger ending with your **1** finger.

TWO RULES TO LEARNING ALL 12 MAJOR SCALES …

As stated earlier, the goal of this course is to make every rule, technique, and principle as easy to understand as possible. Therefore, I have chosen to introduce to you a few rules that will simplify the process of learning all **12 major scales.** I also encourage you to practice these scales often, as you will soon memorize them. (However, memorization is not required).

I also recommend using the **"Piano Player Plus 1.0"** Software to test yourself on the different scales. With this program, you will be able to select random major scales while using your ear to depict which major scale it is. Very helpful when trying to build your ear-skills!

It is also important that you note the order in which we will learn each major scale.

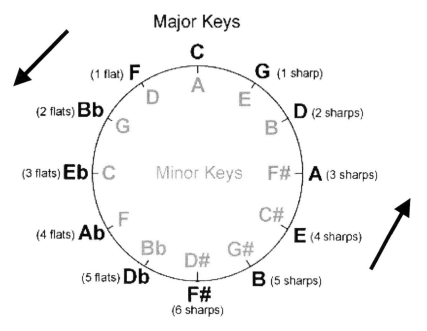

We will be learning the scales in a counter-clockwise order. That is, from C to F to B*b*, and so on … I find it much easier for students to learn the major scales using the chart counter-clockwise versus starting clockwise. Let's get started!

Note: If you already know all 12 major scales, how they are formed, when to use them, and how to turn them into chords, you can skip this lesson.

MAJOR SCALE TECHNIQUES

To explain these two rules, we will start with the major scale that we already know ...

C Major Scale

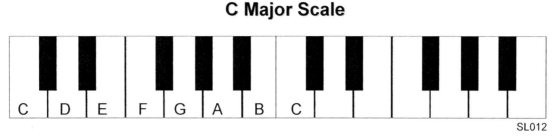

SL012

The whole point of these two rules is to rely on one scale to form another. For example, the next scale to be learned on the Circle of Fifths chart is the **F Major Scale** ...

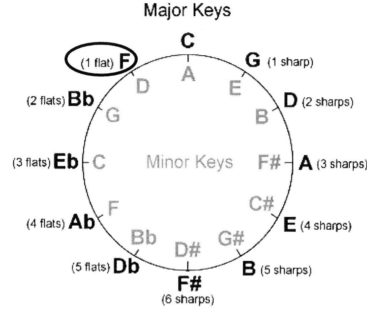

So then, the problem is turning a **C Major Scale** into an **F Major Scale.** How do we do it? **There are two steps which will enable us to perform this simple task:**

STEP #1:

Identify the seventh degree (note) of the current scale and lower it by **one half step** (refer to Lesson 3A if you do not understand the term "half step").

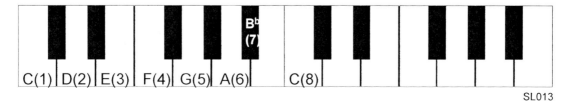

SL013

36

STEP #2:

After lowering the 7ᵗʰ note of the scale **one half step**, change the starting and ending note to the next scale on the chart …

*In this case, we have lowered the 7ᵗʰ note of a C Major Scale and wish to play an F Major Scale. Therefore, all we must do is start and end on **F** instead of **C**.*

EXPLANATION OF TWO STEPS

By lowering the seventh note of the C major scale (or any scale from which you want to form the next scale), we are no longer playing a C major scale. In actuality, we are playing a C Mixolydian Scale (you will learn the different modes of a scale later). In addition, when lowering the 7ᵗʰ degree of C major, we are playing the same exact notes of the F major scale. That is, the only note difference between C major and F major is the [B --Bb]. That is why they are neighboring keys on the "Circle of Fifths" chart. Keep in mind that simply lowering the 7ᵗʰ note does not complete the process of changing from one scale to another. The process is only complete when the scale is played starting and ending on the first note of the *new scale.*

In this case, we would take our C Major Scale (with the lowered 7ᵗʰ note) and play the same exact notes of the scale starting and ending on F:

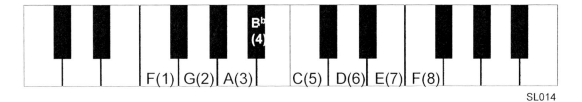

SL014

HearandPlay.com

37

SUMMARIZATION

STEP ONE

We started with a C Major Scale …

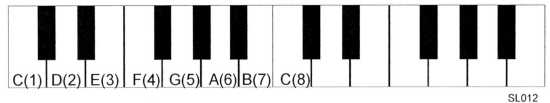

SL012

We identified the 7th note of the scale and lowered it **one half step …**

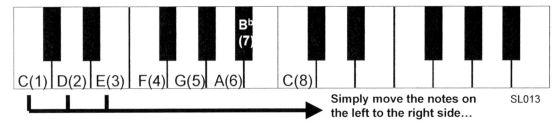

Simply move the notes on the left to the right side…

SL013

STEP TWO

We played the same scale (in step one) *starting and ending on F* (instead of C)

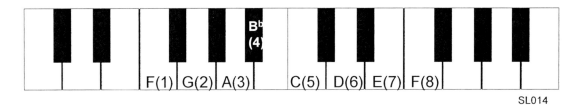

SL014

F Major Scale

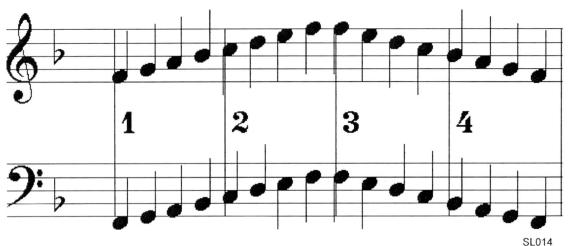

SL014

38

MAJOR SCALES WORKSHEET – 4.1

These exercises will assist you in using the *two rules* to learn the rest of the major scales …

1. Mark the notes of the F Major Scale below:

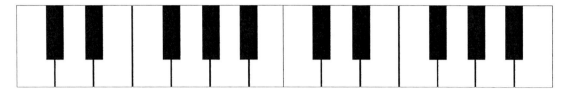

1a. Lower the 7th note of the F Major Scale:

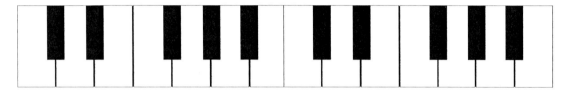

1b. Write the previous scale below starting and ending on B♭

B♭ Major Scale

2.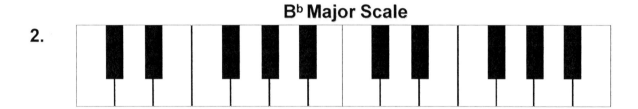

2a. Lower the 7th note of the B♭ Major Scale:

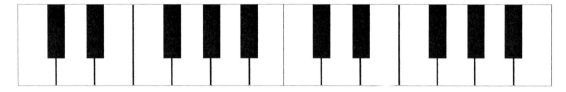

2b. Write the previous scale below starting and ending on E♭

E♭ Major Scale

3.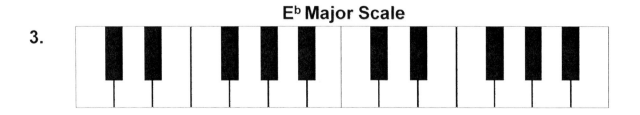

MAJOR SCALES WORKSHEET – 4.2

3a. Lower the 7th note of the E^b Major Scale:

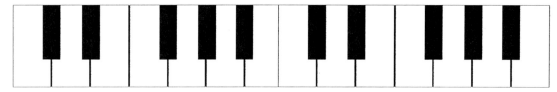

3b. Write the previous scale below starting and ending on A^b

A^b Major Scale

4.
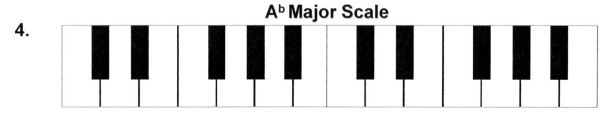

4a. Lower the 7th note of the A^b Major Scale:

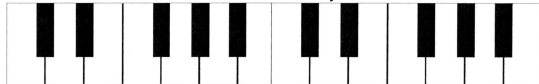

4b. Write the previous scale below starting and ending on D^b

D^b Major Scale

5.
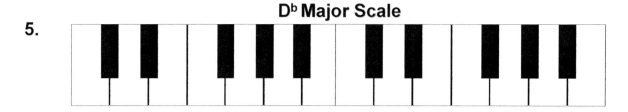

5a. Lower the 7th note of the D^b Major Scale:

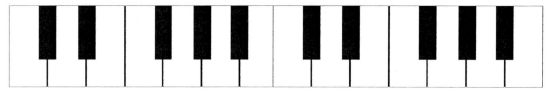

MAJOR SCALES WORKSHEET – 4.3

5b. Write the previous scale below starting and ending on Gb / F#

Gᵇ / F# Major Scale

6.

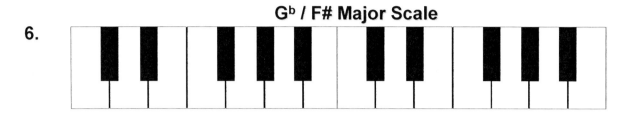

6a. Lower the 7ᵗʰ note of the Gᵇ / F# Major Scale:

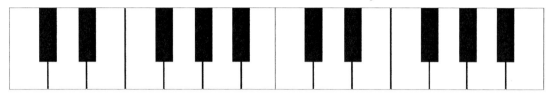

6b. Write the previous scale below starting and ending on B

B Major Scale

7.

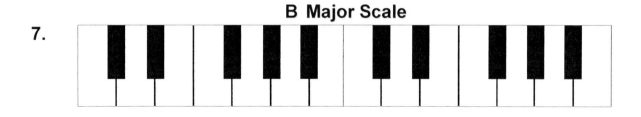

7a. Lower the 7th note of the B Major Scale:

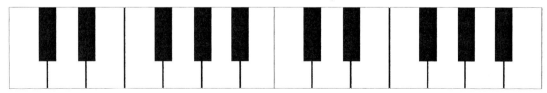

7b. Write the previous scale below starting and ending on E

E Major Scale

8.

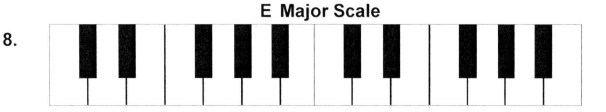

MAJOR SCALES WORKSHEET – 4.4

8a. Lower the 7th note of the E Major Scale:

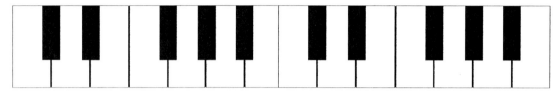

8b. Write the previous scale below starting and ending on A

A Major Scale

9.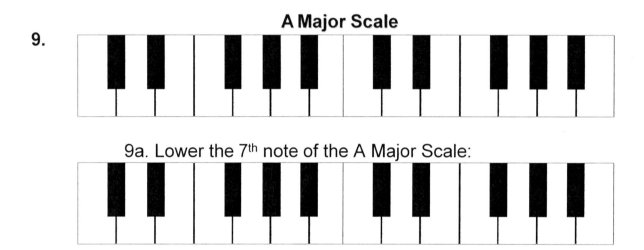

9a. Lower the 7th note of the A Major Scale:

9b. Write the previous scale below starting and ending on D

D Major Scale

10.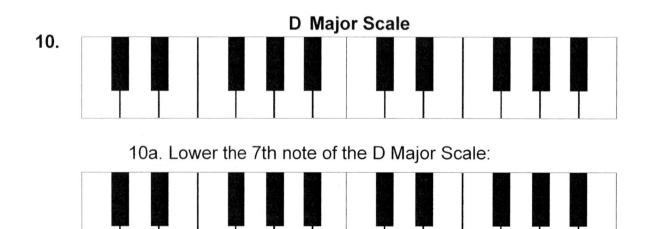

10a. Lower the 7th note of the D Major Scale:

MAJOR SCALES WORKSHEET – 4.5

10b. Write the previous scale below starting and ending on G

G Major Scale

11.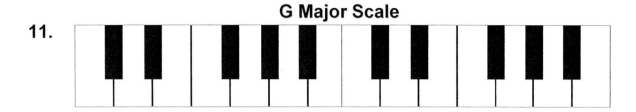

11a. Lower the 7th note of the G Major Scale:

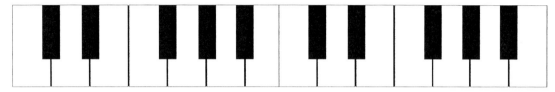

11b. Write the previous scale below starting and ending on C

ENDING THE CIRCLE ...

C Major Scale

12.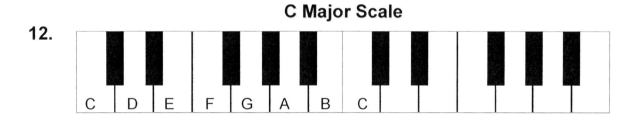

*If you have completed the circle, by lowering the 7th note of the **G Major Scale**, you should be able to successfully return back to the **C Major Scale**.*

Answers are at the end of this section…

A NOTE ABOUT READING MUSIC ...

You should of noticed that the number of flats and sharps increased as you progressed through the *circle.* For example, C major has no sharps or flats, but F major has one flat (B♭). When reading music in a certain key, it will not indicate the flat right by the note (in some cases, it will ...). However, the sheet music will show the amount of flats and sharps in a key (using either # or *b*). You will find these located by the treble / bass clef and time signature symbols.

In F Major, you will only see one flat displayed. But in a key like D flat major, you will see five flats because D♭ has 5 flats in it's scale.

This chart as well as the following pages will help you to understand how to find what key a song (or chord progression) is in by looking at the number of # or *b* displayed.

# of Flats	Which means...
b	You are in the key of F Major and this means that every time a note is on the "B" line or space, you play B flat
bb	You are in the key of B Flat Major and this means that every time a note is on the "B" or "E" line or space, you play B flat and E flat
bbb	You are in the key of E Flat Major and this means that every time a note is on the "B" , "E", or "A" line or space, you play B flat, E flat, and A flat
bbbb	You are in the key of A flat Major which means that "B", "E", "A", and "D" are all flatted
bbbbb	You are in the key of D flat Major which means that "B", "E", "A", "D" and "G" are all flatted
bbbbbb	You are in the key of G flat Major which means that "B", "E", "A", "D" ,"G" and "C" are all flatted. Note: *C flat* = "B" (but since B is already used as B♭, we must use C♭). **REMEMBER ...** you can never put two different notes on one line.

# of Sharps	Which means...
# # # # # #	You are in the key of F# Major and the F, C, G, D, A and E are sharp. Just as in the Gᵇ Major Scale, two notes cannot be on the same line. Since F# occupies the "F" line or space, E# must be used in it's place.
# # # # #	You are in the key of B and the F, C, G, D and A are sharp
# # # #	You are in the key of E and the F, C, G, and D are sharp
# # #	You are in the key of A and the F, C, and G are sharp
# #	You are in the key of D and the F and C are sharp
#	You are in the key of G and only one key is sharp (F). That is, whenever you see an F note, you play F# (unless otherwise noted).

The **"Circle of Fifths"** chart also shows the difference in the # of sharps and flats used in different keys...

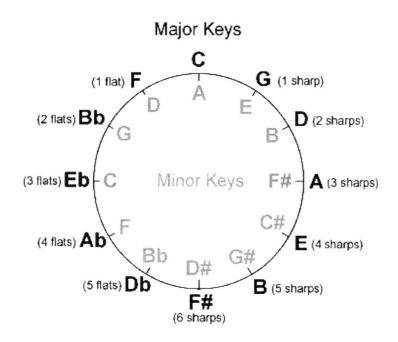

HearandPlay.com

B♭ Major Scale

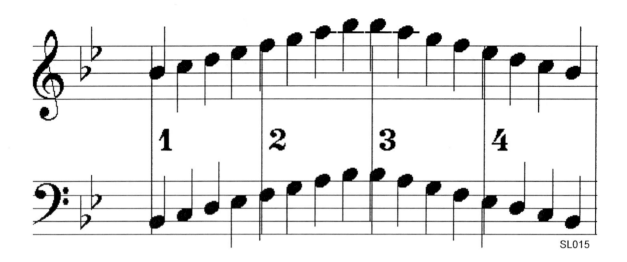

SL015

E♭ Major Scale

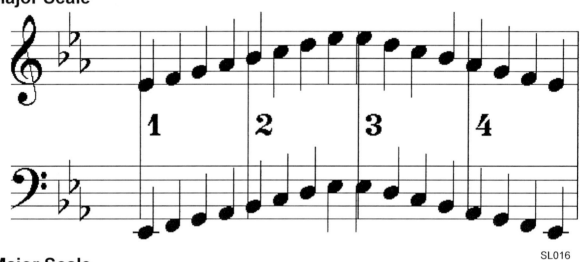

SL016

A♭ Major Scale

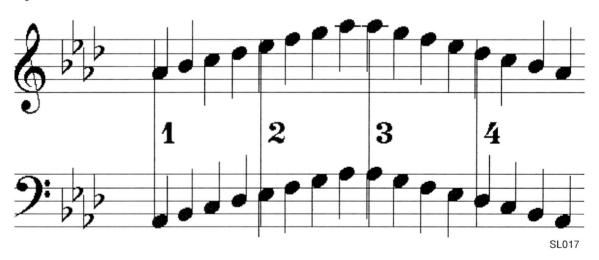

SL017

46

D♭ Major Scale

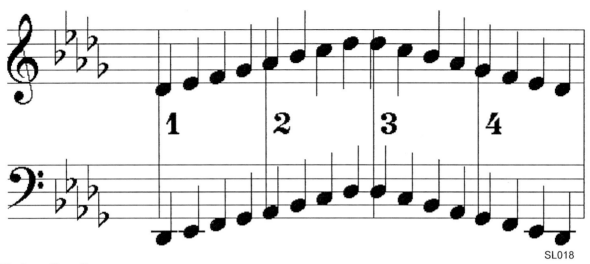

SL018

F# Major Scale

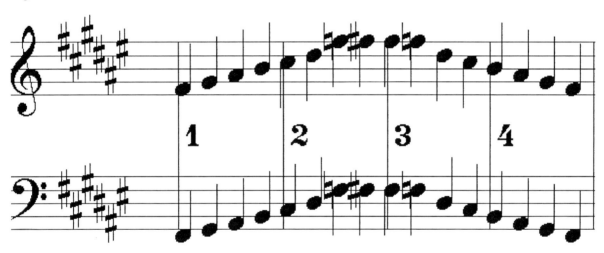

SL019

B Major Scale

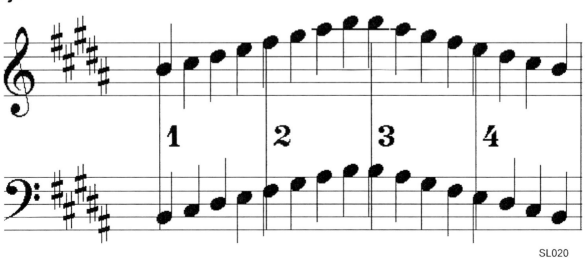

SL020

E Major Scale

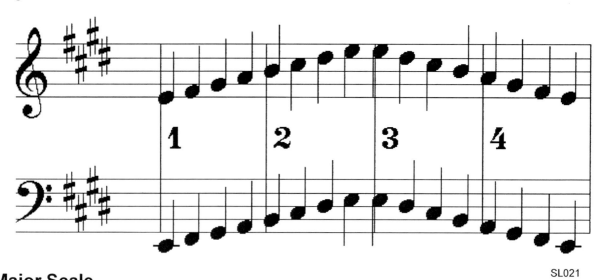

SL021

A Major Scale

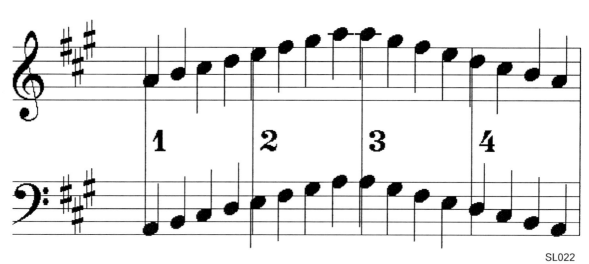

SL022

D Major Scale

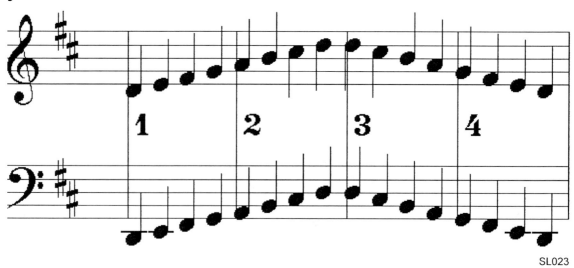

SL023

48

G Major Scale

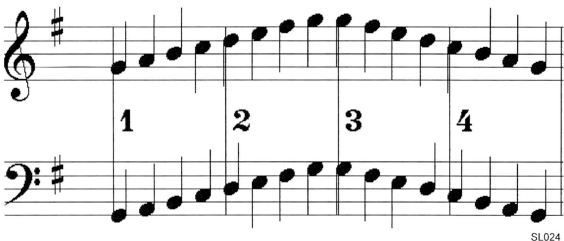

SL024

EXERCISE 4.6

ALL 12 MAJOR SCALES: Label the major scales below…

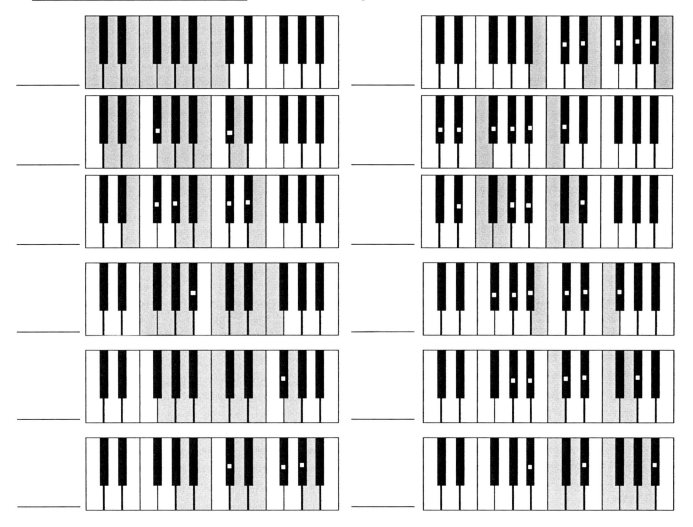

Note: There are also several ear-training exercises available on the **"Piano Player Plus 1.0"** Software to test yourself on the different scales. With this program, you will be able to build your ear skills by testing yourself on scales. The software program will keep track of your progress.

Lesson Five

"Intervals, Major Chords & Inversions"

In this lesson, we will study the **major chord.** In the previous lesson, you've already learned how to form a major scale. With a few easy *techniques*, I am going to show you how to easily transform a major scale into a major chord, when major chords are most likely to be played, and a few major chord progressions.

WHAT ARE CHORDS?

A chord can be characterized by the following:

A group of notes when played together produce a certain type of sound.

Chords, as defined, include a combination of tones which blend harmoniously when sounded together. The chord with the least amount of tones is a three note chord, sometimes called a TRIAD.

Again, the three-toned chord is called a *Triad,* a four-toned chord a *Seventh,* a five-toned chord a *ninth,* a six-toned chord an *Eleventh,* and a seven-toned chord a *Thirteenth.*

# of notes	Type of Chord	
Three	**Triad**	SL025
Four	**Seventh**	SL026
Five	**Ninth**	SL027
Six	**Eleventh**	SL028
Seven	**Thirteenth**	SL029

Prerequisites for this lesson: Must understand whole/half step intervals (Lesson 3A) & Major Scales (Lesson 4); have basic sight reading skills (lesson 2)

INTERVALS

An **INTERVAL** in music is the distance in pitch between two notes. The interval is counted from the lower note to the higher one, with the lower counted as 1.

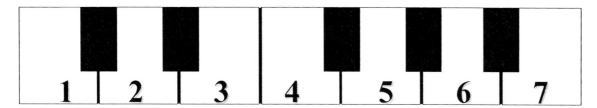

Intervals are named by the number of the upper note (2nds, 3rds, etc.) with two exceptions: The interval between notes that are identical is called **UNISON** (also called a **PRIME INTERVAL**); the interval of an 8th is called an **OCTAVE**. The intervals below are all shown with C as the lower note:

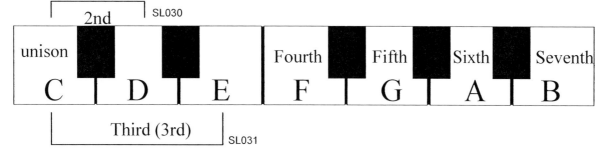

Melodic and Harmonic Intervals

Intervals are called **MELODIC INTERVALS** when they are sounded separately and **HARMONIC INTERVALS** when they are sounded together. Because we are studying chords, we will be dealing with **HARMONIC INTERVALS**. When melodies are played, this involves the study of **MELODIC INTERVALS**.

Mary had a little lamb = E - D - C - D - E - E - E (**Melodic Intervals**) SL032

C Major Chord = C + E + G (played together; **Harmonic Interval**) SL033

Note: As you will learn later, **3rd** and **5th** intervals make up the major chord. A lowered 3rd interval (minor interval) and 5th interval make up the minor chord.

Intervals (cont.)

PERFECT AND MAJOR INTERVALS

The interval between the keynote of a major scale and the unison, 4th, 5th, or octave of that scale is called a **PERFECT INTERVAL.**

For example, the difference from C to G (in a C major scale) is called a **Perfect 5th.** The difference from C to F is called a **Perfect 4th.** The 8th note of the scale is referred to as the **Perfect Octave.** The difference between the same note is called the **Perfect Unison.**

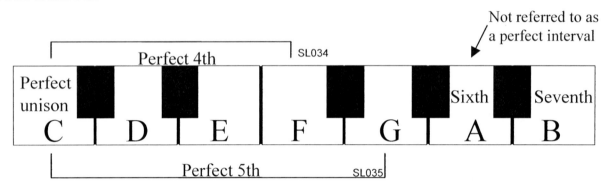

The interval between the keynote of a major scale and the 2nd, 3rd, 6th or 7th of that scale is called a **MAJOR INTERVAL.**

For example, the difference from C to D (in a C major scale) is called a **Major 2nd.** The difference from C to E is called a **Major 3rd.** The difference from C to A is called a **Major 6th** and the difference from C to B is called a **Major 7th.**

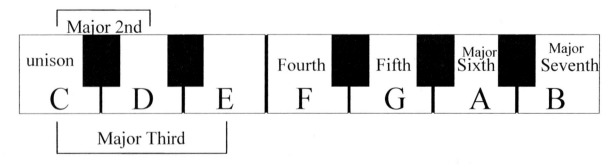

PERFECT INTERVALS	MAJOR INTERVALS
Unison	2nd
4th	3rd
5th	6th
Octave	7th

Intervals (cont.)

MINOR INTERVALS
When the interval between two notes of a major interval (2nd, 3rd, 6th or 7th) is decreased by a *half step*, they become **MINOR INTERVALS.**

For example, a major 3rd becomes a minor 3rd when decreased by a half step. In a C major scale, the major third interval is from C to E. Changing the major third to a minor third would simply mean lowering the E to an E flat. A minor 2nd would be D flat instead of D. A minor 6th would be A flat instead of A. The minor 7th interval would include B flat instead of B.

NOTE: **ONLY MAJOR INTERVALS MAY BE MADE INTO MINOR INTERVALS --** PERFECT INTERVALS MAY NOT (for example, a minor perfect does not exist)

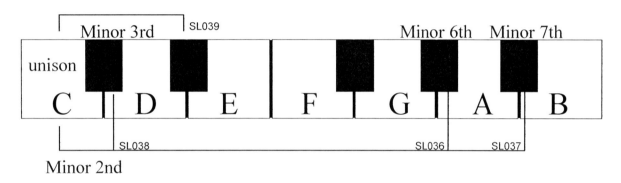

AUGMENTED AND DIMINSHED INTERVALS
The word *augmented* means "made larger." When a perfect or major interval is made larger by a *half step*, it becomes an **AUGMENTED INTERVAL.** For example, a perfect 5th can become an augmented 5th by raising the 5th one half step.

In a C major scale, the perfect 5th is the interval from C to G. By simply raising G to G#, the interval has been expanded, which makes it an **Augmented 5th.**

The word *diminished* means "made smaller." When a perfect or minor interval is made smaller by a *half step*, it becomes a **DIMINISHED INTERVAL.** For example, a perfect 4th can become a diminished 4th by lowering the 4th a half step.

HearandPlay.com

<u>Intervals</u> (cont.)

AUGMENTED AND DIMINSHED INTERVALS (cont.)

In the C Major scale, G is the perfect 5th. By simply lowering G to G$^\flat$, it has been made the diminished 5th.

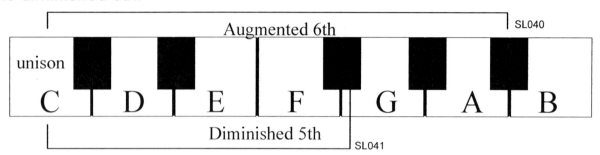

CHROMATIC INTERVAL

When the keynote and the upper note of an interval are not from the same major scale, it is called a **CHROMATIC INTERVAL**. Minor, diminished, and augmented intervals are always chromatic intervals in major keys.

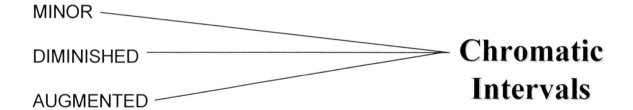

MINOR

DIMINISHED   **Chromatic**

AUGMENTED   **Intervals**

SELF EVALUATION

You should fully understand the following concepts before moving on:

- What an Interval is
- Unison (Prime Interval) and Octave
- Melodic/Harmonic Intervals
- Perfect Unison, 4th, 5th and Perfect Octave
- Major 2nd, 3rd, 6th, and 7th
- Minor Intervals
- Augmented and Diminished Intervals
- Chromatic Intervals

MAJOR CHORDS

PRIMARY AND MAJOR TRIADS

The most important triads of a key are built on the 1st, 4th, and 5th scale degrees of the major scale. They are called the **PRIMARY TRIADS** or **PRIMARY CHORDS** of the key and are identified by the ROMAN NUMERALS **I (1), IV (4) and V (5).** These three triads contain every tone in the major scale.

For example, the C Major Scale is: C - D - E - F - G - A - B - C
Out of those 8 notes (excluding the perfect octave; C), *3 of them are Primary or Major Triads.* **C** is one of them; **F** the next; and **G** the last.

As you will learn later, the other notes of the scale are associated with other types of chords. (like minor and diminished).

The primary triads are **MAJOR TRIADS** because they consist of the *root,* a major 3rd, and a perfect 5th.

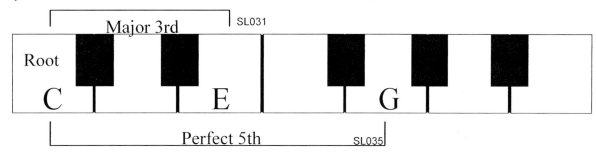

The above diagram displays a major triad chord in the key of C. The chord pictured above is known as the **C MAJOR CHORD.** Because the IV and V degree are also major triads, they are called **F MAJOR** and **G MAJOR CHORDS.**

MAJOR THIRD + PERFECT FIFTH = MAJOR CHORD

Primary and Major Triads (cont.)

Why are major scales important in understanding this section?

If we hadn't known the C major scale, how would we have known that E is the major third and G is the perfect 5th of C major? It is important to know all the major scales!!

HOWEVER... there are **two ways** of forming a major triad:

1. Select the 1st, 3rd, and 5th notes of a major scale

This is the easiest way if you know your major scales. In the key of **F Major**, *F* is the 1st note, *A* is the 3rd note, and *C* is the 5th note. **F, A, & C make up an F major chord.** *THE SAME RULE APPLIES IN ALL 12 KEYS.*

C MAJOR CHORD

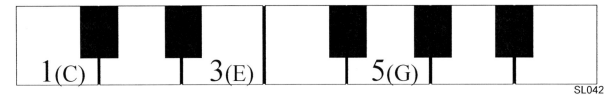

SL042

D MAJOR CHORD

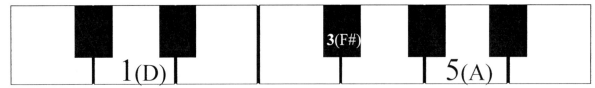

SL043

Another way of forming a major chord (triad) is....
2. Add the interval of a minor 3rd on top of a major third

If you know that a **minor 3rd** equals **3 half steps** and a **major third** equals **4 half steps** (or 2 whole steps), then you can cheat the major scale method.

For example, from **C to E flat** (minor third) is **3 half steps**. *** C to C# = **1** half step ; C to D = **2** half steps; and C to E flat = **3** half steps.

So... to make a major chord, just put a minor 3rd on top of a major third....

Primary and Major Triads (cont.)
Here's the secret....

Let's say you want to build a G major chord.

1) Start at G (the root)
2) Add a major third (4 half steps)
      G + B
3) Add a minor third (3 half steps) on top of that (from B)
      G + B + D

Let's examine it....

From G to B is a major triad and from B to D is a minor triad. THIS MAKES A **G MAJOR CHORD**. This is idea is illustrated with a C major chord below:

C MAJOR CHORD

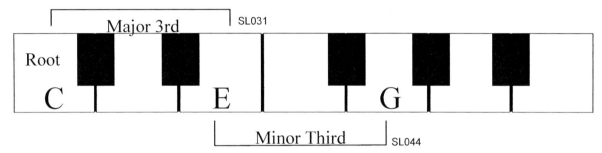

In the key of C major, the

> **I**   triad (or chord) is the C triad (C - E - G)
> **IV** triad (or chord) is the F triad (F - A - C)
> **V**   triad (or chord) is the G triad (G - B - D)

C Major Scale

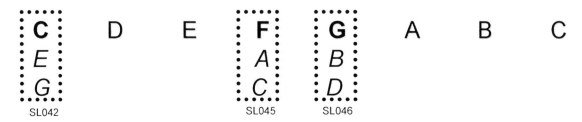

Note: In the key of C Major, D, E & A are associated with the Minor Chord. B is associated with the diminished chord.

Primary and Major Triads (cont.)

EXERCISE 5.1

•Play a C Major Chord (C - E - G)

Describe the sound of the chord below:

_____

_____

_____

_____

Think of songs that have this chord as it's starting note. Write them below:

_____

_____

_____

_____

Songs that start with major chords
Mary had a little lamb, Are you sleeping?, Go tell it on the mountain……

INVERSIONS

We are currently studying *triads* -- or three toned chords. As you learned earlier, there are 4-toned, 5-toned, 6-toned, and even 7-toned chords called thirteenths.

THE NUMBER OF TONES = THE NUMBER OF WAYS THE CHORD CAN BE PLAYED

Since a triad is three-toned, it can be played three different ways: the **root,** the **first inversion**, and the **second inversion**.

Inversions (cont.)

If the *ROOT* (Chord name) is the *lowest tone* of the chord, it is said to be in the *Root* or *Fundamental position.*

For example, if you are playing a **C major chord** with C as the lowest note, it is being played in Root or Fundamental position.

If another tone of the chord is the lowest tone, the chord is said to be **INVERTED.**

The *First Inversion* would have the *Third* of the chord as the lowest note
The *Second Inversion* would have the *Fifth* of the chord as the lowest note
The *Third Inversion* would have the *Seventh* of the chord as the lowest note

C MAJOR CHORD (ROOT)

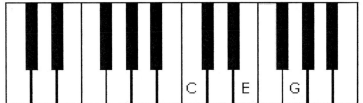

SL042

Since C is the lowest note, it is said to be in it's root position.

C MAJOR (1ST INVERSION)

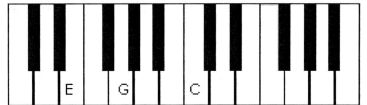

SL042a

Since E (the third of C major) is the lowest note, it is said to be in it's First Inversion

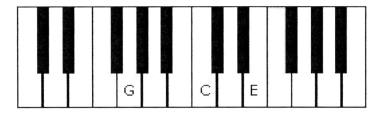

SL042b

Since G (the fifth of C major) is the lowest note, it is said to be in it's Second Inversion

HearandPlay.com

Exercises 5.2

1. Shade the root position of a G major Chord

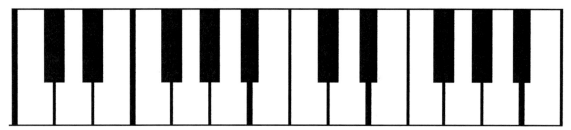

2. Shade the 2nd inversion of an F# major Chord

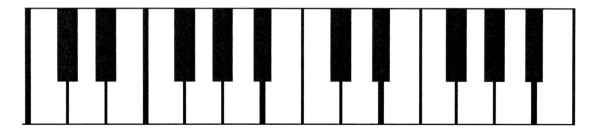

3. Shade the 1st inversion of a B major chord

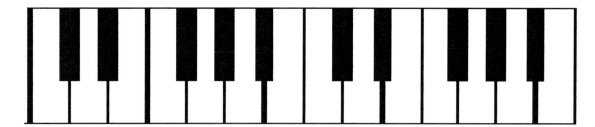

4. Shade the root position of an E major chord

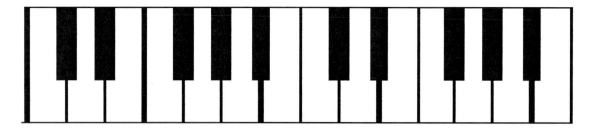

The following pages display the **root position, 1st & 2nd inversion of all twelve major chords.** Try playing all the chords on the next page. Refer to the fingering chart in Lesson 4. Use fingers 1, 3 and 5 on the right hand. (you can use 2 instead of 3 depending on the size of your hand)

MAJOR CHORDS

C MAJOR

1st Inversion   *Root Position*   *Second Inversion*

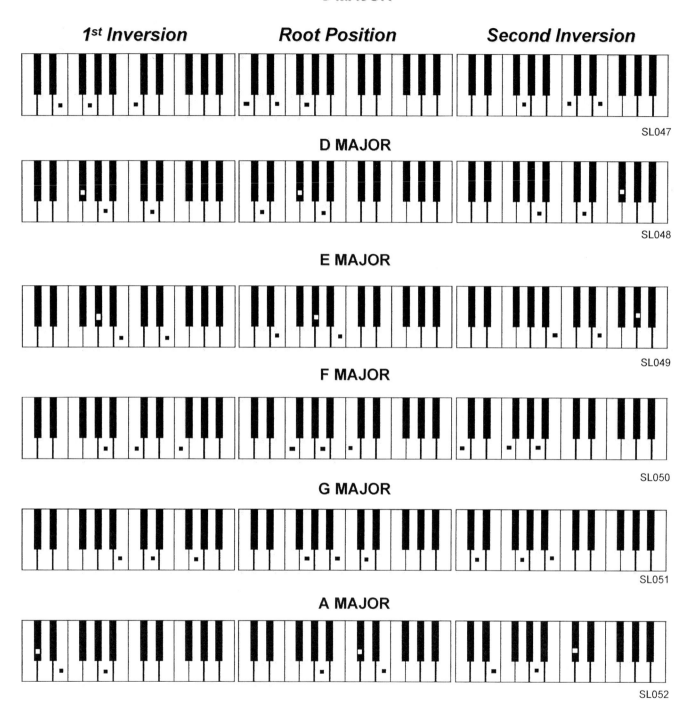

SL047

D MAJOR

SL048

E MAJOR

SL049

F MAJOR

SL050

G MAJOR

SL051

A MAJOR

SL052

Notice: When a chord is played in it's **root position**, the keynote is always on the bottom. When a chord is played in it's **first inversion**, the keynote is always on the top. When a chord is played in it's **second inversion**, the keynote is always in the middle.

MAJOR CHORDS (cont.)

B or C♭ MAJOR

1ˢᵗ Inversion   **Root Position**   **Second Inversion**

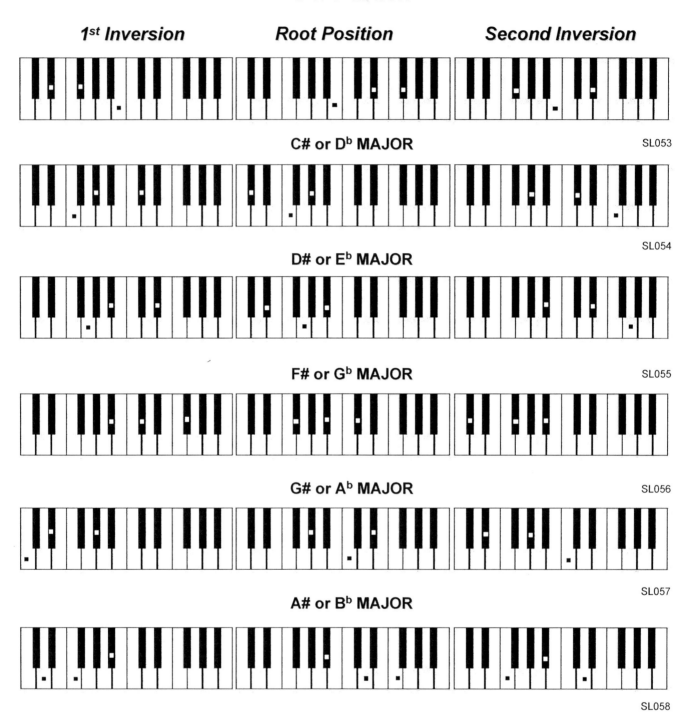

C# or D♭ MAJOR

SL053

D# or E♭ MAJOR

SL054

SL055

F# or G♭ MAJOR

SL056

G# or A♭ MAJOR

SL057

A# or B♭ MAJOR

SL058

Note: I also recommend using the **"Piano Player Plus 1.0"** Software to test yourself on the different sounds of the major chords and inversions. With this program, you will be able to build your ear skills by testing yourself on chords and inversions. The software program will keep track of your progress.

HearandPlay.com

EXERCISE 5.3

Label the following chords

	CHORD NAME	INVERSION

EXERCISE 5.4

Draw the following chords

	CHORD NAME	INVERSION
	C Major	Root
	F Major	Second
	B♭ Major	First
	A Major	Second
	B Major	Root
	E Major	First

Lesson Six

"Major Chord Progressions"

In this lesson, we will study **major chord progressions.** In the previous lesson, you've already learned how to form and invert major chords. In this lesson, we will use the major chords learned to create usable progressions.

MAJOR CHORD PROGRESSIONS

Chords that move from one to another are called a **Chord Progression.** Because the **I, IV** and **V** chords contain all the notes of the major scale, they can be used to accompany (play along with) most simple melodies.

I, IV & V CHORDS

The 1st, 4th & 5th degree of a major scale are associated with the **Major** Chord. As you will learn later, the 2nd, 3rd & 6th degree of a major scale are associated with the **Minor** Chord. Lastly, the 7th degree of a major scale is associated with the **diminished** chord.

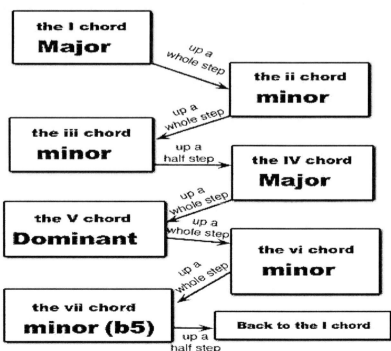

Note: In many chord progressions, a V7 (dominant) chord is used in place of the V chord (you will learn V7 chords later).

65

Since we have learned all 12 **Major Chords,** we will only cover *major chord progressions* in this lesson. However, the chart below gives you an idea of how each note of a major scale corresponds to either a major, minor, or diminished chord:

I	ii	iii	IV	V	vi	Vii	I
Major Chord	Minor Chord	Minor Chord	Major Chord	Major Chord	Minor Chord	Diminished Chord (or min7^{b}5)	Major Chord

For example, in **C Major,** the following scale tones and chords correspond together:

I	ii	iii	IV	V	vi	vii	I
C Major Chord	D Minor Chord	E Minor Chord	F Major Chord	G Major Chord	A Minor Chord	B Diminished Chord (or min7^{b}5)	C Major Chord

SL059

Since the I, IV & V chords are major, we will concentrate on the chord progressions that involve only those three chords (we will cover other chords and progressions in further chapters).

I – IV – I – V – I Progression   SL060
This progression simply changes from the I chord to the IV (fourth) chord; back to the one chord; then, to the V (fifth) chord resolving back to the I chord.

In the key of **C Major,** this would be: **Cmaj -- Fmaj -- Cmaj -- Gmaj -- Cmaj**

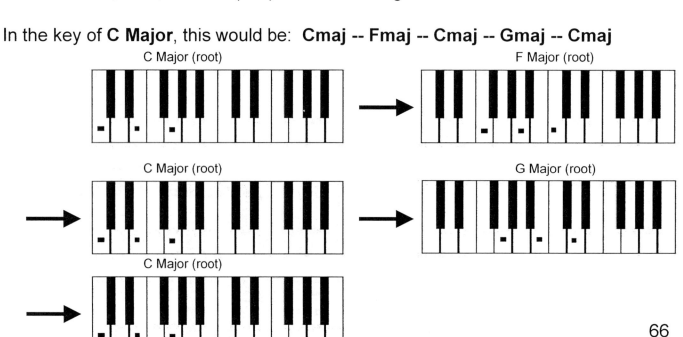

66

I – IV – I – V – I (1 A)

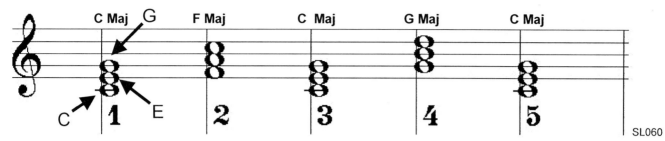

SL060

When the IV and V chords are in root position, the progression sounds choppy. To make it easier to play and sound smoother, the IV chord is often moved to the 2nd inversion, and the V chord is often moved to the 1st inversion. Notice, how easier it is to play the progression when using these inversions …

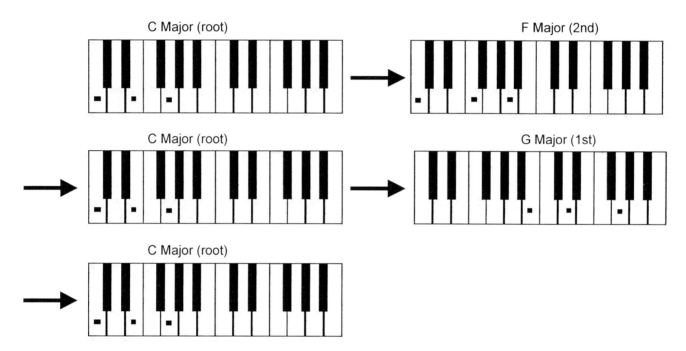

I – IV – I – V – I (1 B)

Compare the inverted progression (fig 1B) to the original progression (fig 1A). Remember, when playing the I chord to the IV chord, simply convert from the root to the 2nd inversion to create a smoother transition. When playing the I chord to the V chord, simply convert from the root to the 1st inversion to create a smoother transition between the two chords. As compared to the original chart, this progression is obviously easier and smoother to play…

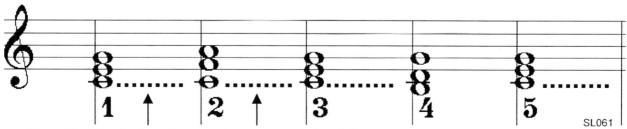

SL061

Note: The "I" note stays the same in measures 1, 2, 3 & 5

Relationship between the I and V Chords ... (V -- I)

As you become more experienced in playing various chord progressions, you will notice that one commonly used progression is the **V** chord to the **I** chord. Notice in the previous chord progression (I – IV – I – *V* – *I*) how the **V** chord leads back to the **I** chord; this is also the case in many other progressions. **Ex** - [I – vi – ii – V – I], [ii – V – I]

Because the **V** chord is most commonly used when resolving back to the **I** chord, it is often found at the end of verses, songs, and parts of a song that resolve to a major chord.

For example, towards the end of *"Mary Had a Little Lamb,"* you will find a **V – I** progression:

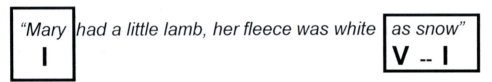

> *"Mary* | *had a little lamb, her fleece was white* | *as snow"*
> **I**   **V -- I**

Notice that the verse begins and ends on a **I** chord. However, the ending **I** chord is preceded by a **V** chord. In the key of **C major**, the **I** chord is C major and the **V** chord is G major.

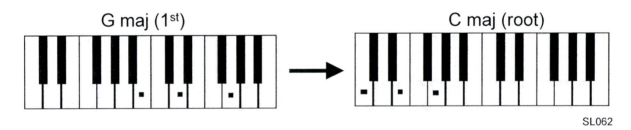

G maj (1st)   →   C maj (root)

SL062

•Play the I – IV – I – V – I progression in any key of your choice. To do this, simply take the major chords of the 1st, 4th, and 5th degree of any major scale. For example, in F Major, this progression would use F major, B flat major, and C major chords; in B flat major, this progression would use B flat major, E flat major and F major chords.

•Note how many songs you know that end with this progression. You will find that most of the songs that you recall end with this progression (or some type of similar alteration). Most likely, if a song ends on the I chord (the keynote), it is preceded by a V chord. Again, this is the most common type of progression towards the end of a verse or song. Keep this in mind when you start attempting to figure out the chords of various progressions!

•Test yourself. I recommend that you use the **"Piano Player Plus 1.0"** Software to test yourself on different major chord progressions. With this program, you will be able to select random major chord progressions while using your ear to depict which key the progression is derived from. Check it out!

HearandPlay.com

Relationship between the I and V Chords ... (V -- I) [cont.]

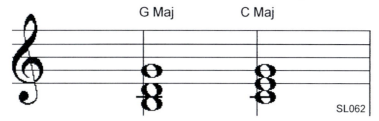

The bass (left hand) for the progression above is simply the root of each chord. That is, if you are playing a *C* major chord, then the bass is *C*; if you are playing an *F* major chord, the bass is *F*; *G major chord* = *G* ... and so on...

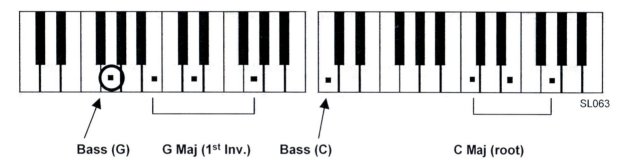

Bass (G)   G Maj (1st Inv.)   Bass (C)   C Maj (root)

Another approach to the V -- I Progression

By now, you should already understand the concept of the V chord leading to the I chord (in most cases). We will now introduce another type of V -- I progression ...

Instead of playing the V chord to resolve back to the I chord, play the IV chord. Please note that the bass (left hand) for the V -- I progression will remain the same. That is, the keynote of the V chord will remain the bass note even though you're playing the IV chord. For example, in C major this progression would look like this:

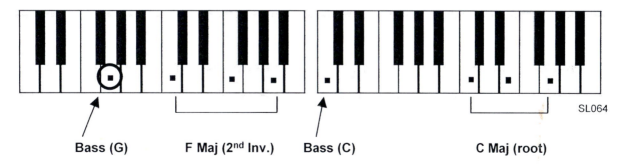

Bass (G)   F Maj (2nd Inv.)   Bass (C)   C Maj (root)

Note: Notice, that we used the F major (2nd Inversion) chord to lead back to C major (root inversion) chord because it's the easiest transition. However, any inversion of the IV chord (or F major in this case) will work and produce a similar sound. Try playing and comparing all three inversions.

EXERCISE 6.1

Compare the sounds of the V --I Chord Progressions

_____

_____

List examples of songs that end in a V -- I Chord Progression

_____

_____

Name each chord tone and their corresponding chord (_V, vi, major, minor, diminished, etc_)

_____

_____

Why did we invert the (I – IV – I – V – I) Progression?

_____

_____

EXERCISE 6.2 Fill in the following chart with the scale degree and corresponding chord for each key…

key	I	ii	iii	IV	V	vi	vii	I
C	C maj	D min	E min	F maj	G maj	A min	B dim	C maj
D	D maj	E min	F# min	G maj	A maj	B min	C# dim	D maj
E	E maj	F# min	G# min	A maj	B maj	C# min	D# dim	E maj
F					C maj			
G	G maj	A min	B min	C maj	D maj	E min	F# dim	
A	A maj	B min	C# min	D maj	E maj	F# min	G# dim	
B								

More approaches to the V -- I Progression ...

You have already learned that the V and IV chord can be used along with the V *bass note* to resolve back to the I chord. We will now learn another approach to produce the same type of progression. Keep in mind that any **three** of these chord progressions can be used depending on the type of sound you want to produce.

As you know, the iii tone of a scale corresponds to the minor chord. For example, in C major, the iii tone is **E.** Thus, it's chord is **E min.** However, for this progression, we will use the third tone as a **major chord** (along with the *same* "V" bass note).

In C Major, this progression would look like this:

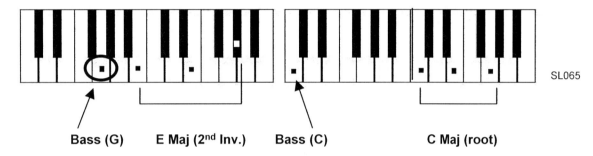

Bass (G)   E Maj (2nd Inv.)   Bass (C)   C Maj (root)

Note: Notice, that we used the E major (2nd Inversion) chord to lead back to C major (root inversion) chord because again, it's the easiest transition. However, any inversion of the III chord (or E major in this case) will work and produce a similar sound. Try playing and comparing all three inversions.

V -- I Summarization

Here is a diagram of all *three* progression that we have covered which lead to a **I** chord:

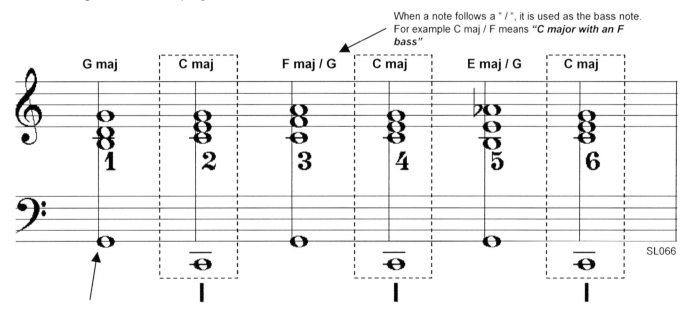

When a note follows a " / ", it is used as the bass note. For example C maj / F means *"C major with an F bass"*

This chord does not need a " / " because it is already implied that **G** is the bass note since we are playing a **G major chord**

71

Relationship between the I and V Chords ... (V -- I) [cont.]

We have already studied various progressions where the **V chord** (or **v** bass note with another **major chord**) leads to the **I chord**. The following chart shows the different types of progressions and the sounds they produce:

Bass / Major Chord	Sound	
V / V	Sounds happy; used for most endings	SL067
V / IV	Sounds suspenseful; makes listener await for the ending chord (**I chord**)	SL068
V / III	Sounds jazzy & smooth; usually transitions into a maj7 or maj9 chord (you will learn those later ...)	SL069

Now, we will study chord progressions where the **I chord** leads to the **V chord** (or some type of alteration of the V chord as in the previous chord progression)

I -- V Chord Progression

The "I -- V" is also a commonly used **chord progression.** Contrary to the "V -- I" progression, the "I -- V" progression is commonly used in the middle of songs where the beginning is repeated.

Mary had a little lamb[1]	*little lamb*[2]	*little lamb*[3]
I Chord ⟶	V Chord ⟶	I Chord

I -- V		V -- I

Try singing "Mary had a little lamb" while holding down the chords above. The "V" (or *G* when in the key of *C* major) is used as the chord for the *second*[2] "little lamb." Also, observe where in the song this chord appears. It is located right before you repeat "Mary had a little lamb"...

I -- V ┆ V -- I

Beginning is repeated ...   *Mary had a little lamb[1], little lamb[2], little lamb[3]*
Mary had a little lamb, her fleece was white as snow

Here's an example of the "I" -- "V" progression in C major:

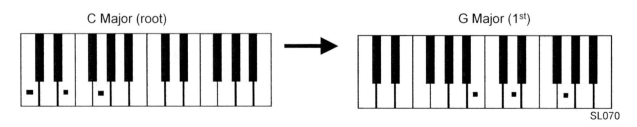

C Major (root)   G Major (1st)

SL070

72

EXERCISE 6.3

List the (a) key of the chord progression, (b) each chord of the progression, and (c) its inversion

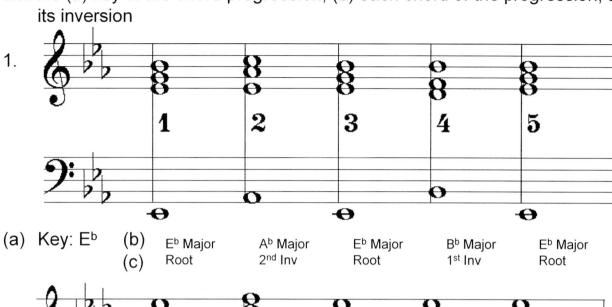

1.

(a) Key: E♭   (b)   E♭ Major   A♭ Major   E♭ Major   B♭ Major   E♭ Major

           (c)   Root   2nd Inv   Root   1st Inv   Root

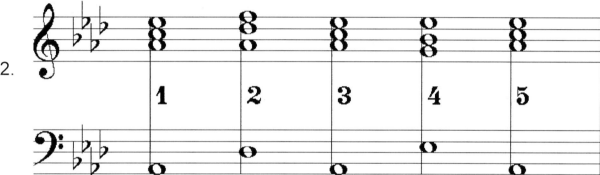

2.

(a) Key: A♭   (b)   A♭ major   D♭maj   A♭ maj   E♭ Major   A♭ maj

           (c)   Root   2nd Inv   Root   1st Inv   Root

3.

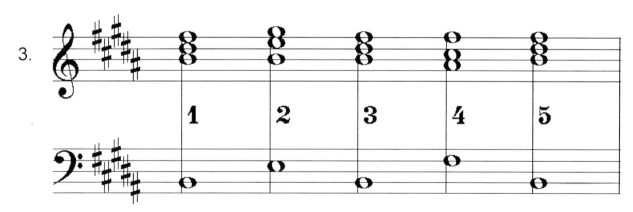

(a) Key: B   (b)   B major   E major   B major   F maj   B major

          (c)   Root   2 Inv   Root   1st Inv   Root

Relationship between the I and IV Chords …

Another common progression is the "I -- IV". It is commonly used in gospel, jazz, and blues music.

Here's an example of a "I-IV" progression in C major …

SL071

Again, notice that we use F major (2nd inversion) because of its easy transition from C major (root inversion). Below is a chart which shows the *easiest transitions* between ALL inversions in the "I-IV" progression.

"I" Chord	"IV" Chord
Root	2nd
1st	Root
2nd	1st

In the chart above, when a "I" chord is played in root inversion, the easiest transition is the 2nd inversion of the "IV" chord. When the "I" chord is played in its 1st inversion, the easiest transition is the root inversion of the "IV" chord. When the "I" chord is played in its 2nd inversion, the easiest transition is the 1st inversion of the "IV" chord.

Note: The keynote of the "I" chord is shared in the "IV" also. Thus, the same note is played both in the "I" and "IV" chord. For example, in C major, the "I" chord is: [C] [E] [G] (root) and the "IV" chord is: [C] [F] [A] (2nd inversion). The [C] note does not move; only the two higher notes in this instance.

Root -- 2nd	Bottom note does not move
1st -- Root	Top note does not move
2nd -- 1st	Middle note does not move

Try playing the different inversions. Notice that in each example, one note will always stay stationary. This is useful in helping you to play chords easier and without much thinking as playing all chords in root will require you to jump from chord to chord.

EXERCISE 6.4

One chord will be displayed (I or IV chord). Draw the missing chord which allows you to transition from the shown chord the easiest. (choose the best inversion)...

Note: Refer to the chord inversion chart earlier in the course if needed. Also, remember the tips on which inversions of "I" chords convert to "IV" the easiest …

"I" Chord	"IV" Chord
This is a **B Major** (2nd Inv) because **B** is in the middle. Because the B major chord is played in its second inversion, the IV chord should be played in it's first inversion for smooth transitioning.	The fourth tone of the **B** Major scale is **E.** Thus, our "IV" chord is **E major.** Because the "I" chord is played in it's second inversion, the "IV" (E major) should be played in it's first inversion for smooth transition (as displayed in picture above).

EXERCISE 6.5

Complete the charts below filling in the missing chords for each progression ...

KEY	"I" (root)	"IV" (2nd)	"I" (root)	"V" (1st)	"I" (root)
C	C – E – G (c)	C – F – A (F)	C – E – G (C)	B – D – G (G)	C – E – G (c)
D	D – F# – A (D)	D – G – B (G)	D – F# - A (D)	C# – E – A (A)	D – F# – A (D)
E	E – G# – B (E)	E – A – C# (A)	E – G# – B (E)	D# – F# – B (B)	E – G# - B (E)
F	F – A – C (F)	F – Bb – D (Bb)	F – A – C (F)	E – G – C (C)	F – G – C (F)
G	G – B – D (G)	G – C – E (C)	G – B – D (G)	F# – A – D (A)	G – B – D (G)
A	A – C# – E (A)	A – D – F# (D)	A – C# - E (A)	G# – B – E (E)	A – C# – E (A)
B	B – D# – F# (B)	B – E – G# (E)	B – D# – F# (B)	A# - C# - F# (F#)	B – D# – F# (B)
C# / Db	C# - F – G# Db – F – Ab	Db – Gb – Bb (Gb)	Db – F – Ab (Db)	C – Eb – Ab (Ab)	Db – F – Ab (Db)
D# / Eb	Eb – G – Bb (Eb)	Eb – Ab – C (Ab)	Eb – G – Bb (Eb)	D – F – Bb (Bb)	Eb – G – Bb (Eb)
F# / Gb	F# - A# - C#				
G# / Ab	Ab – C – Eb (Ab)	G# - C# - F Ab – Db – F (Db)	Ab – C – Eb (Ab)	G – Bb – Eb (Eb)	Ab – C – Eb (Ab)
A# / Bb	Bb – D – F (Bb)	Bb – Db – E (Db)	Bb – D – F (Bb)	A – C – F (F)	Bb – D – F (Bb)

Key	"V" (1st)	"I" (root)
C	B – D – G	C – E - G
D	C# – E – A	D – F# – A
E		E – G# - B
F		
G		
A	G# - B - E	
B		

Key	"I" (root)	"IV" (2nd)
C	C – E – G	C – F – A
D	D – F# - A	
E		
F		F – Bb - D
G		
A		
B	B – D# - F#	

More Major Chord Progressions...

The last chord progression we will study within the major chords of a scale is the **"I – IV – V – IV – I"**.

This chord progression is commonly heard in rock, gospel, and jazz music. Try playing this progression in C major:

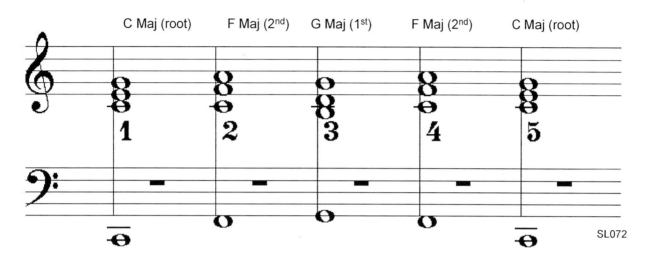

Also, try the same progression with two *small* alterations ...

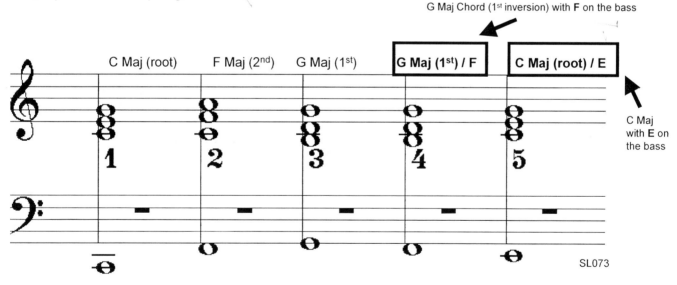

•Piano Player Plus v1.0: Included on the *PPP v1.0* are audio examples of **all** the chord progressions mentioned in this lesson. In addition, you will be able to train your ear by listening and taking quizzes on each chord progression allowing you to be better equipped to recognize these chord progressions in other songs. Check it out!

PianoPlayerPlus.com

EXERCISE 6.9

"Circle of Fifths" Exercise: Play the "I" major chord of each major key in the order in which they appear on the "Circle of Fifths" chart below. For example, **C maj -- F maj -- B^b** maj … and so on …

If you look closely, you'll notice that this exercise consists of playing a series of **"I – IV"** progressions which means that you should be able to play each chord quickly and easily by choosing the right inversion. **TIP:** You should never have to move all three fingers at once as each chord will share **one** note from the previous chord. Simply move the other two notes to the appropriate notes of the new chord keeping the third note the same. Example: C maj (**C** – E – G) -- F maj (**C** – F – A)

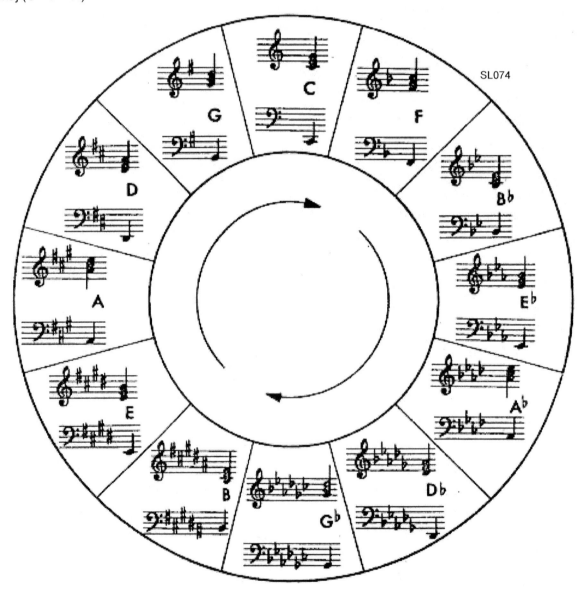

This concludes lesson seven on **Major Chord Progressions.** In the next few lessons, we will study the *minor scale, minor chord, and minor chord progressions …*

Lesson Seven

"Modes & Minor Scales"

As you should remember, the tones of the major scale correspond to either a major, minor, or diminished chord. We have already studied the major chord and various major chord progressions. We will now study the minor scale as this will help us to easily play minor chords and various minor chord progressions.

Prerequisites for this lesson: Must understand whole/half step intervals (Lesson 3A), Major Scales (Lesson 4), and have basic sight reading skills

"Modes of a Scale"

Before we study minor scales, it is important that we understand the "**modes of a scale.**"

MODES are a system of scales that began in ancient Greece. Just like a major or minor scale, a mode is a scale of eight notes in alphabetical order. A mode can begin on any scale degree of a major scale using the key signature of the parent scale.

For example, in the key of C, a mode can begin and end on C (I), on D (ii), on E (iii), and so on. There are **SEVEN** modes altogether and each has a Greek name.

MODES OF A SCALE

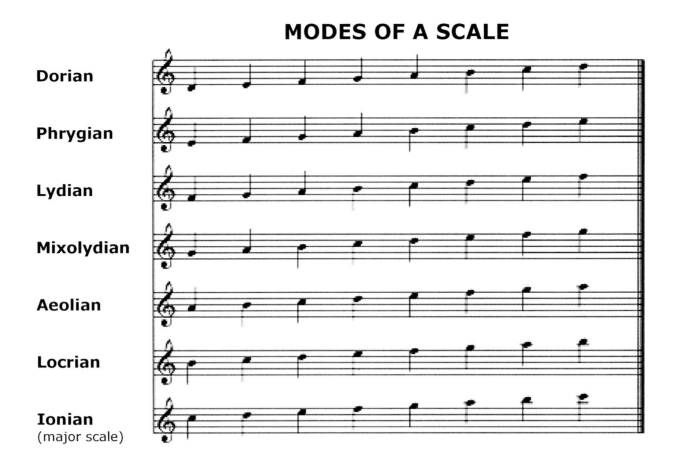

Dorian

Phrygian

Lydian

Mixolydian

Aeolian

Locrian

Ionian
(major scale)

"Modes of a Scale" (cont.)

Here is a chart to better help you understand the modes of a scale …

Scale Degree	I	ii	iii	IV	V	vi	vii
MODES:	Ionian	Dorian	Phrygian	Lydian	Mixolydian	Aeolian	Locrian
	SL075	SL076	SL077	SL078	SL079	SL080	SL081

(1) IONIAN MODE: 1st scale degree of a major scale to its octave note (also known as a Major Scale because it starts and ends on the 1st tone of the scale). In C major, this would be the C major scale from C to C.

(2) DORIAN MODE: 2nd scale degree of a major scale to its octave note. In C major, this would be the C major scale from D to D.

(3) PHRYGIAN MODE: 3rd scale degree of a major scale to its octave note. In C major, this would be the C major scale from E to E.

(4) LYDIAN MODE: 4th scale degree of a major scale to its octave note. In C major, this would be the C major scale from F to F.

(5) MIXOLYDIAN: 5th scale degree of a major scale to its octave note. In C major, this would be the C major scale from G to G. (also known as a Major Scale with a flatted 7th note)

(6) AEOLIAN MODE: 6th scale degree of a major scale to its octave note (also known as a Natural Minor scale). In C major, this would be the C major scale from A to A.

(7) LOCRIAN: 7th scale degree of a major scale to its octave note. In C major, this would be the C major scale from B to B.

EXAMPLES OF MODULAR SCALES

C Mixolydian: (1) *Since the Mixolydian scale starts on the 5th degree, we must determine what major key has "C"* as it's 5th tone. (2) Once we have determined which major key "C" is the fifth tone of, we must play that particular major key starting from C ending on C (not a C major scale, but the scale from which C is the 5th tone). In this case, F major would be the parent scale from which C major is the 5th tone. By simply playing an F major scale from **C** to **C**, we are playing a C major scale with one difference – the lowered 7th note. Thus, **C Mixolydian** is a major scale with a lowered 7th note. This goes for all Mixolydian scales …

F Dorian: (1) Since we know that the Dorian mode deals with the second degree of a major scale, we must find what major key has **F** as it's second tone. In this case, E^b would be the parent major scale. By simply playing an E^b major scale from F to F, we have played an **F Dorian Scale.**

MODES RELATED TO THE MAJOR SCALE:

Ionian mode is simply a major scale

Mixolydian mode is simply a major scale with the 7th tone lowered a half step.

Lydian mode is simply a major scale with the 4th tone raised a half step

MODES RELATED TO THE MINOR SCALE:

Aeolian mode is simply a natural minor scale.

Dorian mode is a natural minor scale with the 6th tone raised a half step.

Phrygian mode is a natural minor scale with the 2nd tone lowered a half step.

Locrian mode is a natural minor scale with the 2nd and 5th tone lowered a half step.

THE AEOLIAN MODE

The Aeolian mode is the mode that we will refer to the most in this lesson (because it is the natural minor scale).

NATURAL MINOR SCALES SL080

We've already learned all 12 major scales with unique key signatures. Now, we will learn a new concept which deals with minor scales.

For every **MAJOR KEY,** there is a **RELATIVE MINOR KEY** that also shares the same key signature.

Each relative minor scales begins on the 6th degree (Aeolian) of the **RELATIVE MAJOR SCALE.** The 6th note is the keynote (first note played) of the minor scale and the note from which the scale gets its name.

"MINOR SCALES"

MAJOR KEY	RELATIVE MINOR
C Major	A Minor
D Major	B Minor
E Major	C# Minor
F Major	D Minor
G Major	E Minor
A Major	F# Minor
B Major	G# Minor
D Flat / C# Major	B Flat Minor
E Flat / D# Major	C Minor
G Flat / F# Major	E Flat Minor
A Flat / G# Major	F Minor
B Flat / A# Major	G Minor

2 STEPS TO PLAYING A MINOR SCALE ...

1) **Find the relative major key of the minor scale that you want to play.** (either refer to the chart above or find what scale has the keynote of the minor scale you want to play as it's 6th tone ... since the minor scale is also the Aeolian mode of a scale ...)

2) **Play the relative major key starting and ending on the sixth degree.** (the sixth degree of the relative major key should be the keynote of the minor scale that you want to play. You can also verify the relative major key by counting 3 half steps to the right. If it takes more or less than 3 half steps to get to the relative major key, then the relative major key that you have chosen is not correct.)

C MAJOR SCALE
("A" Minor Scale displayed also)

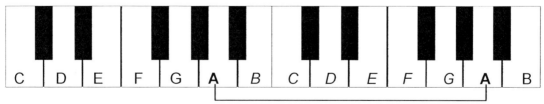

Sixth Degree of the major scale; **"A" minor Scale**

MINOR SCALES WORKSHEET – 7.1

These exercises will assist you in using the *two steps* to learn the rest of the minor scales …

1. B MINOR: Draw the relative major scale below (circle the 6th degree):

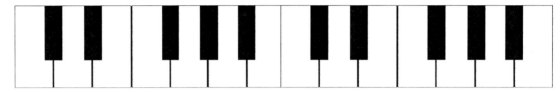

Re-draw the relative major scale starting and ending on B Minor

B Minor Scale

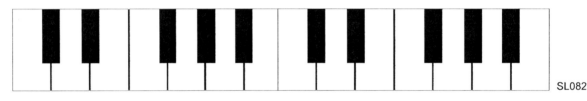

SL082

2. C MINOR: Draw the relative major scale below (circle the 6th degree):

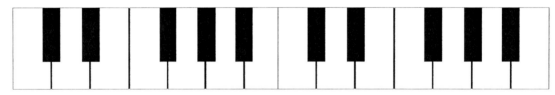

Re-draw the relative major scale starting and ending on C Minor

C Minor Scale

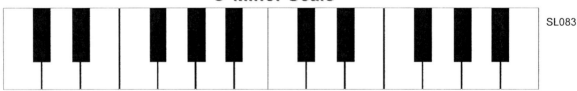

SL083

3. D MINOR: Draw the relative major scale below (circle the 6th degree):

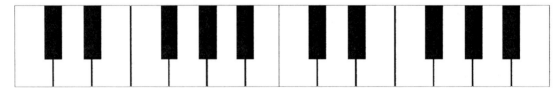

MINOR SCALES WORKSHEET – 7.2

Re-draw the relative major scale starting and ending on D Minor

D Minor Scale

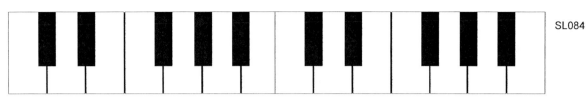

SL084

4. E MINOR: Draw the relative major scale below (circle the 6th degree):

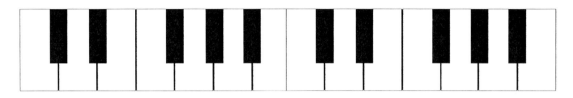

Re-draw the relative major scale starting and ending on E Minor

E Minor Scale

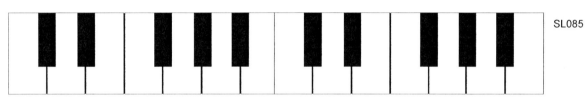

SL085

5. F MINOR: Draw the relative major scale below (circle the 6th degree):

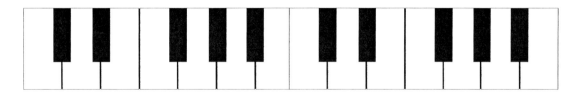

Re-draw the relative major scale starting and ending on F Minor

F Minor Scale

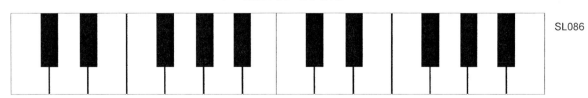

SL086

MINOR SCALES WORKSHEET – 7.3

6. G MINOR: Draw the relative major scale below (circle the 6th degree):

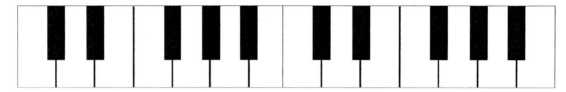

Re-draw the relative major scale starting and ending on G Minor

G Minor Scale

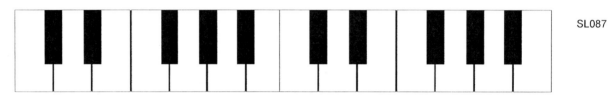

SL087

7. C# / D♭ MINOR: Draw the relative major scale below (circle the 6th degree):

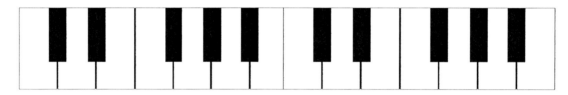

Re-draw the relative major scale starting and ending on C# / D♭ Minor

C# / D♭ Minor Scale

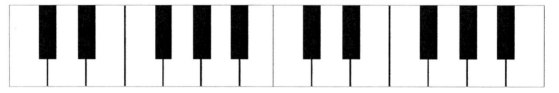

SL089

8. D# / E♭ MINOR: Draw the relative major scale below (circle the 6th degree):

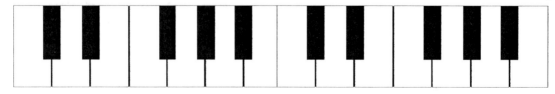

MINOR SCALES WORKSHEET – 7.4

Re-draw the relative major scale starting and ending on D# / E♭ Minor

D# / E♭ Minor Scale

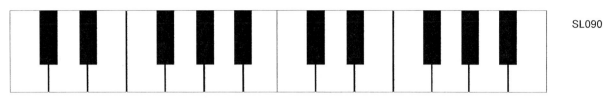

SL090

9. F# / G♭ MINOR: Draw the relative major scale below (circle the 6th degree):

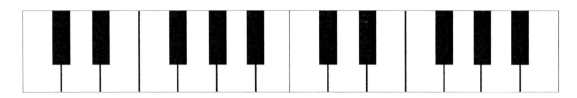

Re-draw the relative major scale starting and ending on F# / G♭ Minor

F# / G♭ Minor Scale

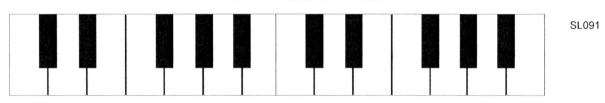

SL091

10. G# / A♭ MINOR: Draw the relative major scale below (circle the 6th degree):

Re-draw the relative major scale starting and ending on G# / A♭ Minor

G# / A♭ Minor Scale

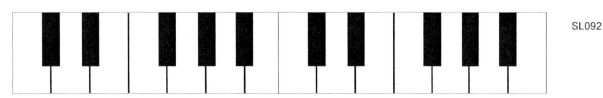

SL092

MINOR SCALES WORKSHEET – 7.5

11. A# / B♭ MINOR: Draw the relative major scale below (circle the 6th degree):

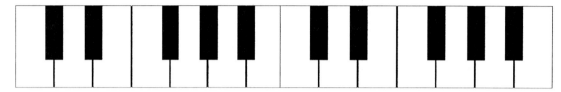

Re-draw the relative major scale starting and ending on A# / B♭ Minor

A# / B♭ Minor Scale

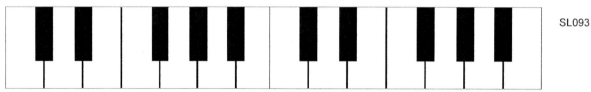

SL093

Natural Minor Scales

MINOR SCALES

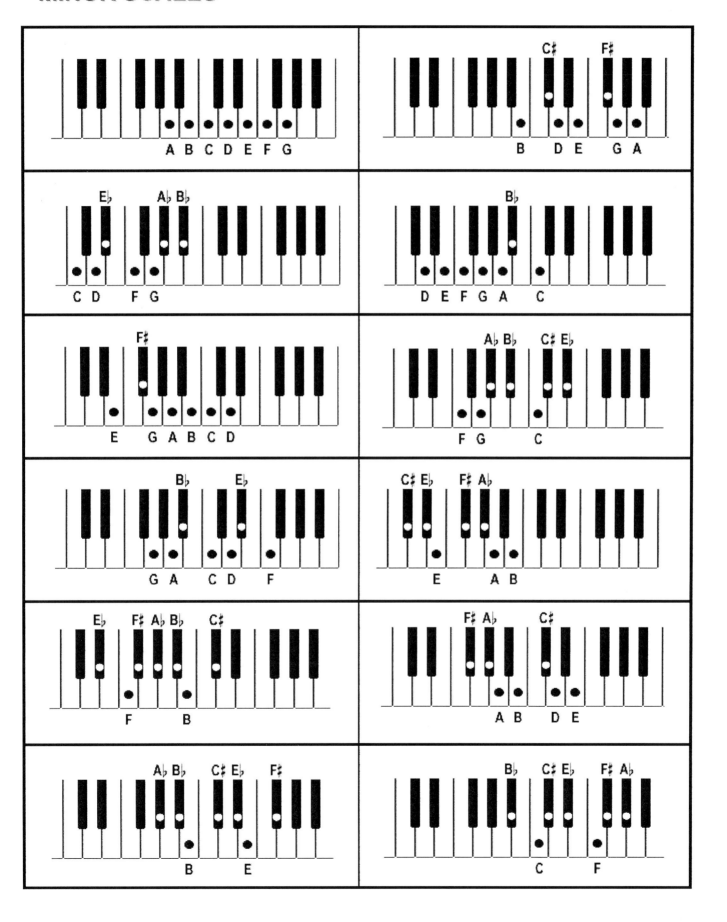

EXERCISE 7.6
Answer the following questions…

1.Compare the sounds of the major and minor scales. In what ways are they different? How are they the same?

_____

_____

_____

2. Summarize the two steps to playing a minor scale:

_____

_____

_____

3. List all the modes of a major scale

_____

_____

_____

4. Which mode is also known as the natural minor scale?

_____

5. Which modes are related to the major scale and why?

_____

_____

6. Which modes are related to the minor scale and why?

_____

_____

Lesson Eight

"Minor & Diminished Chords"

In this lesson, we will study the **minor chord.** In the previous lesson, you've already learned how to form a minor scale. With a few easy *techniques*, I am going to show you how to easily transform a minor scale into a minor chord, when minor chords are most likely to be played, and a few minor chord progressions.

# of notes	Type of Chord
Three	**Triad**
Four	**Seventh**
Five	**Ninth**
Six	**Eleventh**
Seven	**Thirteenth**

We will study minor triads in this lesson … (3-toned chords)

Prerequisites for this lesson: Must understand whole/half step intervals (Lesson 3A) & Minor Scales (Lesson 7); have basic sight reading skills (lesson 2)

MINOR CHORDS

Minor Triads

Just as a major triad can be built from the 1st, 3rd and 5th scale degrees of a major scale, a **MINOR TRIAD** can be built from the 1st, 3rd and 5th scale degrees of a minor scale.

C MAJOR SCALE
A *"C Major"* Scale is: C - D - E - F - G - A - B - C

A *"C Major"* Chord is: **C**   **E**   **G**
                       1   3   5

C MINOR SCALE
Like **major scales & chords**, it's just as important to know your minor scales in constructing **minor chords**.

There are 3 ways to build a minor chord:
        1. Select the 1st, 3rd, and 5th notes of a minor scale
        2. Add the interval of a major third on top of a minor 3rd (opposite of major triad)
        3. Lower the major third of a major chord a half step

---

1. If you know the minor scale of a key, simply take the 1st (root), the 3rd degree and the 5th degree to create the minor chord of that key.

For example, the C MINOR SCALE IS: C - D - E flat - F - G - A flat - B flat - C.
The 1st, 3rd, and 5th notes are: C - E flat - G.

> **The *C Minor Chord* is C - E^b - G.**

Minor Triads (Cont.)

2. By now, you know that a **major third** equals **4 half steps** (or 2 whole steps) and a **minor third** equals **3 half steps**. Earlier, you learned that a major chord is a minor third on top of a major third.

A **MINOR CHORD** consists of a *Major third* on top of a *Minor third* (simply the opposite of the major chord).

C MINOR CHORD

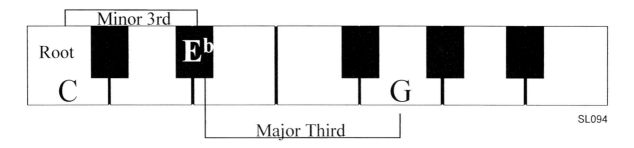

3. The last method for building a minor chord is the lowering of the major third in a major chord. A **C MAJOR CHORD** is: C - E - G. Lowering E to E flat would make this C major chord a **C MINOR CHORD (C - E flat - G).**

C MAJOR CHORD LOWERED TO A *"C MINOR CHORD"*

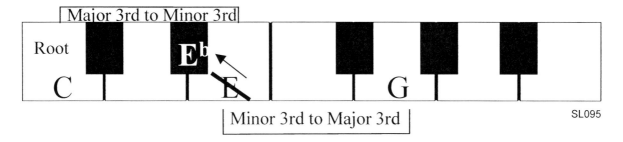

MAJOR AND MINOR TRIADS IN THE MAJOR SCALE
In a major scale, only triads with the roots on the 1st, 4th, and 5th scale degrees are *major triads.* Triads with the root on the 2nd, 3rd and 6th scale degrees are *minor triads.*

MAJOR TRIADS	MINOR TRIADS
I , IV & V	II, III & VI

C Major Scale

| MAJOR | MINOR | MINOR | MAJOR | MAJOR | MINOR | DIMINISHED | SL096 |

INVERSIONS

The same rules apply to **Minor chords**. If the root (chord name) is the lowest note of the chord, it is said to be in the **root** position. If the minor third is the lowest note, it is in the **First** inversion. If the fifth is the lowest note, it is in the **Second** inversion.

C MINOR CHORD (ROOT)

SL094

C MINOR CHORD (1ST INVERSION)

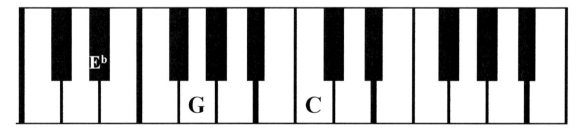

SL094a

C MINOR CHORD (2ND INVERSION)

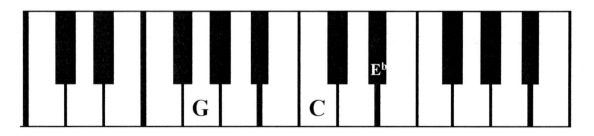

SL095a

MINOR CHORDS

C MINOR

1st Inversion **Root Position** **Second Inversion**

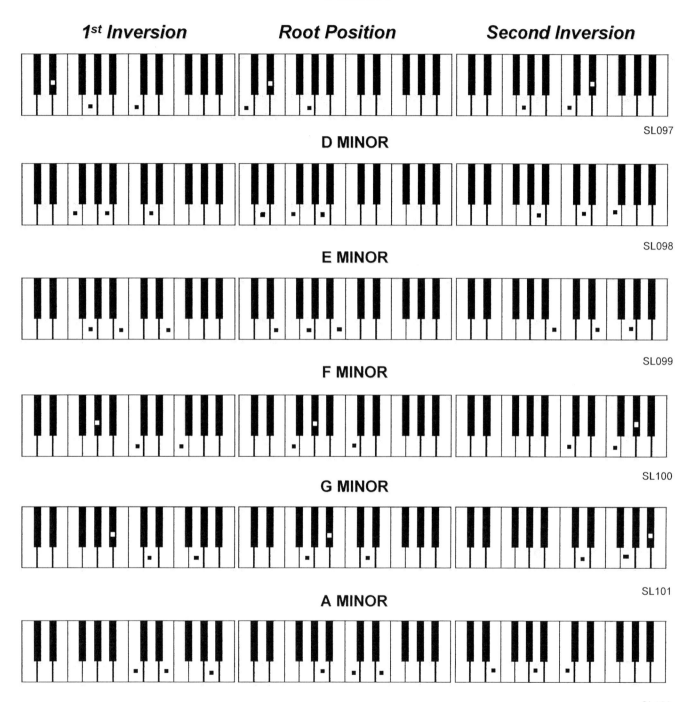

SL097

D MINOR

SL098

E MINOR

SL099

F MINOR

SL100

G MINOR

SL101

A MINOR

SL102

Notice: When a chord is played in it's **root position**, the keynote is always on the bottom. When a chord is played in it's **first inversion**, the keynote is always on the top. When a chord is played in it's **second inversion**, the keynote is always in the middle.

MINOR CHORDS (cont.)

B or C♭ MINOR

1st Inversion **Root Position** **Second Inversion**

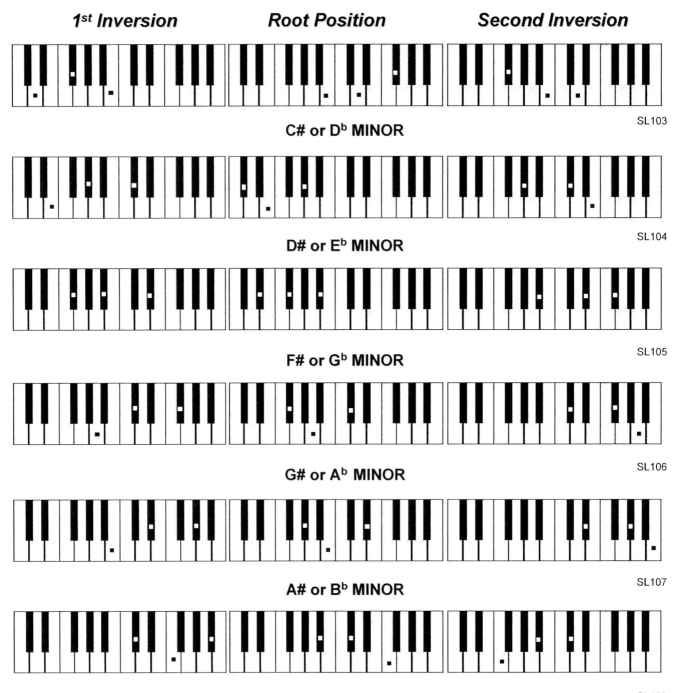

SL103

C# or D♭ MINOR

SL104

D# or E♭ MINOR

SL105

F# or G♭ MINOR

SL106

G# or A♭ MINOR

SL107

A# or B♭ MINOR

SL108

Note: I also recommend using the **"Piano Player Plus 1.0"** Software to test yourself on the different sounds of the minor chords and inversions. With this program, you will be able to build your ear skills by testing yourself on chords and inversions. The software program will keep track of your progress.

HearandPlay.com

EXERCISE 8.1

Answer the following questions:

1. Shade the root position of an E flat minor Chord

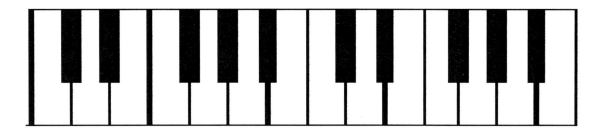

2. Shade the 2nd inversion of an F minor Chord

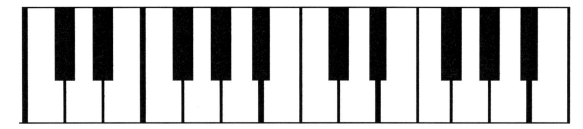

3. Shade the 1st inversion of a D minor chord

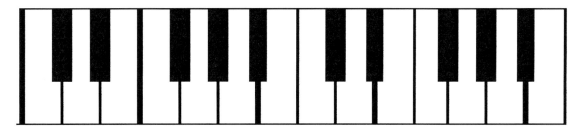

4. Shade the root position of a B flat minor chord

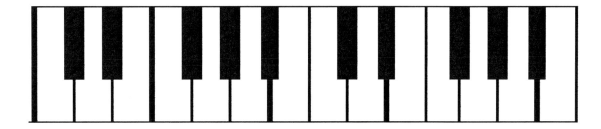

EXERCISE 8.2

Answer the following questions:

1. Play a C minor scale and describe it's mood below:

_____

_____

_____

2. Play a C minor chord followed by a C major chord. Compare the sounds of the two chords below:

_____

_____

_____

3. List songs that share this mood (minor chord):

_____

_____

_____

4. What are the three methods of forming a minor chord?

_____

_____

_____

5. What are six-toned chords called?

_____

6. What notes form a **D minor** chord (2nd Inversion)?

_____

Note: I also recommend using the **"Piano Player Plus 1.0"** Software to test yourself on the sounds of minor and major chords and inversions. With this program, you will be able to build your ear skills by testing yourself on the differences between major and minor chords. This will be very helpful in helping you distinguish the different chords in various songs and progression. Check it out!

PianoPlayerPlus.com

EXERCISE 8.3

Label the following chords

	CHORD NAME	INVERSION

EXERCISE 8.4
Label the following chords (Minor & Major chords ...)

	CHORD NAME	INVERSION

DIMINISHED CHORD

As you learned earlier, the word *diminished* means "made smaller." When a perfect or major interval is made smaller by a *half step*, it becomes a **DIMINISHED INTERVAL.** The Diminished Chord is a Minor Chord with the 5th made smaller by one half step. (Minor Chord shown below)

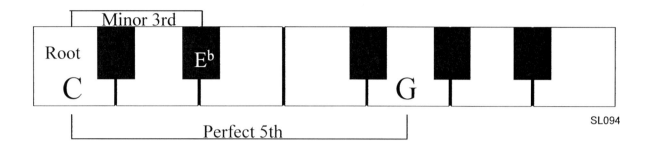

By simply *lowering* the 5th, a minor chord becomes a **Diminished Chord**

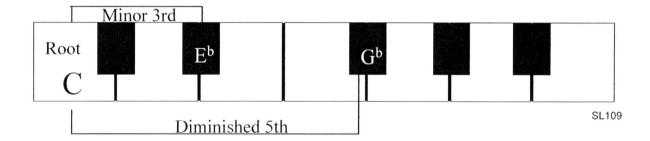

A **Diminished chord** consists of a minor third on a minor third:

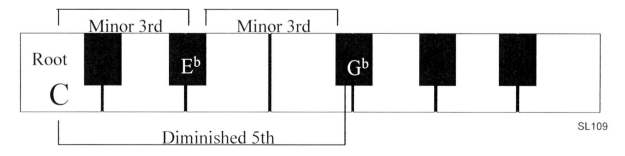

REMEMBER ...

Major = Major Third + Minor Third
Minor = Minor Third + Major Third
Diminished = Minor Third + Minor Third

101

EXERCISE 8.5

Draw the following diminished chords (root position):

C DIMINISHED

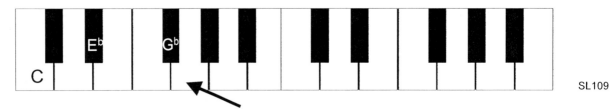

SL109

A *"C Minor"* scale with a lowered 5th note

D DIMINISHED

SL110

E DIMINISHED

SL111

F DIMINISHED

SL112

G DIMINISHED

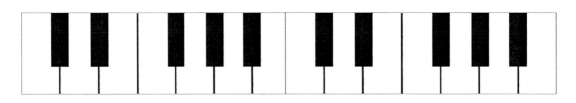

SL113

102

EXERCISE 8.6

Draw the following diminished chords (root position):

A DIMINISHED

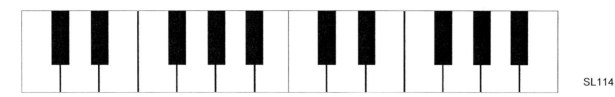

SL114

B DIMINISHED

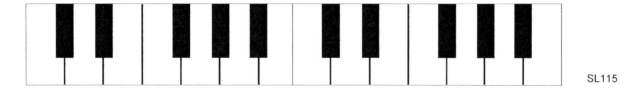

SL115

C# / D♭ DIMINISHED

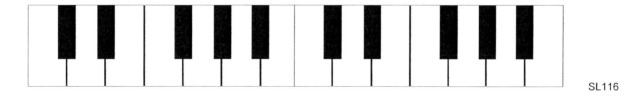

SL116

D# / E♭ DIMINISHED

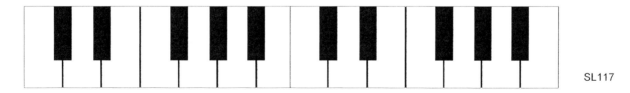

SL117

F# / G♭ DIMINISHED

SL118

EXERCISE 8.7

Draw the following diminished chords (root position):

G# / A♭ DIMINISHED

SL119

A# / B♭ DIMINISHED

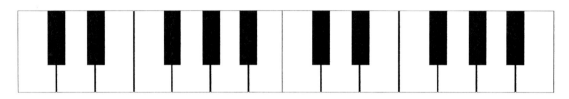

SL120

EXERCISE 8.8

Describe the sound of a diminished chord:

_____

_____

_____

How does a diminished chord differ from a major or minor chord?

_____

_____

_____

How is a minor chord transformed into a diminished chord?

_____

_____

Which diminished triad is formed by three white keys?

_____

Lesson Nine

"Minor, Diminished & Major Chord Progressions"

In this lesson, we will study **minor, diminished and major chord progressions.** In previous lessons, you've already learned how to form and invert minor, diminished and major chords. In this lesson, we will use these various chords to create usable progressions.

CHORD PROGRESSIONS

You've already learned various chord progressions that deal only with major chords. As you know, each tone of the scale corresponds with a different type of chord. The **I**, **IV & V** tones correspond with the major chord while the **ii, iii & vi** tones correspond with the minor chord. The seventh tone is the only degree of the scale that corresponds to the diminished chord.

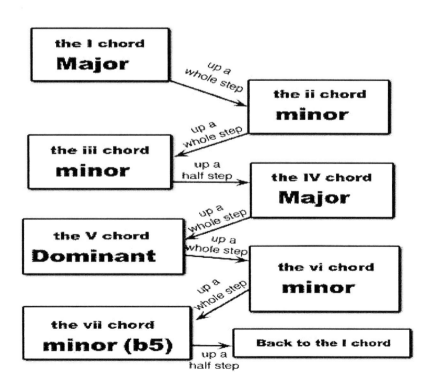

WHY DO CERTAIN TONES OF THE SCALE CORRESPOND WITH DIFFERENT CHORDS?

Consider a **C Major Scale:**

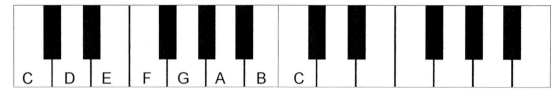

By taking every other note of the scale (starting on C), **we form a C Major Chord**

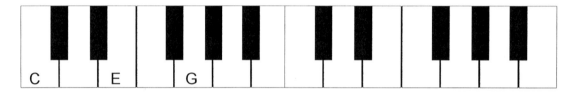

This is also true for <u>all</u> other major scales. Thus, the (1) degree of a scale is always associated with the major chord.

IV & V Degree
The fourth and fifth degree of a scale also form major chords. Thus, they are also associated with the major chord:

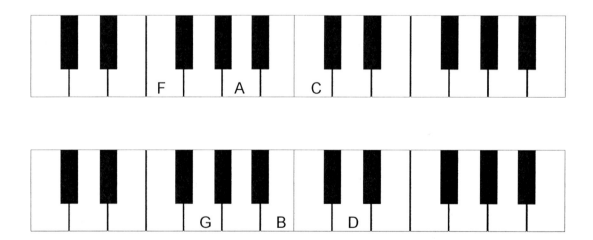

However, by starting on the 2nd degree (D), taking every other note of the scale, we form a **D Minor Chord.**

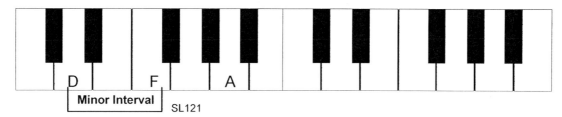

SL121

In order for this chord to be major, the "F" must be "F#" instead (to satisfy the "major third" rule). Since the first interval is minor (from D -- F), the chord is considered a minor chord.

iii & vi Degree

This is also true for the 3rd and 6th degree of any major scale:

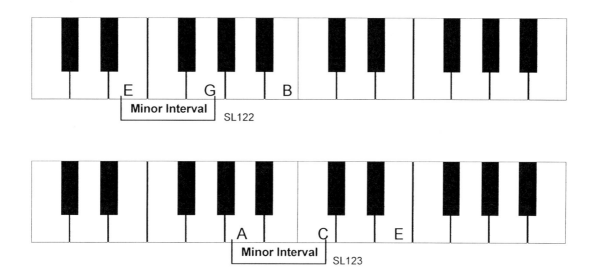

SL122

SL123

vii Degree

When starting on the 7th degree, it is the only tone in the scale that does not create a major or minor chord:

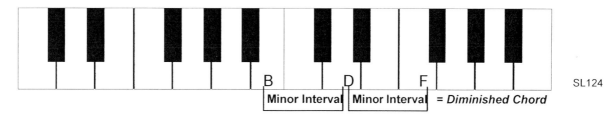

SL124

Therefore, the **vii degree** of a scale is always associated with the diminished chord.

CHORDS OF A MAJOR SCALE ... [In C Major]

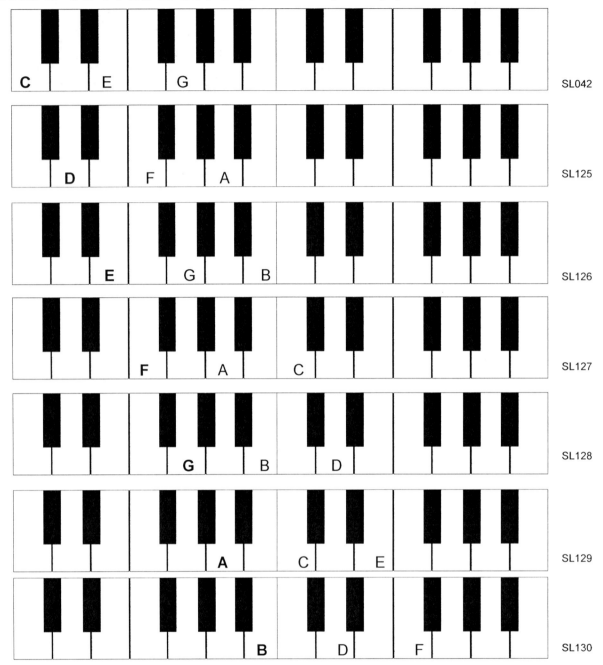

SL042

SL125

SL126

SL127

SL128

SL129

SL130

Cmaj	Dmin	Emin	Fmaj	Gmaj	Amin	Bº	Cmaj
1	2	3	4	5	6	7	8

SL131

SCALE DEGREE NAMES

Each tone of a scale can be identified by a name as well as by a **numbered** scale degree. The most important scale degrees are the same as those on which the primary chords are built: 1, 4 and 5. The three most important scale degree names are the **Tonic (I), Subdominant (IV)** and **Dominant (V).**

TONIC (I)

The keynote of a scale is called the **TONIC**. It is the lowest and highest tone of the scale. Since the tonic is the **1st** degree, it is given the Roman numeral **I**. In C major, C is the tonic note or chord.

DOMINANT (V) and SUBDOMINANT (IV)

The tone a 5th **above** the tonic is called the **DOMINANT**. Since the dominant is the **5th** scale degree, it is given the Roman numeral **V**. In C major, G is the dominant note (or dominant chord).

The tone a 5th **below** the tonic is called the **SUBDOMINANT**. Since the subdominant is the **4th** scale degree, it is given the Roman numeral **IV**. In C major, F is the subdominant note or chord. The prefix "sub" means under or below.

MEDIANT (III) and SUBMEDIANT (VI)

The tone a 3rd degree **above** the tonic (midway between the tonic and the dominant) is called the MEDIANT (a Latin word meaning "in the middle"). Since the mediant is the **3rd** scale degree, it is given the Roman numeral **III**. In C major, E is the mediant note or chord.

The tone a 3rd degree **below** the tonic (midway between the tonic and the subdominant) is called the **SUBMEDIANT**. Since the submediant is the **6th** scale degree, it is given the Roman numeral **VI**. In C major, A is the submediant note or chord.

EXERCISES

There are several exercises available on the **"Piano Player Plus 1.0"** Software to test yourself on the different scale degree names and sounds. With this program, you will be able to build your ear skills by testing yourself on various chords, inversions, rhythms, and key signatures.

HearandPlay.com

SUPERTONIC (II) and LEADING TONE (VII)

The tone a 2nd degree **above** the tonic is called the **SUPERTONIC**. Since the supertonic is the **2nd** scale degree, it is given the Roman numeral **II**. In C Major, D is the supertonic note or chord. The prefix "super" means over or above.

The tone a 2nd degree **below** the tonic is called the **LEADING TONE** - sometimes called the **SUBTONIC**. Leading tone is most often used since the note has a strong tendency to "lead" to the tonic, as it does in an ascending scale. Since the leading tone is the **7th** scale degree, it is given the Roman numeral **VII**. In C major, B is the leading tone or chord.

In scale degree order, the name and Roman numeral of each scale tone is:

| TONIC | SUPERTONIC | MEDIANT | SUBDOMINANT | DOMINANT | S UBMEDIANT | LEADING TONE |

USING SCALE DEGREE TO DETERMINE THE *KEY CENTRE* OF A SONG

The tonic (I) chord establishes the **key center** (the key in which a song is played in…)

The best method for finding the key center of a progression of chords is to list possible keys to which each chord can belong.

Consider the following chord progression:

Dmin --Gmaj -- C maj -- A min -- Dmin -- Gmaj -- C maj   SL132

a)   First, we can look at the ending chord. The ending chord can be a useful clue to finding what key a song is played in. However, not all songs end on the Tonic, or "I" chord. Therefore, this rule alone cannot be used to effectively find the key of a song (some exceptions apply).

b)   Next, we can look at the type of chords that are used. Since we know that a **minor** chord falls on the ii, iii, & vi degree, this can hint us to possible keys. The following chart can better help us understand the use of certain chords in various progressions …

Tonic Chord	**I** chord of a particular key. It's keynote is also the **key center**.	Example: *A song ending on Dmaj.*
Minor Chords	**ii** chord of one key, the **iii** of a second key, or the **vi** of a third key.	Example: A **Dmin** chord could be the **ii** chord in a **C** major chord progression, the **iii** chord in a **B♭ major** chord progression, or the **vi** chord in an **F** major chord progression.
Major Chords	**I** chord of one key, the **IV** of a second key, or the **V** of a third key.	Example: A **Gmaj** chord could be the **I** (or tonic) in a **G major** chord progression, the **IV** chord in a **D major** chord progression, or the **V** chord in a **C major** chord progression.
Diminished Chord x°	**Vii** chord of a particular key. Also known as the *leading tone* to the tonic.	Example: A song with a **D°** chord leading to an **E♭** major chord is most likely to have **E♭** as the key center because the vii chord usually leads back to the I chord.

c)   After observing what chords are in the progression, we can now look for certain progressions (as you will learn many in this course). For example, a G7 (haven't learned it yet) to a Cmaj7 chord hints us to think that the song is in C major because of the dominant G chord. An Emin -- Amin -- Dmin --G7 (dominant) -- Cmaj would let us know that the song is most likely in C major because **C major** is the only key that has an E min, A min, Dmin, G7 and a Cmaj chord in one scale.

d)   To confirm that we have chosen the right **key center**, we can hold down the key center while playing the chord progression. Using our ear, the key center should sound like a perfect match to the chord progression. There isn't too much more principle to this technique than simply using your ear to verify that the key center *matches* the chord progression.

I also recommend using the **"Piano Player Plus 1.0"** Software to test yourself on finding the **key center** of a song. With this program, you will be able to select random songs and chord progressions while using your ear to depict which key the song or progression is being played in. Very helpful when trying to build your ear-skills!

PianoPlayerPlus.com

EXERCISE 9.1

Answer the following questions ...

1. What tones of the major scale are associated with the minor chord?

_____

_____

2. What tones of the major scale are associated with the major chord?

_____

_____

3. Summarize the different scale degree names below:

_____

_____

_____

_____

_____

_____

_____

4. Summarize the technique of using scale degree to determine the key center of a song:

_____

_____

_____

_____

_____

_____

_____

5. If B♭, C & F were all minor chords in a particular scale, what would the suggest key center be?

_____

EXERCISE 9.2

Complete the following table...

The *Key Center* is listed below. Simply insert the tones that are minor, major and diminished for each scale in the table below:

Minor Chords	Major Chords	Diminished Chord	Key Center
E, A, D	C, F, G	B	**C**
			G
			F
			A
			B
			D
			E
			F#
			E^b
			D^b
			G#
			Bb

"2 – 5 – 1" Chord Progression

You have already studied the "5 -1" chord progression:

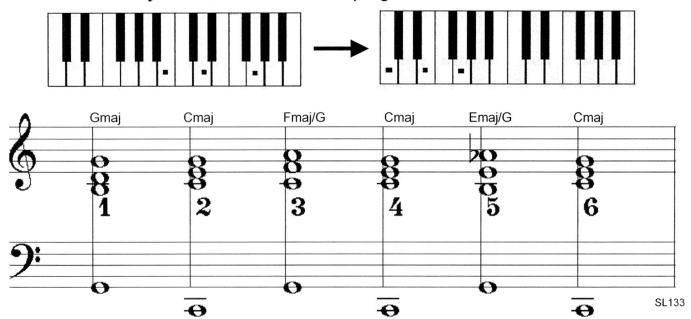

We will now use our knowledge of the different scale degrees to play a very well known progression called "2 – 5 – 1."

We know that the V chord creates a sound which pulls us toward the tonic (I) chord. Now the question is, "what pulls us toward the dominant chord?"

DOMINANT PREPERATION

When a particular chord pulls us toward a dominant chord, it is known as a **dominant preparation**. It is called the **dominant preparation** because it "prepares" us for the **V** chord.

The "ii – V - I" chord progressions gives a perfect example of the **ii** chord acting as a preparer to the **V** chord which acts as a dominant to the **I** chord. In other words, the ii connects to the V chord which conclusively connects back to the tonic chord (I).

The following chart shows some of the most common chord relationships ….

ii (supertonic) ⟶	V (dominant)
iii (mediant) ⟶	vi (submediant)
vii (leading tone) ⟶	iii (mediant)

Families of Chords

> **Tonic -- the tonal center**
> I (i), or vi (VI) following a V
>
> **Dominant -- points to the tonal center**
> V or vii°, or related 7th chords
>
> **Dominant preparation -- points to dominant**
> ii (ii°), IV (iv), or vi (VI) preceding a V

Harmonic Direction

Tonic is the point of repose (last)

That is, the tonic chord (I) is usually the "resting" chord; the chord that ends the song or provides the "desired" sound during a certain part of a song or progression.

Dominant precedes Tonic

The dominant chord (V) usually comes before the tonic (or some other type of variation that points back to the tonic). It provides an unsettling feeling that is fulfilled only when the tonic chord is played after.

Dominant preparation implies Dominant

The dominant preparation (ii, iv, or vii) leads to the dominant. For example, in a "2-5-1" progression, the 2 acts as a dominant preparation.

Thus, the serial order of chords in a *functional* progression is :

> Dominant Preparation --Dominant --Tonic

USING 2 – 5 – 1 TO RESOLVE TO THE TONIC

In the key of C major, a "ii – V – I" progression would simply be the chords that fall on each of those scale degrees. (D -- G -- C)

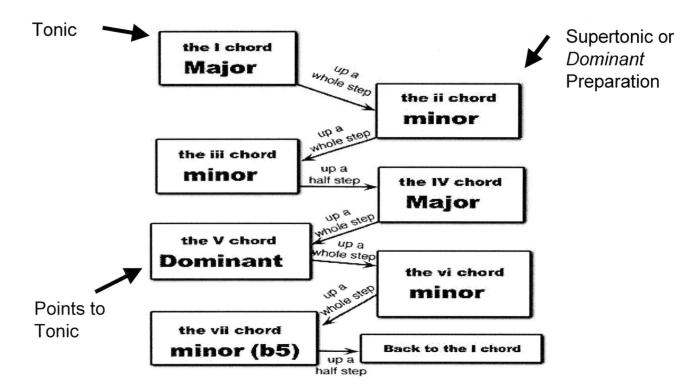

Tonic

Supertonic or *Dominant* Preparation

Points to Tonic

Since the **ii** is a minor chord, the **V** is a major (dominant) chord, and the **I** is a major chord, the following progression shows a "2-5-1" in C major:

Dmin -- Gdom -- Cmaj

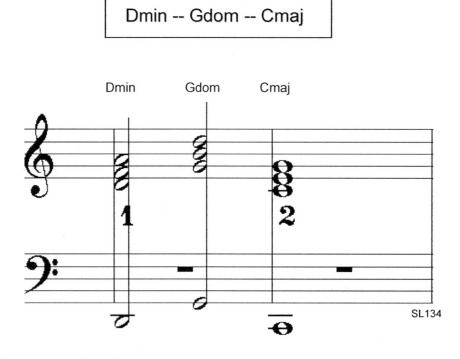

SL134

Try playing a 2-5-1 progression. Note what songs you've heard this type of progression in. If possible, try to find the key center of a song and play the 2-5-1 progression in the appropriate key.

EXERCISE 9.3
Answer the following questions

1.What is a Dominant Preparation?

_____

_____

_____

2. Name three of the most common chord relationships:

_____

_____

_____

3. List the family of chords and explain their functions:

_____

_____

_____

4. What is the order of chords in a functional progression?

_____

_____

_____

5. List the correct scale degrees in the key of B♭ for the chord progression below:

_____ min -- _____ dom -- _____ maj

6. What chord would be a dominant preparation in the key of F major?

_____

EXERCISE 9.4

One chord will be displayed (I, ii or V chord). Draw the missing chords of the "2-5-1" progression below:

"ii" Chord	"V" Chord	"I" Chord

As you've noticed, playing from a ii min chord (root position) to a V maj chord can be rather strenuous (especially when playing at fast tempos).

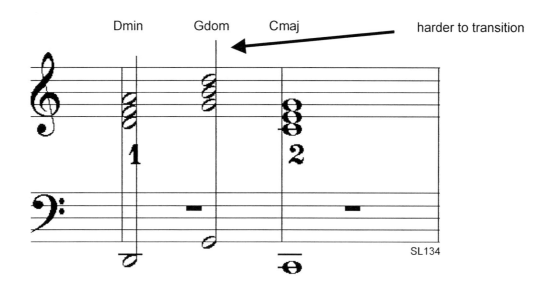

By simply using the 1st inversion for the *ii* chord and the 2nd inversion for the *I* chord, the progression becomes more smoother and easier to play (you will learn the minor seventh chord later which will be used mostly in playing this progression).

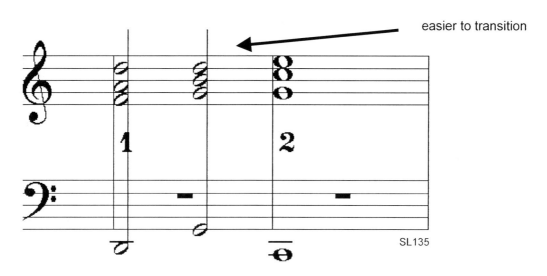

EXERCISE 9.5

One chord will be displayed (I, ii or V chord). **Draw the missing chords of the "2-5-1" progression below using the easiest** *inversions*:

"ii" Chord	"V" Chord	"I" Chord

"6 – 2 – 5 - 1" Chord Progression

You have already studied the "5 -1" and "2-5-1" chord progressions:

Types of Root Progressions

•A progression of chords that ends with the tonic is a *closing progression*

•A progression that moves away from the tonic (generally toward the dominant) is an *opening progression*

•A progression that begins and ends with chords from the same family is a *circular progression*

The **"6-2-5-1" is considered a circular progression** because the **vi** leads to the **ii** which leads to the **v** which pulls back to the **I** (or tonic chord).

| TONIC | SUPERTONIC | MEDIANT | SUBDOMINANT | DOMINANT | S UBMEDIANT | LEADING TONE |

"6 – 2 – 5 – 1" = *Submediant -- Supertonic -- Dominant -- Tonic*

Since, we've already played the "2-5-1" progression in C major, by simply adding the vi chord (minor), we can play the "6 – 2 – 5 – 1" progression…

It is also common to place a I chord before the 6th tone with either the 1st degree or the 5th degree as the bass note.

For example, in C major:

> Cmaj / G -- A min -- Dmin -- Gdom -- Cmaj

SL136

I recommend using the **"Piano Player Plus 1.0"** Software to test yourself on the different chord progressions. With this program, you will be able to select random chord progressions while using your ear to depict which progression it is. You will also be able to listen to each progression as you attempt to play along. I cannot stress how helpful this tool is when trying to build your ear-skills!

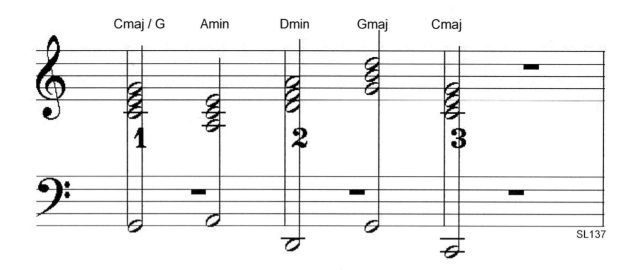

"3 – 6 – 2 – 5 – 1" Chord Progression

Another circular progression which is similar to the "6-2-5-1" progression simply adds another iii chord (minor) before playing the vi (minor):

"3 – 6 – 2 – 5 – 1" = *Mediant -- Submediant -- Supertonic -- Dominant -- Tonic*

ii (supertonic) →	V (dominant)
iii (mediant) →	vi (submediant)
vii (leading tone) →	iii (mediant)

As you can see, this chord progression satisfies the chart above. That is, the Mediant points to the Submediant, the Supertonic to the Dominant, and the Dominant to the Tonic. We will also study a progression which involves the vii chord later.

In C major, this progression would look like this:

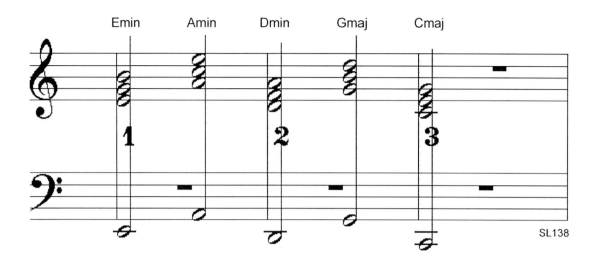

SL138

THESE PROGRESSIONS FOLLOW THE SAME PATTERN AS THE CIRCLE OF FIFTHS DON'T THEY?

If you've already picked up on that, you're absolutely right. Each tone is the dominant of the next. That is, E is the dominant of A major; A is the dominant of D major; D is the dominant of G major; and G is the dominant of C major …

Because dominant chords have a strong pull towards the tonic, it is normal for these chords to have strong pulls toward each other even though neither of them are the tonic of this particular key (only C is the tonic in this case). However, in their own key, these same notes would be their dominant tone:

For example, in A major, E is the **dominant** tone. However, in C major, E is the **mediant** which leads to the **submediant** (A). In both cases, these notes have strong ties. That is why "2-5-1", "6-2-5-1", and "3-6-5-2-1" all work the same way.

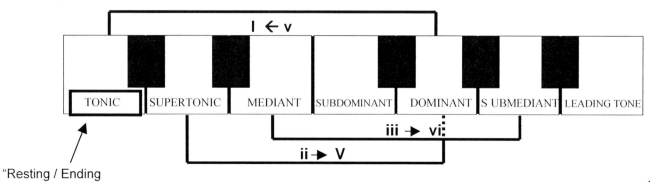

"Resting / Ending Chord"

Note: We will study different *styles* of these progressions in further lessons... (jazz, gospel...)

"7 – 3 – 6 – 2 – 5 – 1 " **Chord Progression** (C Major)

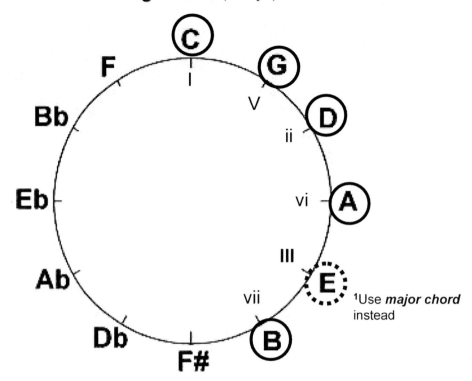

This progression is common in Gospel music

Bdim -- E*maj*[1] -- Amin -- Dmin -- Gdom -- C maj

SL139

This progression is basically a huge turn around starting with the leading tone: From the leading tone to the mediant; from the submediant to the supertonic, from the dominant to the tonic.

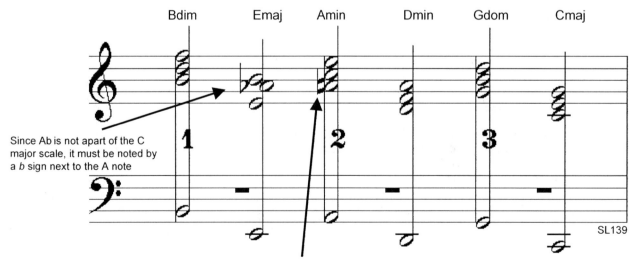

Since Ab is not apart of the C major scale, it must be noted by a *b* sign next to the A note

Symbolizing "A" natural since the "A" was flatted in the last measure

124

EXERCISE 9.6

Complete the charts below filling in the missing chords for each progression …

KEY	"iii"	"vi"	"ii"	"V"	"I"
C	E – G – B	A – C – E	D – F – A	G – B – D	C – E – G
D	F# – A – C#	B – D – F#	E – G – B	A – C# – E	D – F# – A
E	G# – B – D#	C# – E – G#	F# – A – C#	B – D# – F#	E – G# - B
F	A – C – E	D – F – A	G – Bᵇ – D	C – E – G	F – A – C
G	B – D – F#	E – G – B	A – C – E	D – F# - A	G – B – D
A	C# – E – G#	F# – A – C#	B – D – F#	E – G# – B	A – C# – E
B	D# – F# – A#	G# – B – D#	C# – E – G#	F# – A# – C#	B – D# – F#
C# / Dᵇ	F – Aᵇ – C	Bᵇ – Dᵇ – F	Eᵇ – Gᵇ – Bᵇ	Aᵇ – C – Eᵇ	C# - F – G#
D# / Eᵇ	G – Bᵇ – D	C – Eᵇ – G	F – Aᵇ – C	Bᵇ – D – F	Eᵇ – G – Bᵇ
F# / Gᵇ	Bᵇ – Dᵇ – F	Eᵇ – Gᵇ – Bᵇ	Aᵇ – Cᵇ – Eᵇ	Dᵇ – F – Aᵇ	Gᵇ – Bᵇ – Dᵇ
G# / Aᵇ	C – Eᵇ – G	F – Aᵇ – C	Bᵇ – Dᵇ – F	Eᵇ – G – Bᵇ	Aᵇ – C – Eᵇ
A# / Bᵇ	D – F – A	G – Bᵇ – D	C – Eᵇ – G	F – A – C	Bᵇ – D – F

EXERCISE 9.7

What are the three types of root progressions?

_____

_____

What are the differences between the "2 – 5 – 1" -- "6 – 2 – 5 – 1" -- "3 – 6 – 2 – 5 – 1", and "7 – 3 – 6 – 2 – 5 – 1" progressions?

_____

_____

_____

_____

_____

More Chord Progressions...

You've already studied the following chord progressions:

- 1-4-1-5-1
- 1-4-5-4-1
- 5-1
- 1-5
- 1-4
- 2-5-1
- 6-2-5-1
- 3-6-2-5-1
- 7-3-6-2-5-1

We will explore a few more chord progressions in this lesson ...

IVm -- I

Similar to the V -- I progression with the IV degree over the V-bass, this progression takes the minor chord of the IV degree over the V-bass. For example, in C major, we would simply take the subdominant chord (F major) and change it to a minor chord (F minor). The bass will remain the V note (~G).

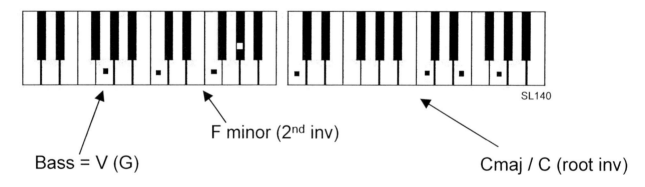

Bass = V (G)

F minor (2nd inv)

SL140

Cmaj / C (root inv)

Variations of the bass

This progression can use various bass notes. Try the following alternatives and choose which one you would prefer to use:

a) Hold the "I" as the bass note for both chords (in this case "C"). -- Used in gospel and worship chord progressions

b) Use D as the first bass note and G as the other. -- Similar to 2-5-1 progression. However, from the G, use another transition such as V -- I to resolve to the tonic chord.

IVm -- I (cont.)

Below are the different variations of the IVm -- I Chord Progression...

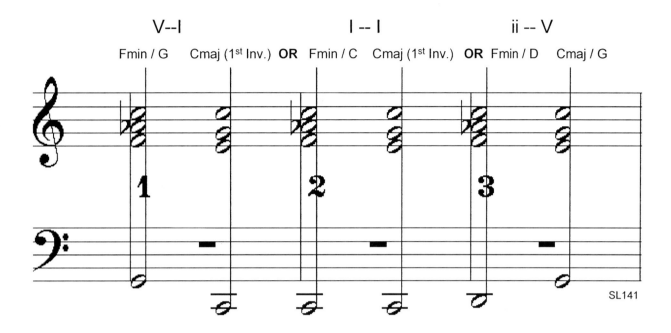

SL141

Gospel Chord Progression
The following progression is very common in up-tempo gospel praise songs. It is commonly used as a turn-around back to the tonic chord.

> vii -- iii -- vi -- ii -- v   -- proceed to "6-2-5-1" turn around...

SL142

I personally prefer altering a few of the chords above to produce more desired transitions. Because we haven't covered seventh chords yet, I will show you some of these alterations <u>just</u> using triads. We will use the key of C major as an example:

Note: The bass notes for this progression will never change. That is, the vii will always be the seventh degree (B), the iii will be E, and so on. However, the chords played on top of those bass notes may be altered as I am about to show you.

vii -- iii -- vi -- ii -- v   -- proceed to "6-2-5-1" turn around…

ALTERATIONS

vii – play the **vi** (minor) chord (root position) over the **vii** bass. This leads to the next chord much smoother than playing the **vii** (diminished chord). However, the diminished chord can be used in some situations.

iii – play the **IVm** (F min; 1st inversion) chord over the iii bass. I find that this chord is a better "*puller*" towards the "vi" chord. However, the iii minor chord can be used in some situations as well as the iii (major) chord to pull towards the vi minor chord.

vi – no alterations. Simply play the sixth chord (minor) in root position

ii – For this chord, play the **IVm** (F min) chord over the **ii** bass. Yes, you'll be playing the **IVm** chord twice. Once, over the **iii** bass, and the second time over the **ii** bass.

same chord *same chord*

Why *can* this chord lead both to the **vi** and the **v?** Because, when played over the right bass, it becomes a "puller" towards the next chord of the "circle." (B -- E -- A -- D -- G … "circle of fifths")

V – For the V chord, play a "I" chord. So, if you're going to play an F min (1st Inv) on the **ii** chord, the easiest "I" chord would be **C** maj (2nd Inv). Usually, the V chord would act as a dominant but not in this case. For this progression, it will act as a *connector* to another progression (which will use the dominant V chord).

Remember, when we studied the "6-2-5-1" progression and noted that it is usually played after a major "I" chord on the V degree? Well, C maj (2nd Inv.) / G serves as the starting point for the "6-2-5-1" progression which will eventually pull us back towards the tonic chord.

6-2-5-1 Alterations
The only chord I usually alter is the "2" (or ii). Instead of playing the "ii" as a minor chord, I usually play it as a major chord. That is, instead of D min -- G maj, I use D maj -- Gmaj.

In actuality, the Dmaj chord in this example is serving as a dominant chord to the Gmaj chord. But since Gmaj is not the tonic (in this case), we call Dmaj a **Secondary Dominant** chord because it serves as a dominant chord to another chord.

6-2-5-1 Alterations (cont.)

Another option is to use the #IV chord as a **Secondary Diminished** Chord.

> **Secondary Diminished of V:** is a diminished chord built on scale degree #4, a half step below the dominant. Like **secondary dominants**, secondary *diminished* chords function as embellishing chords in a harmonic progression.

a) Simply take the **#IV** tone (**F#**) and form a diminished chord. If you remember, diminished chords are formed by adding a minor third on top of a minor third. In other words, by starting on **F#**, simply count a **3-half step** interval followed by another **3-half step** interval.

Here's an example of a **C**dim chord:

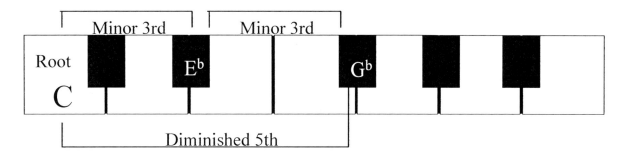

b) Simply play the #4 diminished chord over the **ii** bass. This will create a strong pull towards the dominant chord which will resolve to the **tonic chord.** This is commonly used in all types of gospel progressions.

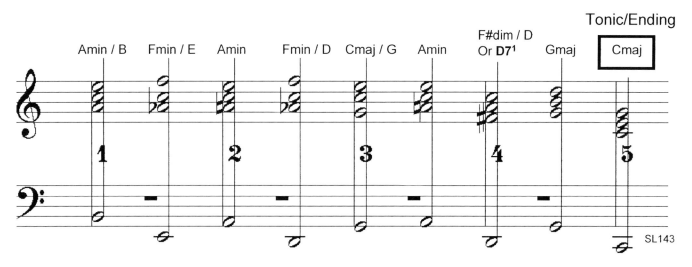

[1] D7 (D Seventh Chord): You will learn this chord in further lessons...

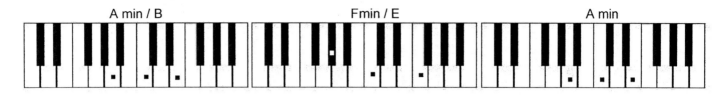

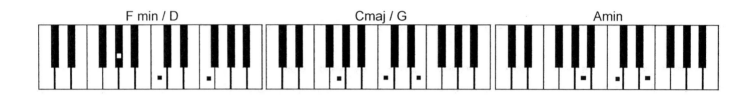

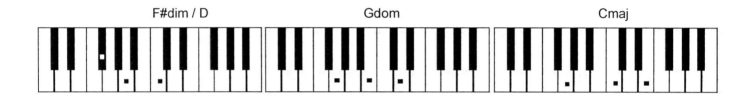

GOSPEL SONGS THAT USE THIS CHORD PROGRESSION

All of these songs are similar in that they share the same type of chord progressions (especially the endings of each song).

Note: Most of these songs are up-beat.

"Can't Nobody Do Me Like Jesus"
"Victory, Victory Shall be Mines"
"I've got a Feeling"
"Praise Him"
"Glory, Glory, Hallelujah"
"Jesus is on the main line"
"Stayed on Jesus"

Try listening to these songs and depicting where the "7-3-2-5 -- 6-2-5-1" progression comes in.

Note: I also recommend using the **"Piano Player Plus 1.0"** Software to listen and test yourself on different chord progressions. With this program, you will be able to build your ear skills by testing yourself on chords progressions and alterations.

Lesson Ten

"Major, Minor & Dominant Seventh Chords"

In this lesson, we will study the **major, minor and dominant seventh chord.** In previous lessons, you've already learned how to form and invert minor, diminished and major triads. In this lesson, we will advance to playing four-toned chords called **Sevenths.**

# of notes	Type of Chord
Three	Triad
Four	Seventh
Five	Ninth
Six	Eleventh
Seven	Thirteenth

"The Seventh Chord"

As you've already learned, the **V** is known as the **Dominant Chord** (or Seventh Chord)

For example, in C major, the dominant tone is **G.** It is also major because the dominant is also a primary chord. The **G major** chord is: G – B – D.

To build a dominant seventh chord, simply add a **minor 3rd to a dominant triad** (or major chord):

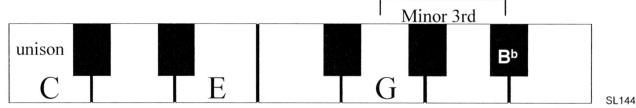

SL144

DOMINANT + MINOR THIRD = DOMINANT 7th

In the key of **C major,** by simply adding a **minor third** to the dominant chord (G), a **dominant seventh chord is created:**

MAJOR THIRD + MINOR THIRD + MINOR THIRD
= **DOMINANT SEVENTH CHORD**

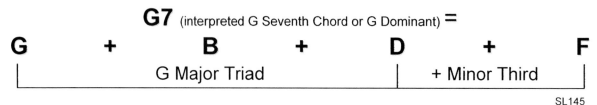

G7 (interpreted G Seventh Chord or G Dominant) =

G	**+**	**B**	**+**	**D**	**+**	**F**
		G Major Triad			+ Minor Third	

SL145

G SEVENTH CHORD

132

"The Seventh Chord" (cont.)

Here is a short-cut to playing a dominant seventh chord in any key:

a) Locate the dominant tone in the scale (V)
b) Add the IV note to the V major chord

For example, in C major, the **V** chord is G major. The **VI** tone is **F**. By simply adding **F** to a **Gmaj** chord, a **G7** chord is created:

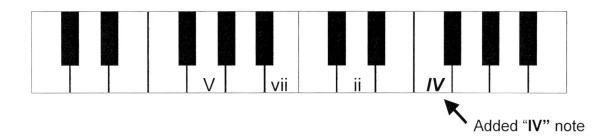

Added "**IV**" note

G7

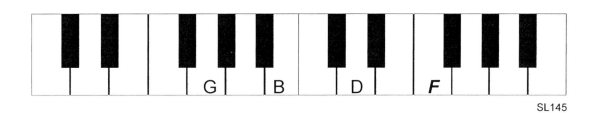

SL145

Note: The V7 chord functions just like the V chord. In fact, it creates an *even* stronger pull towards the tonic as you will notice in later lessons.

EXERCISE 10.1
Fill in the following chart

V7	1st tone	2nd tone	3rd tone	4th tone
G	G	B	D	F
E				
D			A	
A				
Bb		D		
Ab				
C				
D#				C#

133

DOMINANT SEVENTH CHORDS

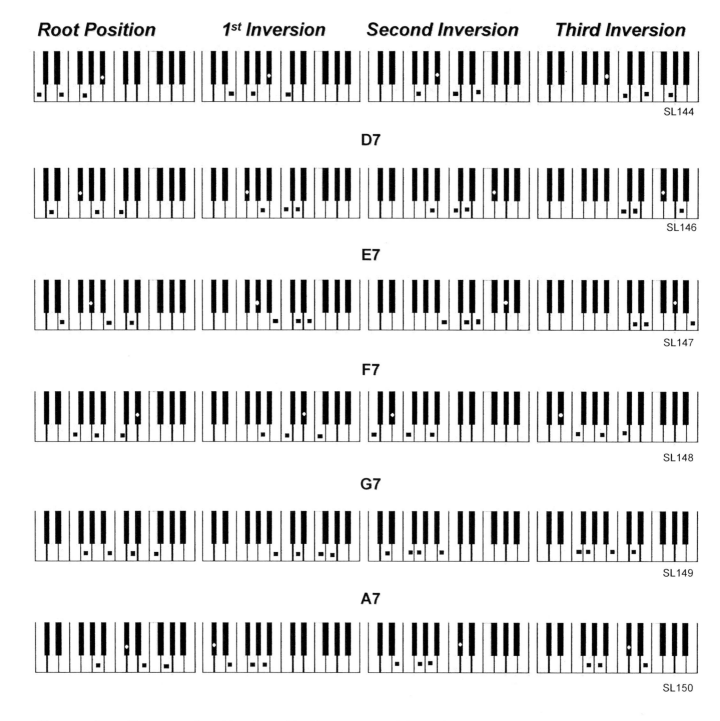

C7

Root Position   **1st Inversion**   **Second Inversion**   **Third Inversion**

SL144

D7

SL146

E7

SL147

F7

SL148

G7

SL149

A7

SL150

Remember: When a chord is played in it's **root position**, the keynote is always on the bottom. When a chord is played in it's **first inversion**, the keynote is always on the top. When a chord is played in it's **second inversion**, the keynote is always in the middle. When a chord is played in it's **third inversion**, the seventh is always on the bottom.

134

DOMINANT SEVENTH CHORDS (cont.)

B7 or C♭7

Root Position **1st Inversion** **Second Inversion** **Third Inversion**

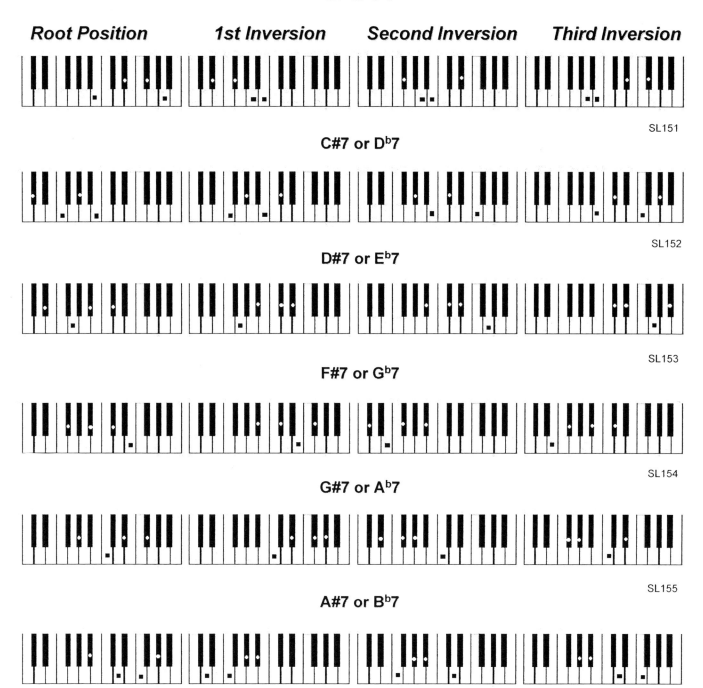

SL151

C#7 or D♭7

SL152

D#7 or E♭7

SL153

F#7 or G♭7

SL154

G#7 or A♭7

SL155

A#7 or B♭7

SL156

Note: I also recommend using the **"Piano Player Plus 1.0"** Software to test yourself on the sounds of the different seventh chords and inversions. With this program, you will be able to build your ear skills by testing yourself on chords and inversions. The software program will keep track of your progress.

PianoPlayerPlus.com

Exercises 10.2

1. Shade the root position of an A7 Chord

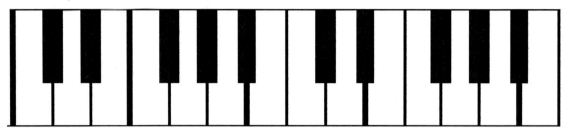

2. Shade the 2nd inversion of an F#7 Chord

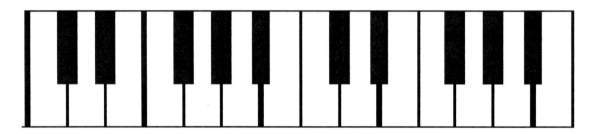

3. Shade the 1st inversion of a D7 chord

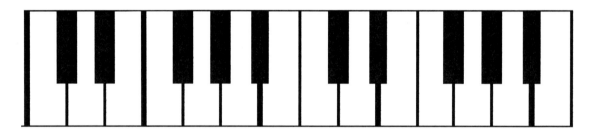

4. Shade the root position of an E$\flat$7 chord

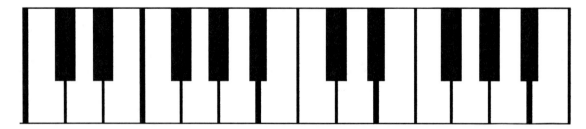

"The Major Seventh Chord"
The Major Seventh Chord is very similar to the Dominant Seventh Chord

The Dominant Seventh Chord:

•a dominant chord (also a *major chord*) with an added minor 3rd

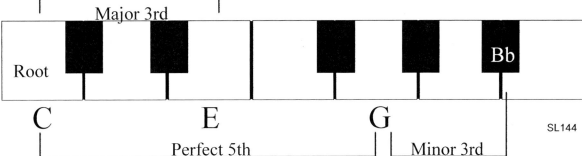

A **Major Seventh Chord** is a major triad with an added major 3rd:

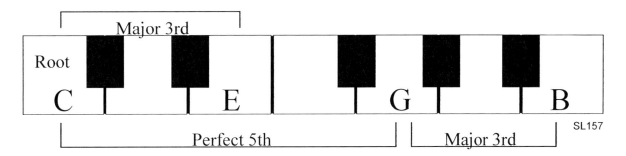

Note: In C and F major, this chord happens to be every other white note. In other keys, it will be a mixture of white and black keys. A **major seventh chord** will never consist of all black keys. However, a major triad *can* be all black keys (ex.-F# maj).

Major Seventh Chords are commonly associated with *"happy"* moods and chord progressions. Like major triads, they are also tonic and subdominant chords in a scale. Play a *C Major Seventh Chord* and write the *feeling* of the chord below:

_____

_____

_____

> MAJOR THIRD + MINOR THIRD + MAJOR THIRD
> = **MAJOR SEVENTH CHORD**

MAJOR SEVENTH CHORDS

Cmaj7

Root Position   **1st Inversion**   **Second Inversion**   **Third Inversion**

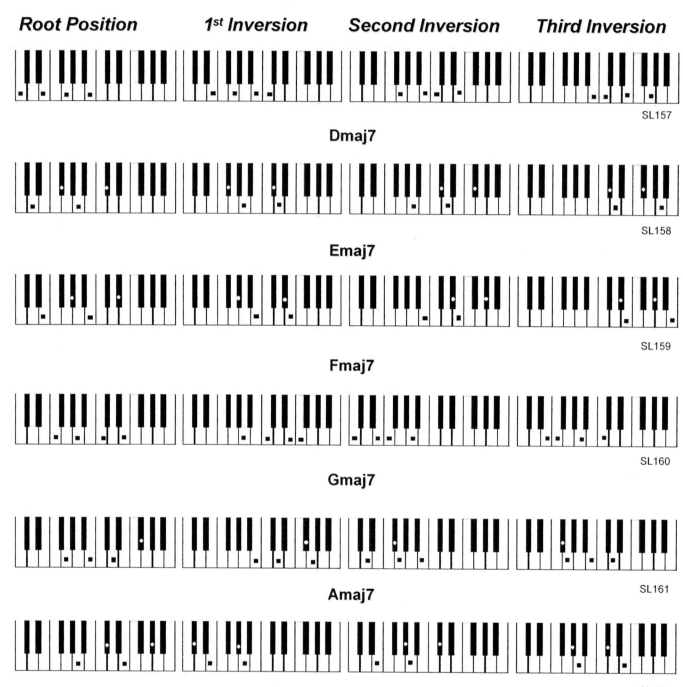

SL157

Dmaj7

SL158

Emaj7

SL159

Fmaj7

SL160

Gmaj7

SL161

Amaj7

SL162

Remember: When a chord is played in it's **root position**, the keynote is always on the bottom. When a chord is played in it's **first inversion**, the keynote is always on the top. When a chord is played in it's **second inversion**, the keynote is always in the middle. When a chord is played in it's **third inversion**, the seventh is always on the bottom.

MAJOR SEVENTH CHORDS (cont.)

Bmaj7 or Cbmaj7

Root Position	1st Inversion	Second Inversion	Third Inversion

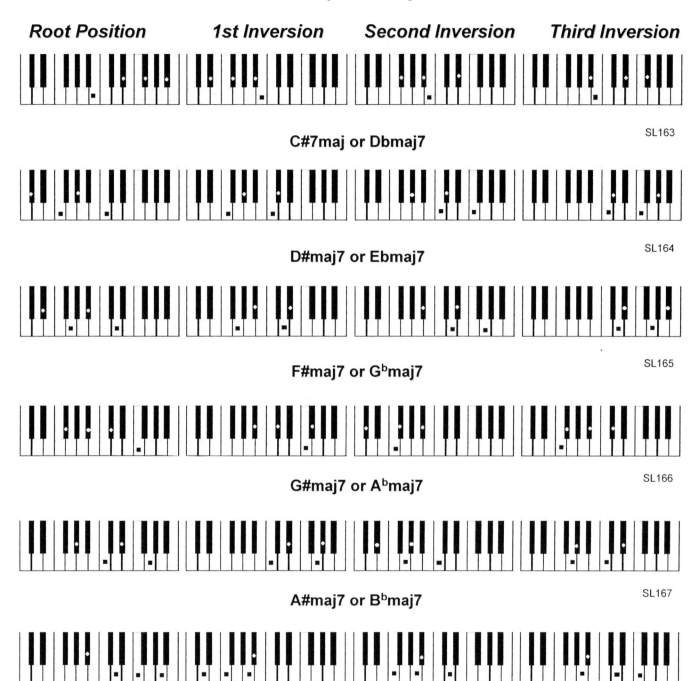

SL163

C#7maj or Dbmaj7

SL164

D#maj7 or Ebmaj7

SL165

F#maj7 or G♭maj7

SL166

G#maj7 or A♭maj7

SL167

A#maj7 or B♭maj7

SL168

Exercises 10.3

1. Shade the root position of a Bmaj7 Chord

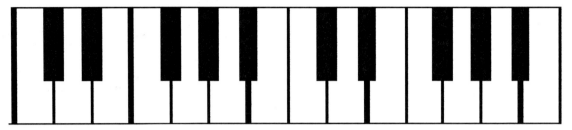

2. Shade the 2nd inversion of an E♭maj7 Chord

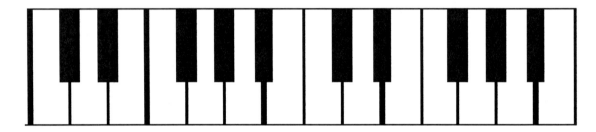

3. Shade the 1st inversion of a Gmaj7 chord

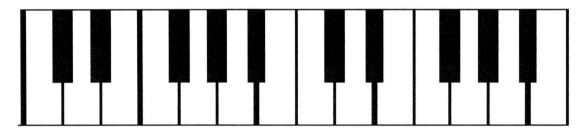

4. Shade the root position of an F#maj7 chord

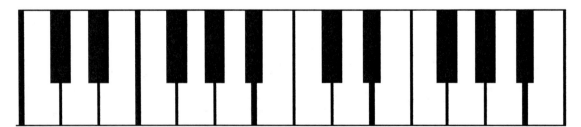

EXERCISE 10.4

Fill in the following chart

maj7	1st tone	2nd tone	3rd tone	4th tone
G				F#
E				
D				
A		C#		
Bb				
Ab			Eb	
C				
D#	D#			
B				
F				
C#				C
F#				

EXERCISE 10.5

Answer the following questions

Describe the sound of the Dominant Seventh Chord:

_____

_____

_____

What is the relationship between the Dominant and Major Seventh Chord?

_____

_____

_____

"The Minor Seventh Chord"

The Minor Seventh Chord is very similar to the Dominant Seventh Chord and Major Seventh Chord. (last section). **The Dominant Seventh Chord**:
•a dominant chord (which is a major chord) with an added minor 3rd

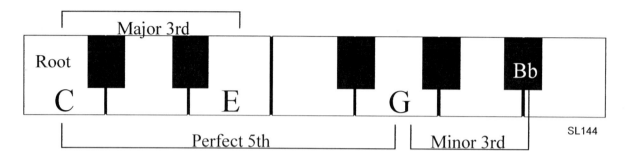

A **Major Seventh Chord** is a major triad with an added major 3rd:

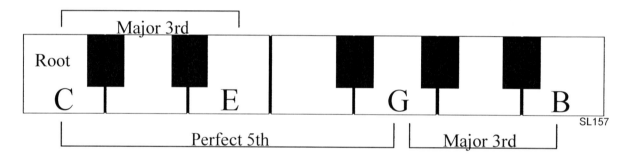

A **Minor Seventh Chord** is simply a minor triad with an added minor 3rd. (or a dominant chord with a flatted 3rd note)

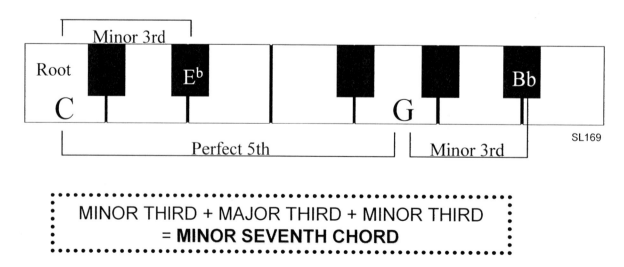

MINOR THIRD + MAJOR THIRD + MINOR THIRD
= **MINOR SEVENTH CHORD**

142

MINOR SEVENTH CHORDS

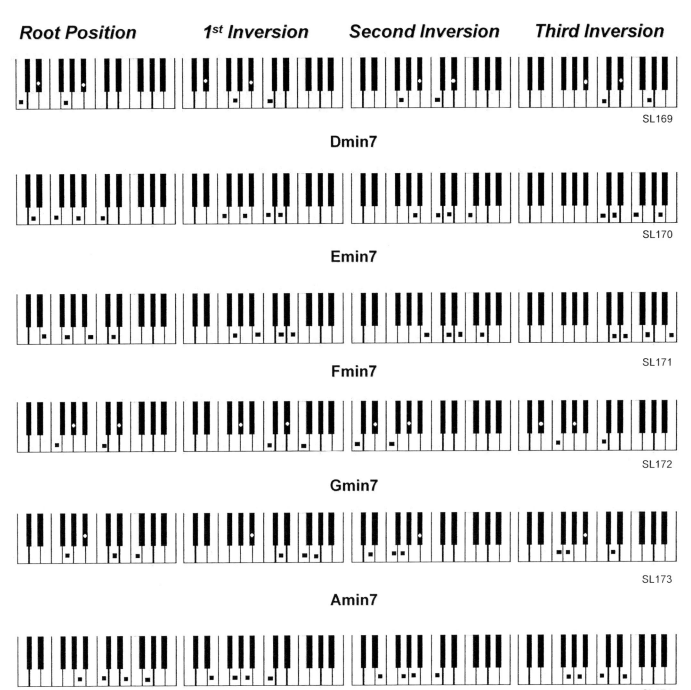

Remember: When a chord is played in it's **root position**, the keynote is always on the bottom. When a chord is played in it's **first inversion**, the keynote is always on the top. When a chord is played in it's **second inversion**, the keynote is always in the middle. When a chord is played in it's **third inversion**, the seventh is always on the bottom.

143

MINOR SEVENTH CHORDS (cont.)

Bmin7 or Cbmin7

Root Position	1st Inversion	Second Inversion	Third Inversion

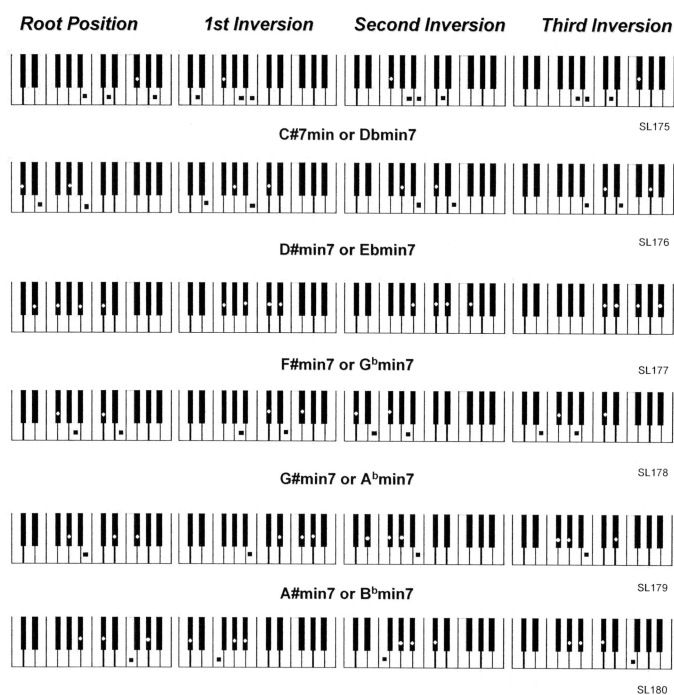

SL175

C#7min or Dbmin7

SL176

D#min7 or Ebmin7

SL177

F#min7 or G♭min7

SL178

G#min7 or A♭min7

SL179

A#min7 or B♭min7

SL180

HearandPlay.com

Exercises 10.5

1. Shade the root position of an Fmin7 Chord

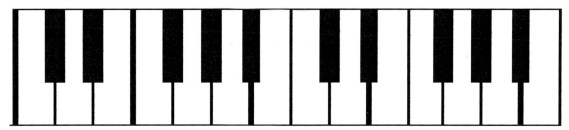

2. Shade the 2nd inversion of a Bmin7 Chord

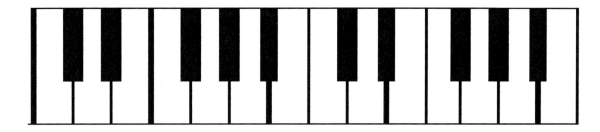

3. Shade the 1st inversion of a B♭min7 chord

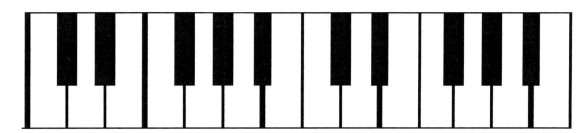

4. Shade the root position of an A#min7 chord

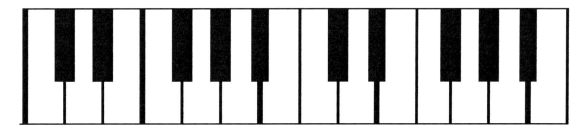

EXERCISE 10.6

Fill in the following chart

min7	1st tone	2nd tone	3rd tone	4th tone
G				F#
E				
D				
A		C		
Bb				
Ab			Eb	
C				
D#	D#			
B				
F				
C#				B
F#				

EXERCISE 10.7

Answer the following questions

Describe the sound of the Minor Seventh Chord:

_____

_____

_____

How does the sound of a Minor Seventh differ from that of the Dominant Seventh Chord?

_____

_____

_____

Lesson Eleven

"Major, Minor & Dominant Seventh Chord Progressions"

In this lesson, we will study **major, minor and dominant seventh chord progressions.** In previous lessons, you've already learned how to form and invert major, minor, and dominant seventh chords. In this lesson, we will use these various chords to create usable progressions.

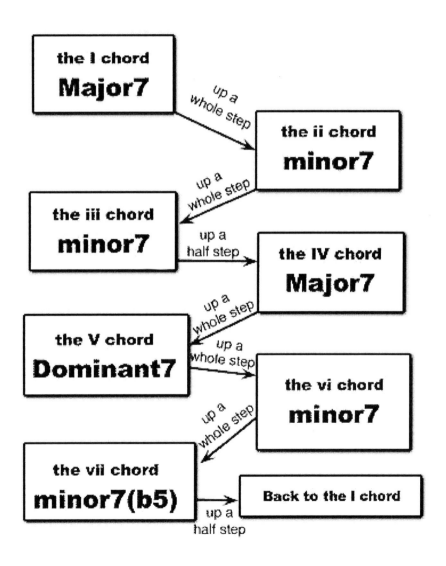

We have already studied how each note of a major scale corresponds to either a major, minor, or diminished chord. We will now study this concept with seventh chords:

I	ii	iii	IV	V	vi	Vii	I
Maj7	Min7	Min7	Maj7	V7	Min7	Min7ᵇ5	Maj7

For example, in **C Major**, the following scale tones and seventh chords correspond together:

I	ii	iii	IV	V	vi	vii	I
C Major7 Chord	D Minor7 Chord	E Minor7 Chord	F Major7 Chord	G Dominant7 Chord	A Minor7 Chord	B Minor7ᵇ5 (or *half diminished*)	C Major7 Chord

SL181

You've already studied the following chord progressions with *triads*:
- •1-4-1-5-1
- •1-4-5-4-1
- •5-1
- •1-5
- •1-4
- •*2-5-1*
- •*6-2-5-1*
- •*3-6-2-5-1*
- •*7-3-6-2-5-1*

By simply replacing the triads with seventh chords, each progression above can be played using 4-toned chords.

Chord Progressions with Seventh Chords

I – IV – I – V – I Progression

By simply adding a **major third** to the **I** & **IV** chords and by adding a **minor third** to the **V** chord, this progression can be played with seventh chords:

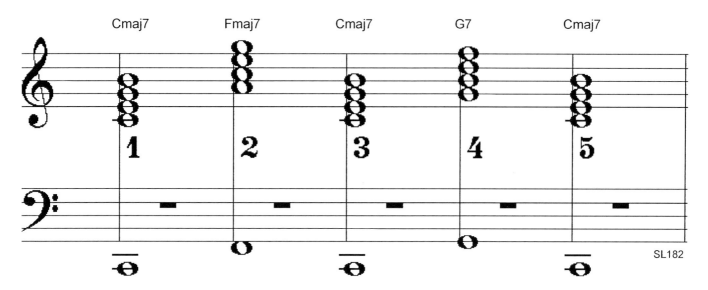

I – IV – I – V – I Progression (Inverted)

Playing the root position of each of the seventh chords above can be rather challenging (especially in fast tempos). By simply using the 2nd inversion of the **IV** chord, and the 1st inversion of the **V** chord, we can transition to each chord more easily.

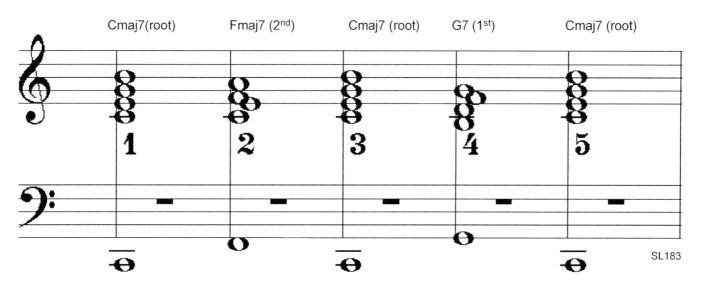

I – IV – V – IV – I Progression

Similar to the previous chord progression, by simply adding a **major third** to the **I** & **IV** chords and by adding a **minor third** to the **V** chord, this progression can be played with seventh chords:

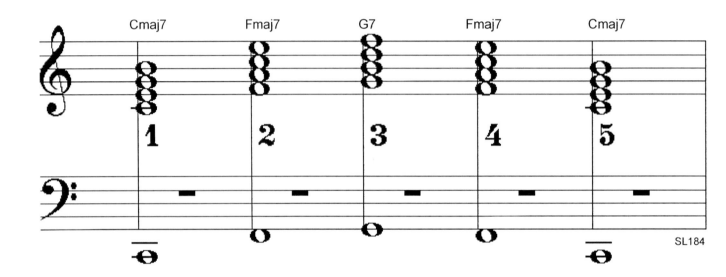

I – IV – V – IV – I Progression (Inverted)

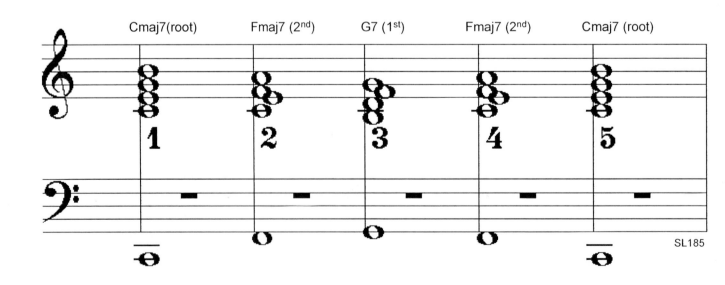

V -- I Progressions

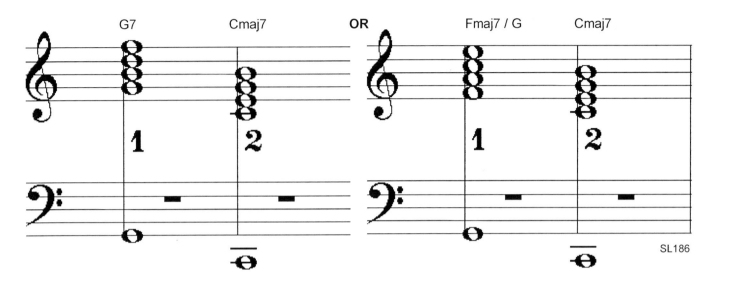

V -- I Progressions (Inverted)

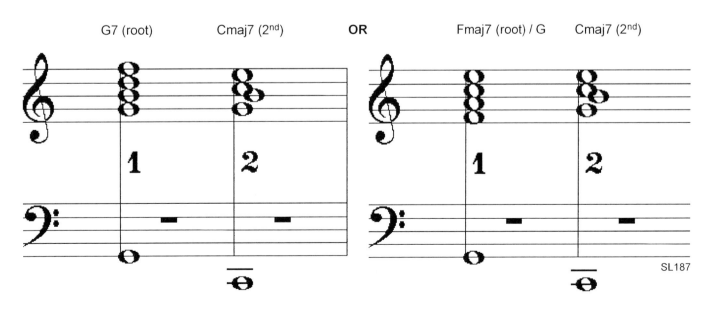

I -- IV Progressions

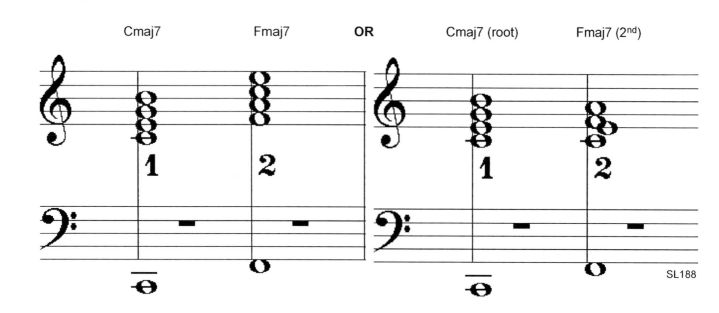

Cmaj7   Fmaj7   **OR**   Cmaj7 (root)   Fmaj7 (2nd)

SL188

Exercise 11.1

Complete the following table:

Chord #1	#2	#3	#4	#5	Key Center	TYPE OF CHORD PROGRESSION
Cmaj7	Fmaj7	Cmaj7	G7	Cmaj7	C	I – IV – I – V – I
		-	-	-	F	V – I
Amaj7					A	I – IV – V – IV – I
Bmaj7		-	-	-	B	I – IV
B^{b}7		-	-	-		V – I
	E^{b}	-	-	-		I – IV
Gmaj7	Cmaj7	D7	Cmaj7	Gmaj7		
					F#	I – IV – I – V – I

152

"ii – V – I" Chord Progression…

As you know, the "2 – 5 – 1" is one of the most commonly used chord progressions in gospel, jazz, and blues music. You have already learned how to play this chord progression with triads:

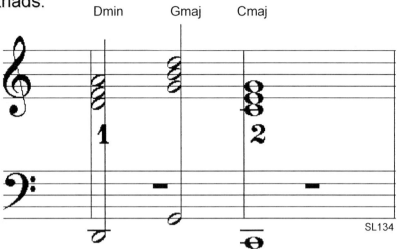

We will now study the "2 – 5 – 1" progression with **Seventh** chords:

Just to review some of the principles … *The **ii** chord is associated with the **min7** chord; the **V** chord is associated with the **dom7** chord and the **I** chord is associated with the **maj7 chord**.*

I	*ii*	iii	IV	V	vi	vii	I
C	D	E	F	G	A	B	C
Major7 Chord	Minor7 Chord	Minor7 Chord	Major7 Chord	Dominant7 Chord	Minor7 Chord	Minor7♭5	Major7 Chord

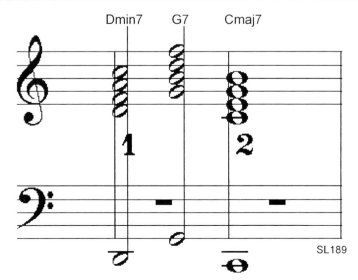

153

"ii – V – I" Chord Progression (cont.) ...

By using another inversion for the **V** chord, this progression can be played much smoother …

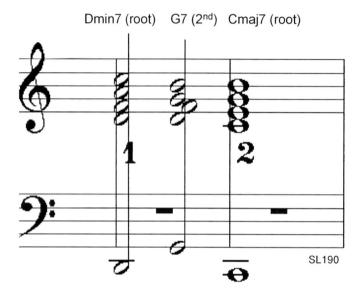

Another approach to the "ii – V – I" Progression…

Instead of playing the "ii" as a minor chord, try playing it as a dominant seventh chord. That is, instead of Dmin7 -- G7, use **D7 -- G7**

In actuality, the **D7** chord in this example is serving as a dominant chord to the **G7** chord. But since Gmaj is not the tonic (but is the dominant chord in C major), we call Dmaj a **Secondary Dominant** chord because it serves as a dominant chord to another chord.

Here are all 12 *"ii -- V"* secondary dominant relationships …

Secondary Dominant	Dominant		Secondary Dominant	Dominant
C7 --	F7		F#7 / Gb7 --	B7
C#7 / Db7 --	F#7 / Gb7		G7 --	C7
D7 --	G7		G#7 / Ab7 --	C#7 / Db7
D#7 / Eb7 --	G#7 / Ab7		A7 --	D7
E7 --	A7		A#7 / Bb7 --	D#7 / Eb7
F7 --	Bb7		B7 --	E7

"ii – V – I" Chord Progression (cont.) ...

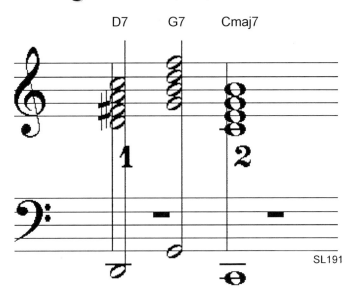

Here is an example of the previous chord progression with the **V** chord inverted:

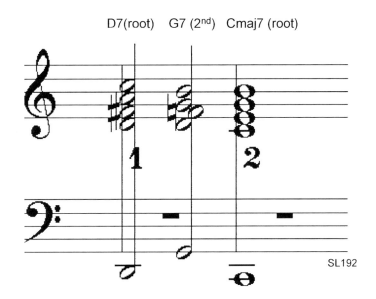

EXERCISE 11.2

One chord will be displayed (Imaj7, iimin7 or V7 chord). Draw the missing chords of the "2-5-1" progression below:

"ii" Chord	"V" Chord	"I" Chord

"vi – ii – V – I" Chord Progression...

Since we've already studied the "ii – V – I" progression with seventh chords, playing this progression simply requires adding one chord: *vi min7*

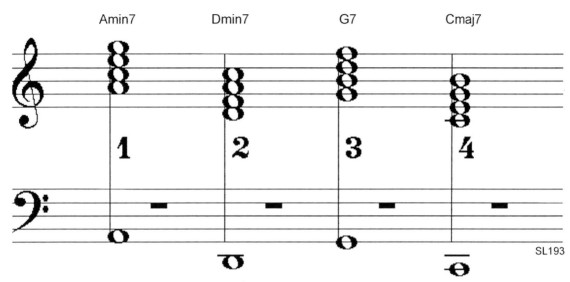

The picture below shows the reason for inverting certain chords. **Inversions** allow musicians to play the *closest* chord available and situate chords with certain notes on top or on the bottom (very helpful when harmonizing a melody).

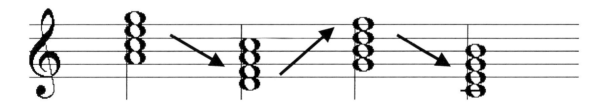

Here is the "6 – 2 – 5 – 1" chord progression with the **I** and **ii** chords inverted:

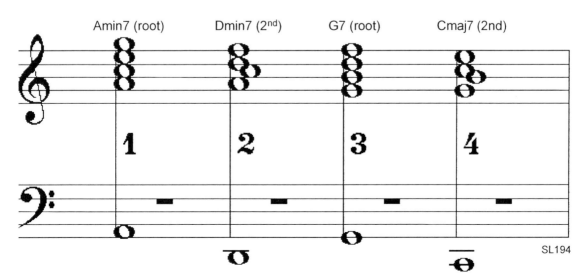

157

Another approach to the "vi – ii – V – I" Progression...

As you know, a chord is called a **Secondary Dominant** when it serves as a dominant chord to another chord. In this example of the "vi – ii – V – I" progression, we will use both the **vi** and the **ii** chords as *secondary dominants.*

For example, instead of playing the **min7 vi chord**, we would play the **vi7 chord**. The same applies to the **ii chord**.

Here's an example of this alteration in C major:

```
A7 -- D7 -- G7 -- Cmaj7
```

SL195

As you've learned in previous lessons, this chord progression is commonly preceded by a **I maj** chord. For example, in **C major,** this chord progression would look like this:

```
Cmaj7 -- A7 -- D7 -- G7 -- Cmaj7
```

SL196

This progression is commonly used at the end of various gospel songs. I call it the *"turn-around"* because it starts at the **I chord** and ends at the **I chord**. Both the **vi** and the **ii** chords serve as secondary dominants. That is, the **vi** chord acts as a dominant to the **ii** chord while the **ii** chord acts as a dominant to the **V** chord.

Keep in mind that only the **V** chord serves as the dominant for a particular key as it is the chord that pulls towards the tonic chord. Any other dominants that pull towards other chords in the scale act as **secondary dominants chords.**

Another approach to the "vi – ii – V – I" Progression (cont.) ...

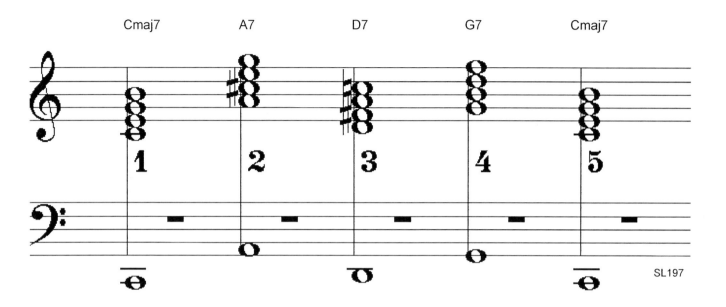

Here is the inverted form of the chord progression above...

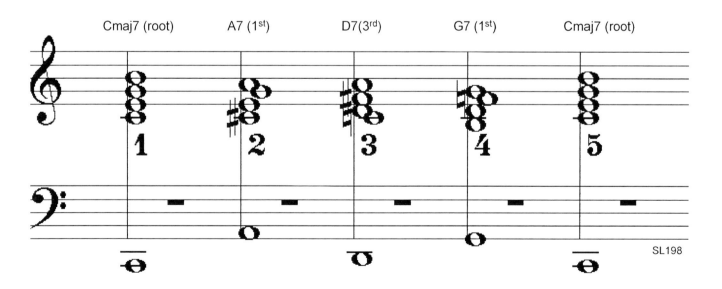

"iii – vi – ii – V – I" Chord Progression…

This progression can be played by simply adding the **iii min7 chord** before the **vi min 7 chord:**

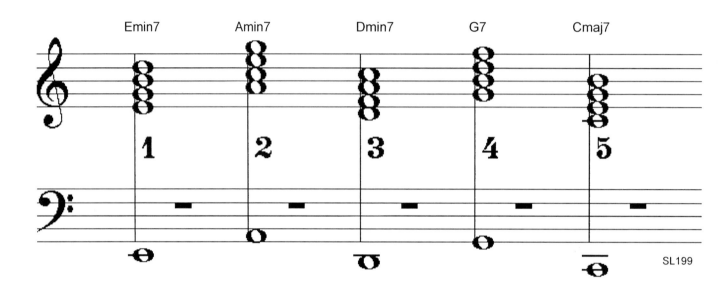

Here is the inverted form of the chord progression above…

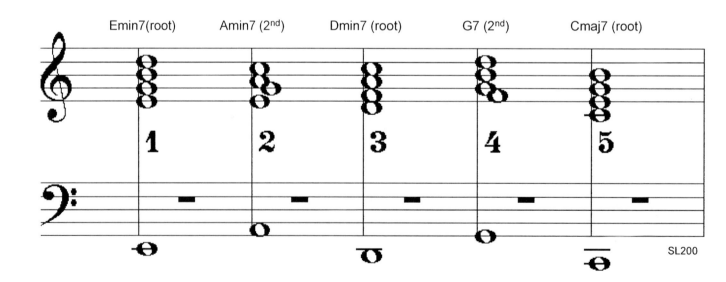

Another approach to the "iii – vi – ii – V – I" Progression (cont.)

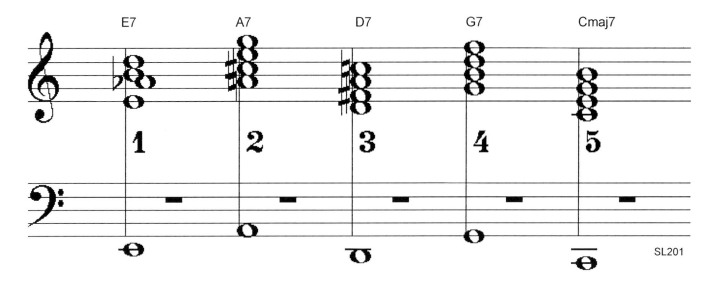

Here is the inverted form of the chord progression above…

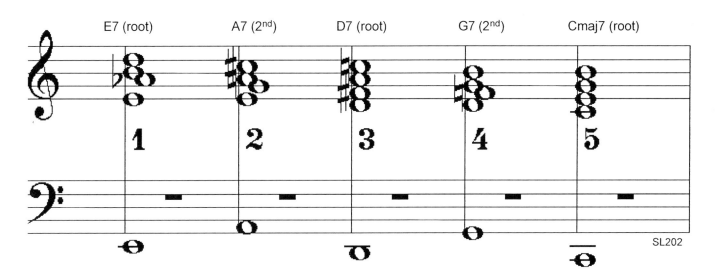

EXERCISE 11.3

Complete the charts below filling in the missing chords for each progression …

KEY	"iii7"	"vi7"	"ii7"	"V7"	"I maj7"
C					C – E – G – B
D		B – D# – F# - A			
E					E – G# - B – D#
F			G – B – D – F		
G				D – F# - A - C	
A					
B					
C# / D♭					C# - F – G# - C
D# / E♭					
F# / G♭					
G# / A♭					
A# / B♭					

EXERCISE 11.4

What are secondary dominant chords?

_____

_____

Why are chords inverted?

_____

_____

_____

_____

_____

12-bar Blues Chord Progression

Don't let the name fool you! This chord progression is common in just about all styles of music including jazz, blues and gospel.

This progression is 12 bars (or measures) long. If you don't remember what bars are, refer back to chapter two.

As you already know, there are three **primary chords** in a given scale: the **I, IV & V**. This chord progression utilizes those three primary chords. In C major, these chords are: **Cmaj (I), Fmaj (IV) & Gmaj (V)**.

However, by using the **dominant chords** of these tones, we can produce the *"bluesy"* sound that we desire.

Personally, I don't prefer playing all 4 tones of the dominant chord. Since most of the time, the bass note **is** the keynote, I choose to omit the **"I"** tone. For example, a C7 chord is: **C – E – G – B^b**. Instead of playing all 4 tones, I leave out the 1st note (which is C, since I'm already playing it on the bass). You will notice that this, too, helps to produce a more *bluesy* feeling.

Lastly, I prefer using the *3rd inversion* when playing the 1st chord of a blues progression. There is no theoretic reason for this other than that I prefer it's sound over the *root* position. For example, in **C major**, after I have omitted the **C** in my right hand, I transform the chord with B^b on the bottom (B^b – E – G). I will leave it up to you how you form your chords (as long as you form the right chord!)

C7 (root)   C7 (3rd inv; ≠ C)

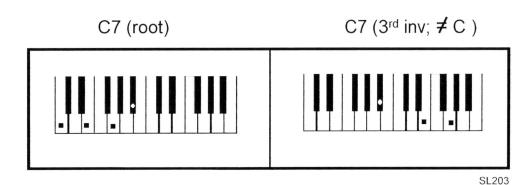

SL203

12-bar Blues Chord Progression (cont.)

I also transform the **IV7 & V7 chords.** However, in order to transition smoothly, the closest inversions of the **IV7 & V chords** must be played (in terms of the **previous chord**)

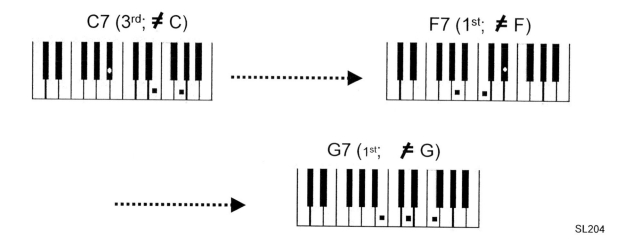

SL204

Now that you know the three chords of this progression, it is now time to learn **when they are played.**

From the title, we know that this progression will have "12 bars." Since each bar has 4 beats, this amounts to 48 beats. The following example shows how the chords are divided in this progression:

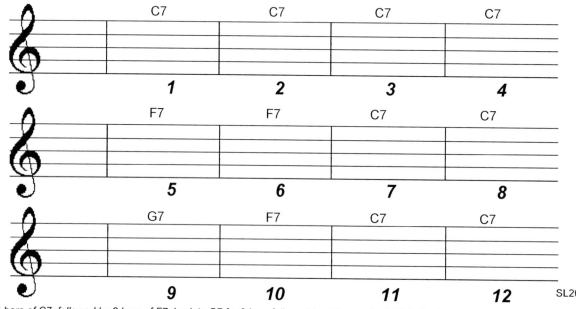

SL205

4 bars of C7, followed by 2 bars of F7; back to C7 for 2 bars followed by 1 bar each of G7 & F7; followed by 2 bars of C7 [ending]
(You may also access an audio example of this progression on **Piano Player Plus v1.0)**

164

EXERCISE 11.5

Write the chords to the following "12-bar Blues" Progressions...

F Major

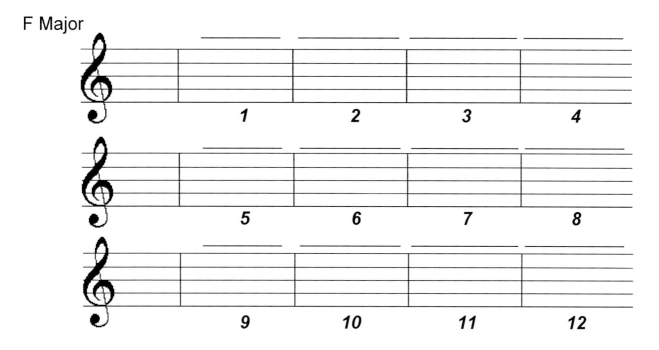

Eb Major

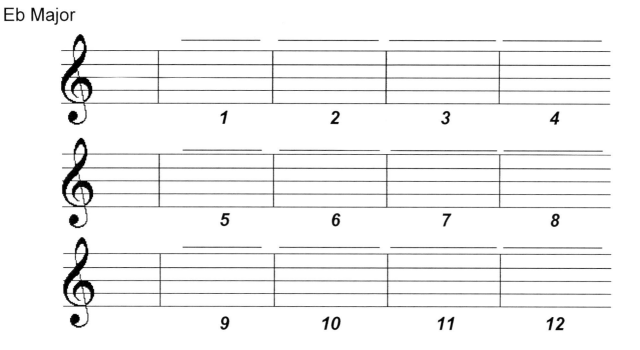

PianoPlayerPlus.com

Lesson Twelve

"Diminished Seventh, Major Sixth & Minor Sixth Chords"

In this lesson, we will study the **diminished seventh, major sixth & minor sixth chords.** In previous lessons, you've already learned how to form and invert major, minor & dominant seventh chords. In this lesson, we will learn three more types of seventh chords.

# of notes	Type of Chord
Three	Triad
Four	*Seventh*
Five	Ninth
Six	Eleventh
Seven	Thirteenth

"The Diminished Seventh Chord"

As you learned earlier, the word *diminished* means "made smaller." When a perfect or major interval is made smaller by a *half step*, it becomes a **DIMINISHED INTERVAL.** The Diminished triad is a Minor triad with the 5th tone made smaller by one half step. (Minor Chord below)

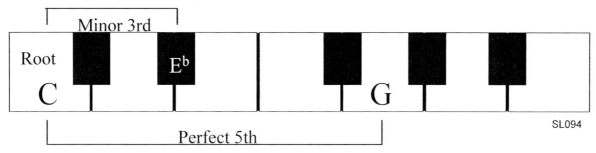

By simply *lowering* the 5th, the chord becomes a **Diminished Chord**

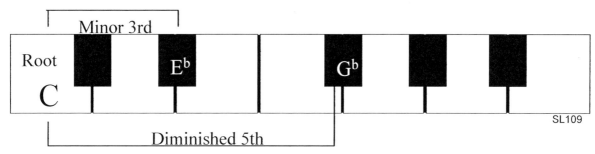

A **Diminished chord** consists of a minor third on a minor third:

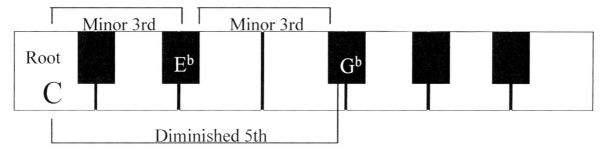

Adding a minor third to the top of a diminished chord creates a **Diminished Seventh Chord:**

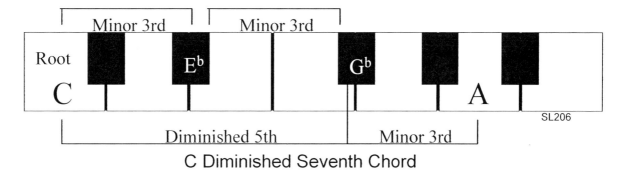

C Diminished Seventh Chord

"The Diminished Seventh Chord" (cont.)

In reality, there are only **three groups** of Diminished Seventh Chords:

1. [A♭dim7, Bdim7, C♭dim7[1], Ddim7, Fdim7 & G#dim7]

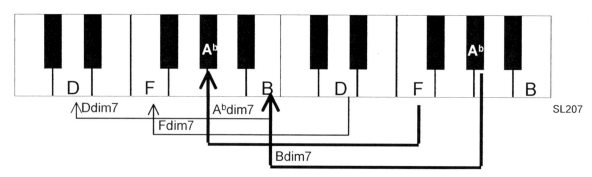

SL207

[1] C♭ sounds the same as B

In other words, these chords all share the same notes. For example, an A♭dim7 chord is simply a Bdim7 chord (third inversion). A Ddim7 chord is an Fdim7 chord (third inversion).

2. [Adim7, Cdim7, D#dim7, E♭dim7, F#dim7 & G♭dim7]

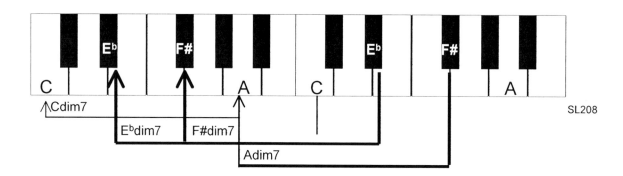

SL208

3. [A#dim7, B♭dim7, C#dim7, D♭dim7, Edim7 & Gdim7]

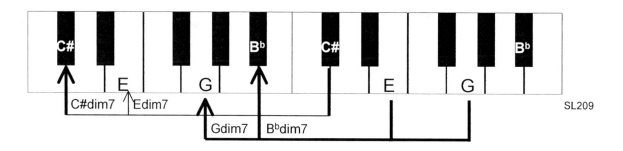

SL209

Exercises 12.1 Answer the following questions and record your observations below:

1. Shade the root position of a Bdim7 Chord

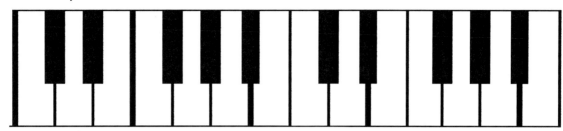

2. Shade the 2nd inversion of an Fdim7 Chord

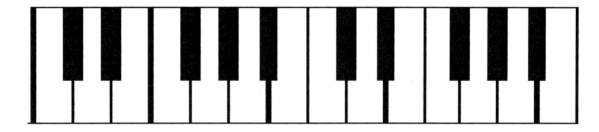

3. Shade the 1st inversion of a Gdim7 chord

4. Shade the root position of a B♭dim7 chord

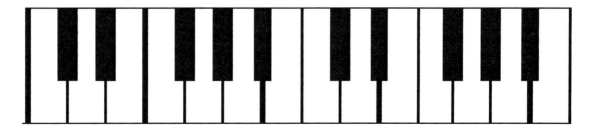

Observations:

_____

_____

_____

_____

Exercises 12.2 Answer the following questions and record your observations below:

1. Shade the root position of an Edim7 Chord

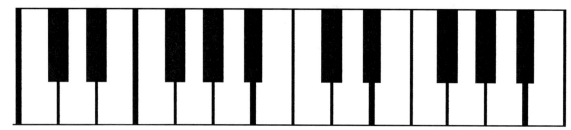

2. Shade the 3rd inversion of a Gdim7 Chord

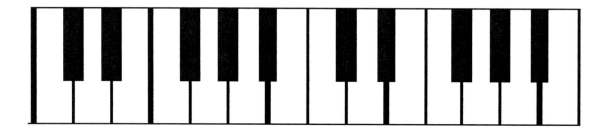

3. Shade the 1st inversion of a Ddim7 chord

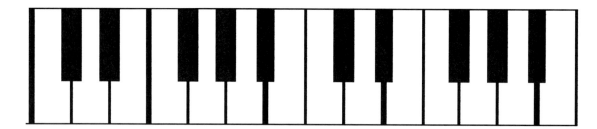

4. Shade the root position of an Fdim7 chord

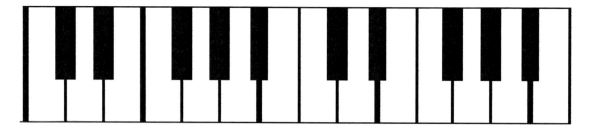

Observations:

_____

_____

_____

_____

DIMINISHED SEVENTH CHORDS

Cdim7

Root Position   **1st Inversion**   **Second Inversion**   **Third Inversion**

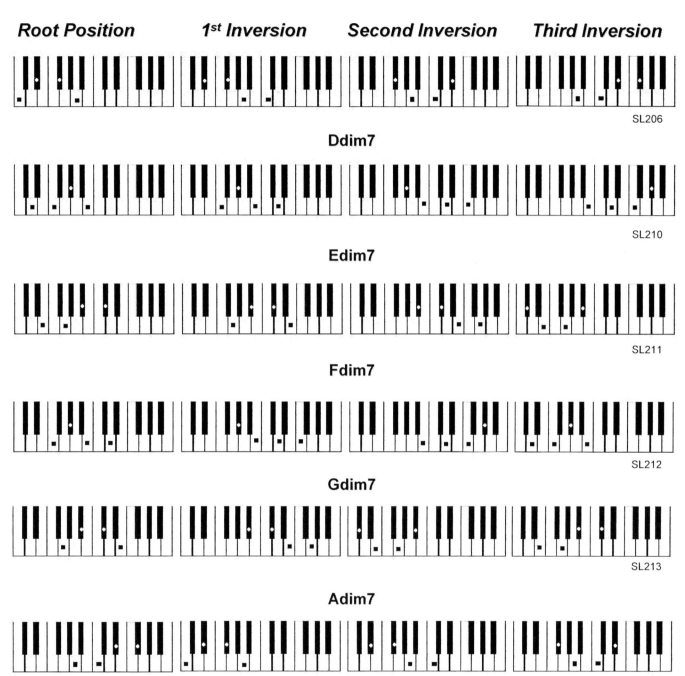

SL206

Ddim7

SL210

Edim7

SL211

Fdim7

SL212

Gdim7

SL213

Adim7

SL214

Remember: When a chord is played in it's **root position**, the keynote is always on the bottom. When a chord is played in it's **first inversion**, the keynote is always on the top. When a chord is played in it's **second inversion**, the keynote is always in the middle. When a chord is played in it's **third inversion**, the seventh is always on the bottom.

DIMINISHED SEVENTH CHORDS (cont.)

Bdim7 or C♭dim7

Root Position	1st Inversion	Second Inversion	Third Inversion

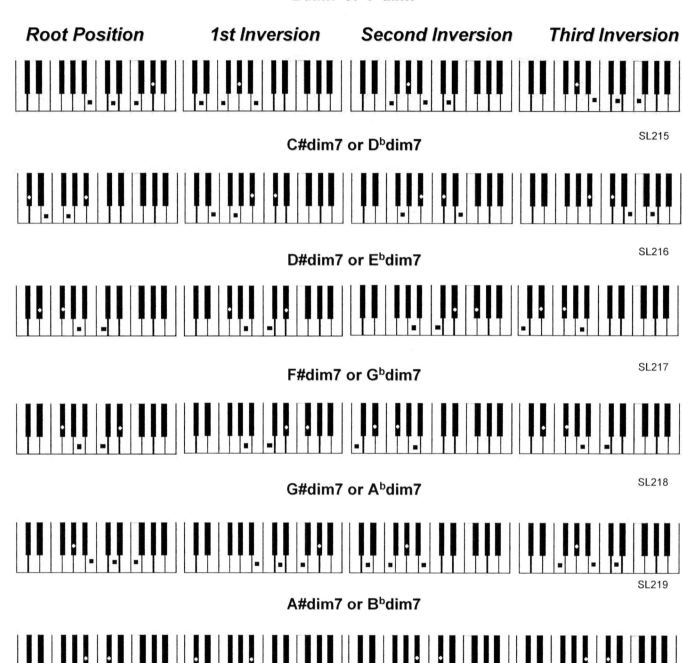

SL215

C#dim7 or D♭dim7

SL216

D#dim7 or E♭dim7

SL217

F#dim7 or G♭dim7

SL218

G#dim7 or A♭dim7

SL219

A#dim7 or B♭dim7

SL220

Note: I also recommend using the **"Piano Player Plus 1.0"** Software to test yourself on the sounds of the different diminished seventh chords and inversions. With this program, you will be able to build your ear skills by testing yourself on chords and inversions. The software program will keep track of your progress.

PianoPlayerPlus.com

"The Half Diminished Seventh Chord"

You've probably been curious about the **vii** chord in a scale (min7b5). It is also known as the **Half Diminished Chord** because one of the intervals is a major third instead of a minor third.

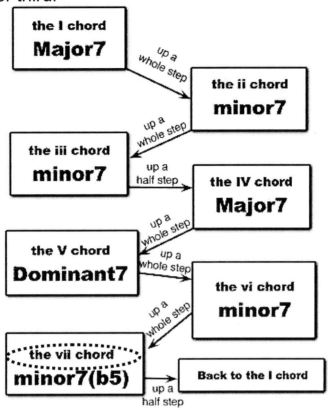

C Diminished Seventh Chord

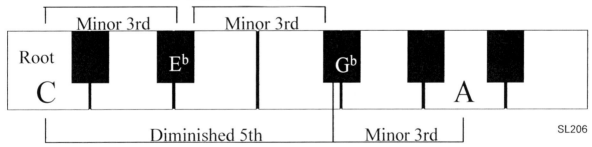

C Half Diminished (C⌀) Seventh Chord (or Cmin7b5)

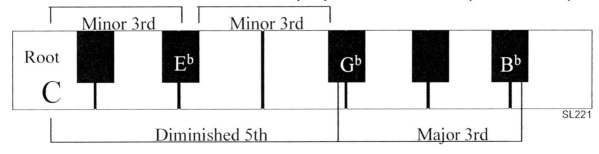

Note: This chord can also be looked at as a Cmin7b5 because the 5th tone **(G)** is lowered one-half step   173

HALF DIMINISHED SEVENTH CHORDS

OR MINOR SEVENTH CHORDS WITH FLAT FIFTH (∅ or min7ᵇ5)

Cmin7ᵇ5

Root Position	1ˢᵗ Inversion	Second Inversion	Third Inversion

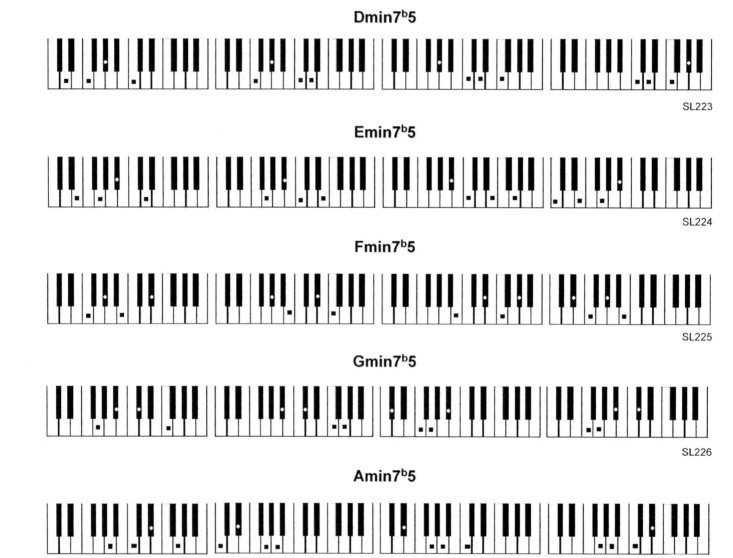

SL222

Dmin7ᵇ5

SL223

Emin7ᵇ5

SL224

Fmin7ᵇ5

SL225

Gmin7ᵇ5

SL226

Amin7ᵇ5

SL227

Remember: When a chord is played in it's **root position**, the keynote is always on the bottom. When a chord is played in it's **first inversion**, the keynote is always on the top. When a chord is played in it's **second inversion**, the keynote is always in the middle. When a chord is played in it's **third inversion**, the seventh is always on the bottom.

174

HALF DIMINISHED SEVENTH CHORDS (cont.)

Bmin⁷♭5 or C♭min⁷♭5

Root Position	1st Inversion	Second Inversion	Third Inversion

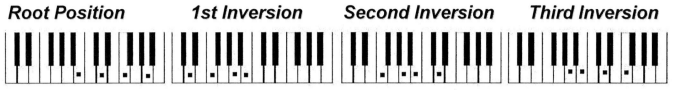

SL228

C#min⁷♭5 or D♭min⁷♭5

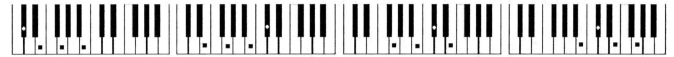

SL229

D#min⁷♭5 or E♭min⁷♭5

SL230

F#min⁷♭5 or G♭min⁷♭5

SL231

G#min⁷♭5 or A♭min⁷♭5

SL232

A#min⁷♭5 or B♭min⁷♭5

SL233

Note: I also recommend using the **"Piano Player Plus 1.0"** Software to test yourself on the sounds of the different half diminished seventh chords and inversions. With this program, you will be able to build your ear skills by testing yourself on chords and inversions. The software program will keep track of your progress.

"Major & Minor Sixth Chords"

The **Major Sixth** Chord is simply a major chord with an added sixth note. For example, in C Major, the 6th degree is: **A.** The C major chord is: C - E - G. Adding an **A** (C-E-G-A) creates a major Sixth Chord.

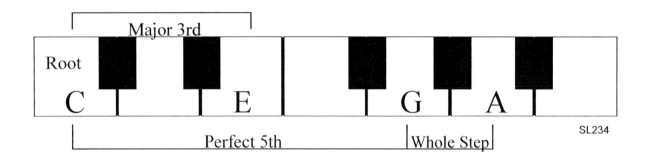

A **Minor Sixth Chord** is a minor triad with an added sixth note. For example in C minor, the sixth degree is: **A.** The C minor chord is: **C - Eb - G.** Adding an **A** creates a minor sixth chord. (C-Eb-G-A)

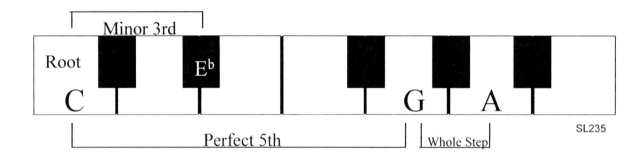

EXERCISE 12.3: Play the two chords. Compare the chords below:

_____

_____

_____

_____

What other chord produces the same sound as a Major Sixth Chord?

_____

"Major & Minor Sixth Chords" (cont.)

In previous chapters, you've studied the Minor Seventh Chord:

Cmin7

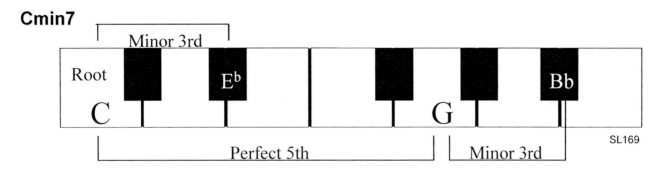

SL169

Notice in the Cmin7 chord above, how an E♭ Major chord (E♭ – G – B♭) is played with an *"added C."* While this chord is still a Cmin7 chord, it is also an E♭6 chord (third inversion) because of the *"added C."*

Note: "C" is the sixth tone degree in an E♭ major scale

With this relationship in mind, it should be easier to remember minor seventh chords. Simply take the *keynote of the minor chord* + the relative major triad ... and there's your minor seventh chord!

For example, in C minor, the relative major is **E♭**. Since I am trying to form a **Cmin7** chord, the keynote is "**C**." Therefore, by simply adding an E♭ major chord on top of the **C**, a **Cmin7** chord is formed.

C + [E♭ – G – B♭]

Here's another example: In A minor, the relative major is **C**. To form an **Amin7** chord, I would simply add the relative major (C) chord on top of the keynote (A).

A + [C – E – G]

Maj6 = Min7

177

"Major & Minor Sixth Chords" (cont.)

In the beginning of this chapter, you studied the Half Diminished Seventh Chord or (Min7♭5):

C∅ or Cmin7♭5

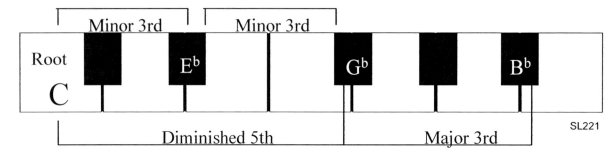

SL221

Notice in the Cmin7♭5 chord above, how an E♭ Minor chord (E♭ – G♭ – B♭) is played with an *"added C."* While this chord is still a Cmin7♭5 chord, it is also an E♭m6 chord (third inversion) because of the *"added C."*

Note: **m6** = minor sixth chord

With this relationship in mind, it should be easier to remember half diminished chords (or min7♭5) . Simply take the *keynote of the half diminished chord* + the minor triad of the relative major key … and there's your minor seventh chord!

For example, in C minor, the relative major is **E♭**. However, instead of taking the major chord of E♭, we're going to take the E♭ minor chord. Therefore, by simply adding an E♭ minor chord on top of the **C**, a **Cmin7♭5** chord is formed.

> C + [E♭ – G♭ – B♭]

Here's another example: In A minor, the relative major is **C**. To form an **Amin7♭5** chord, I would simply add a *Cmin* chord (instead of a Cmaj chord) chord on top of the keynote (A).

> A + [C – E♭ – G]

Min6 = Min7♭5

178

"Major & Minor Sixth Chords" (cont.)

The following table will help you to understand the relationship between major / minor sixth and minor seventh chords:

MAJOR SIXTH CHORD	MINOR SEVENTH CHORD
C6 --	Amin7
C#6 / D♭6 --	A#min7 / B♭min7
D6 --	Bmin7
D#6 / E♭6 --	Cmin7
E6 --	C#min7 / D♭min7
F6 --	Dmin7
F#6 / G♭6 --	D#min7 / E♭min7
G6 --	Emin7
G#6 / A♭6 --	Fmin7
A6 --	F#min7 / G♭min7
A#6 / B♭6 --	Gmin7
B6 --	G#min7 / A♭min7

MINOR SIXTH CHORD	HALF DIMINISHED CHORD (min7♭5)
Cm6 --	Amin7♭5
C#m6 / D♭m6 --	A#min7♭5 / B♭min7♭5
Dm6 --	Bmin7♭5
D#m6 / E♭m6 --	Cmin7♭5
Em6 --	C#min7♭5 / D♭min7♭5
Fm6 --	Dmin7♭5
F#m6 / G♭m6 --	D#min7♭5 / E♭min7♭5
Gm6 --	Emin7♭5
G#m6 / A♭m6 --	Fmin7♭5
Am6 --	F#min7♭5 / G♭min7♭5
A#m6 / B♭m6 --	Gmin7♭5
Bm6 --	G#min7♭5 / A♭min7♭5

EXERCISE 12.4
Label the following chords

	CHORD NAME (s)	INVERSION

EXERCISE 12.5
Label the following chords

	CHORD NAME (s)	INVERSION

Lesson Thirteen

"Major Sixth, Minor Sixth and Diminished Chord Progressions"

In this lesson, we will study **major sixth, minor sixth and diminished seventh chord progressions.** In previous lessons, you've already learned how to form and invert major sixth, minor sixth, and diminished seventh chords. In this lesson, we will use these various chords to create usable progressions.

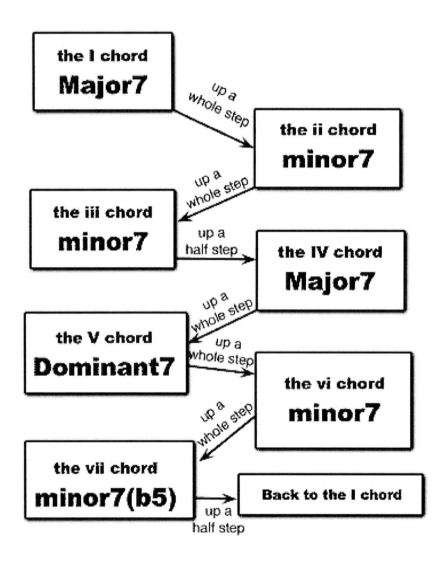

We have already studied how each note of a major scale corresponds to either a major, minor, or diminished chord. We have reviewed every seventh chord of the scale except the **vii**. Since, we have studied the *half diminished (or min7♭5)* chord in the last chapter, we can now **complete** the scale of seventh chords:

I	ii	iii	IV	V	vi	vii	I
Maj7	Min7	Min7	Maj7	V7	Min7	Min7♭5	Maj7

SL059

By now, you should be able to play <u>all</u> of the corresponding chords of any given major scale. Here is an example of the seventh chords of a **C major scale:**

I	ii	iii	IV	V	vi	vii	I
C Major7 Chord	D Minor7 Chord	E Minor7 Chord	F Major7 Chord	G Dominant7 Chord	A Minor7 Chord	B Minor7♭5 (or *half diminished*)	C Major7 Chord

SL181

EXERCISE 13.1
Play the following scales with seventh chords:

C major
F major
B♭ major
E♭ major
A♭ major
D♭ major

EXERCISE 13.2   [KEY RELATIONSHIPS]
Label the following chords

Key	I	ii	iii	IV	V	vi	vii	VIII
C	Cmaj7	Dmin7	Emin7	Fmaj7	G7	Amin7	Bmin7♭5	Cmaj7
F								
B♭								B♭maj7
E♭								
A♭				E♭7				
D♭								
G♭								
B			D#min7					
E								
A								
D				Gmaj7				
G								

OBSERVATIONS

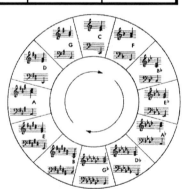

- The keys are listed according to the "**Circle of Fifths**"
- The **IV** chord will always be the **I** chord in the next key
- The **I** chord will always be the **V** chord in the next key
- The **ii** chord will always be the **vi** chord in the next key
- The **iii** chord will always transform to be the min7♭5 **vii** chord in the next key
- The **v** chord will always transform to the be the min7**ii** chord in the next key
- The **vi** chord will always be the **iii** chord in the next key
- The **vii** will always transform to be the maj7**IV** chord

1st Key	2nd Key
I --	V
ii --	vi
iii --	vii
IV --	I
V --	ii
vi --	iii
vii --	IV

184

"2 – 5 – 1" Chord Progression (with the Dim7 chord)

You have already studied the "2 - 5 -1" chord progression with major, minor, and dominant seventh chords:

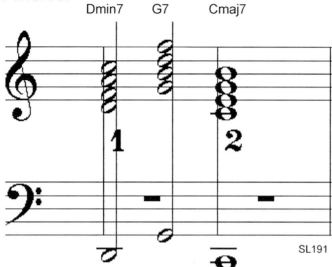

We will now introduce another approach to playing the "2 – 5 – 1 chord progression.

Secondary Diminished of V: is a diminished chord built on scale degree #4, a half step below the dominant. Like **secondary dominants**, secondary **diminished** chords function as embellishing chords in a harmonic progression.

The "2 – 5 – 1" Progression that you're already experienced in playing normally utilizes the min7 (ii), V7 (V), and the maj7 (I)

However, in this approach, we will substitute the **ii min7** chord for a **IV#dim7** chord. For example, in C major, the **IV#** note is F# because **F** is the 4th tone of the C major scale and by raising it a half step, F# is played instead of F.

In addition, instead of playing the V7 chord, we will play the **IVmaj** triad over the V bass. (you've already played this progression in earlier chapters…). For example, this is Fmaj (IV) over G (V – bass).

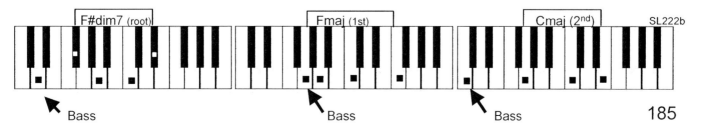

185

"2 – 5 – 1" Chord Progression with the Dim7 chord (cont.)

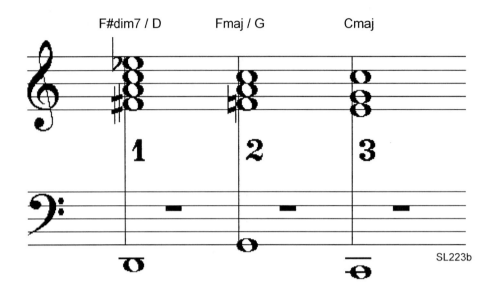

You may also replace the diminished seventh chord with a **half diminished chord seventh chord** to create a "*happier*" feeling …

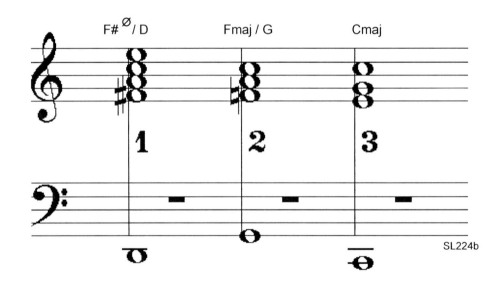

Note the differences in sound between the two progressions. Which progression do you prefer to use when resolving back to the "**I" maj** chord? Write your response below:

_____

_____

_____

186

EXERCISE 13.3

Label the following chord progressions. Note whether each progression uses the dim7 or dim $^\varnothing$ chord.

"Using the dim7 as a Passing Chord"

You've already studied such progressions where the "I" chord leads to the "V" for various reasons. This progressions will utilize the diminished chord as a passing chord to the iimin7 chord which will lead to the V7 chord.

I -- ii -- V

a. Play a cmaj7 chord
b. Play a c#dim7 chord
c. Play a dmin7 chord
d. Play a G7 chord

Note: "b" serves as a passing chord to the dmin7 chord since it is not a chord associated with any of the tones of the major scale.

So, by simply raising the "I" chord a half step and playing the diminished seventh chord, it can act as a "puller" towards the iimin7 chord.

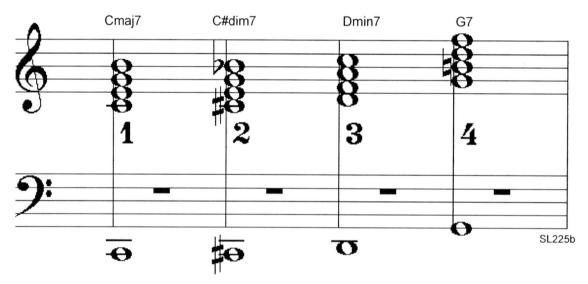

Since the **vi** chord also leads to the **ii** chord, the "I#dim7" can also be played on top of the **vi bass:**

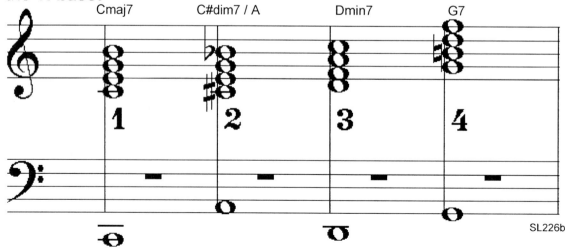

188

EXERCISE 13.4

Complete the chart below filling in the missing chords for the following progression

KEY	"I maj7"	"I # dim7"	"ii min7"	"V7"
C				
D		D# - F# - A - C		
E				
F			G – B^b – D – F	
G				D – F# - A - C
A				
B				
C# / D^b				
D# / E^b				
F# / G^b				
G# / A^b				
A# / B^b				

EXERCISE 13.5

List the corresponding seventh chords for every scale tone below: (I = maj7 ...)

_____

_____

What is a secondary diminished chord of V?

_____

_____

_____

_____

_____

"vii – iii – vi – ii – V – I" Chord Progression…

For this progression, we are going to use an example from chapter 9:

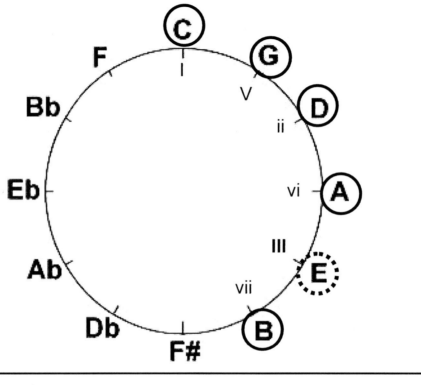

Bmin^b5 (half diminished) -- E7 -- Amin7 -- D7 -- G7 -- C maj

Here is the inverted form of the progression above:

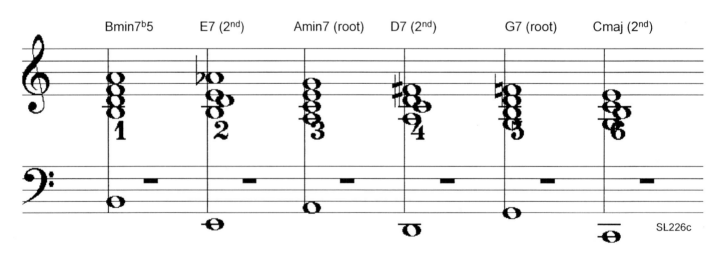

Using Diminished Seventh Chords in gospel progressions

Playing the Dim7 chord to the dom7 is very common in gospel progressions. (especially when music is used during sermons, etc.). For example, in C major, this is simply a Cdim7 -- C7 (bass = C)

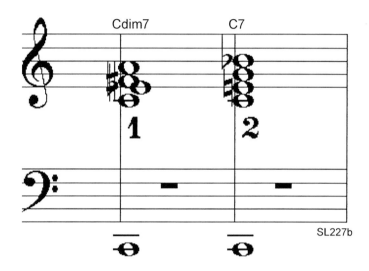

Playing a Dim7 chord in between a IV7 & I maj chord is also very common in gospel progressions. For example, in C major, this is: **F7 -- F#dim7 -- Cmaj / G**

Note: The bass for this progressions simply rises one half step at a time from F to F# to G (or IV -- IV# -- V)

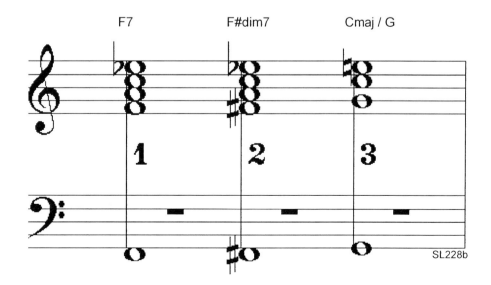

BLUES PROGRESSION WITH DIMINISHED CHORDS ...

Similar to the blues progression learned in earlier chapters, this chord progression includes the diminished chord. Try playing it below:

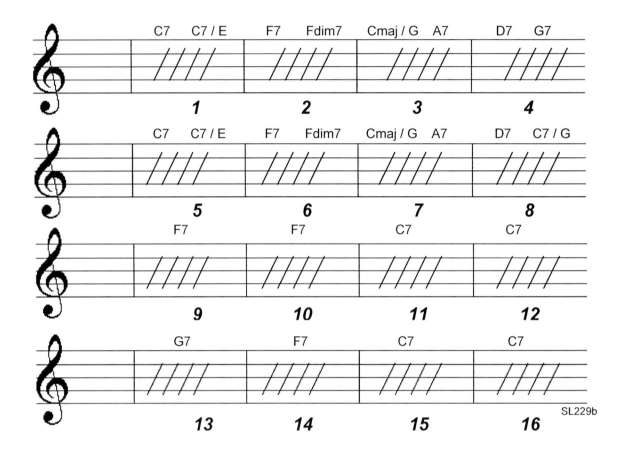

Note: Bars with two chords in them each get "2" counts. (Ta – ah). Bars with only one chord get all "4" counts. (Ta-ah-ah-ah).

(You may also access an audio example of this progression on **Piano Player Plus v1.0**)

PianoPlayerPlus.com

Lesson Fourteen

"Major & Minor Ninth Chords & Progressions"

In this lesson, we will study **major & minor ninth chords.** In previous lessons, you've already learned several three and four-toned chords (triad & seventh chords). **In this** lesson, we will study five-toned chords called *ninths.*

# of notes	Type of Chord
Three	**Triad**
Four	Seventh
Five	**Ninth**
Six	**Eleventh**
Seven	**Thirteenth**

"Major Ninth Chords"

When a chord extends beyond the octave tone (**viii**), any notes that are added above the viii tone are labeled with a number < 8 (greater than).

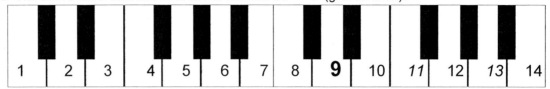

Thus, a major ninth chord is simply a major seventh chord with an added 9th tone.

For example, in C major, the ninth tone is **D:**

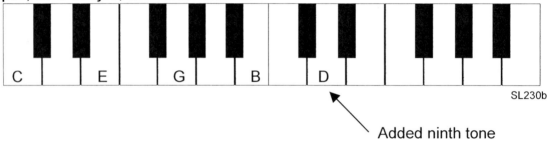

Added ninth tone

I personally prefer playing ninth chords with the 9th tone embedded in the middle of the chord:

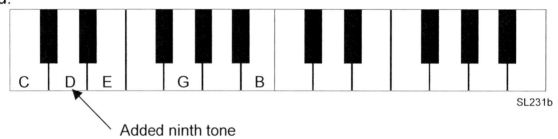

Added ninth tone

You can also create a maj9 chord by playing the iii min7 chord on top of the keynote bass. For example, to form a Cmaj9, simply take the iii tone (E), form an Emin7 chord on top of C (bass):

Cmaj9

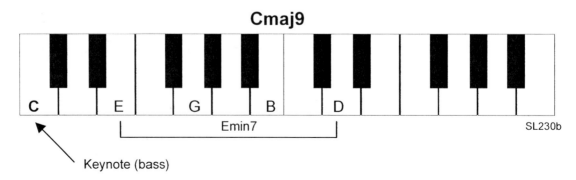

Keynote (bass)

194

Exercises 14.1

1. Shade a Gmaj9 Chord

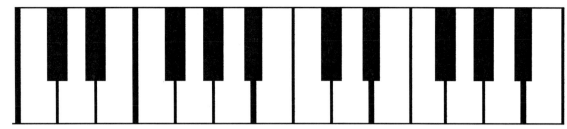

2. Shade an Fmaj9 Chord

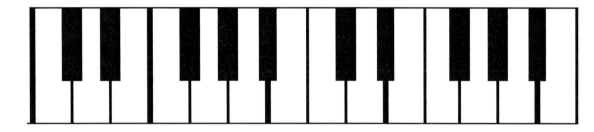

3. Shade an E♭maj9 Chord

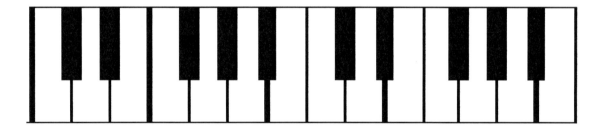

4. Shade a Dmaj9 Chord

Exercises 14.2

1. Shade an Emaj9 Chord

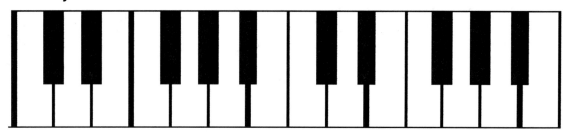

2. Shade an Amaj9 Chord

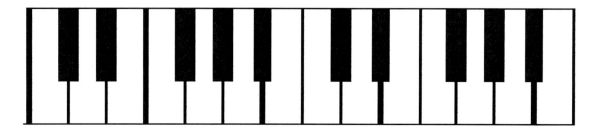

3. Shade an C#maj9 Chord

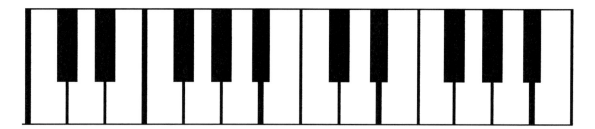

4. Shade a A♭maj9 Chord

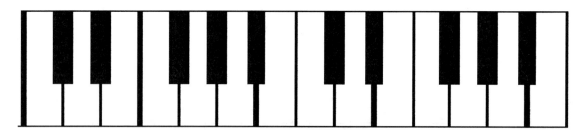

"Minor Ninth Chords"

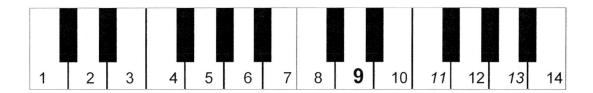

A minor ninth chord is simply a **minor seventh chord** with an added **ninth tone.** It can also be remembered by this:

Keynote + Relative Major Seventh Chord

For example, in C minor, the relative major key is **E♭.** So by simply adding an **E♭maj7 chord** on top of a **C** (bass), a Cmin9 chord is formed.

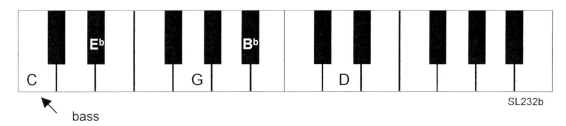

I personally prefer playing ninth chords with the 9th tone embedded in the middle of the chord:

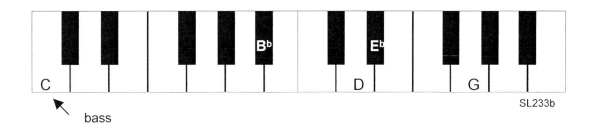

197

Exercises 14.3

1. Shade a Cmin9 Chord

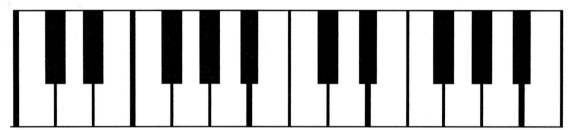

2. Shade an Fmin9 Chord

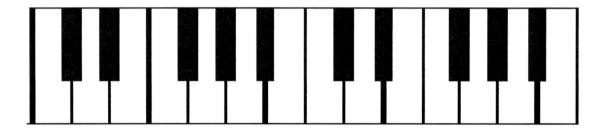

3. Shade an Amin9 Chord

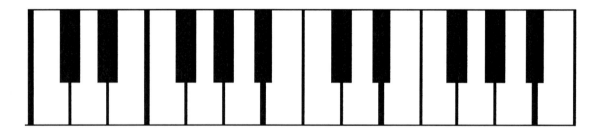

4. Shade a G♭min9 Chord

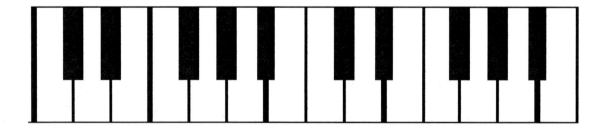

Exercises 14.4

1. Shade a Dmin9 Chord

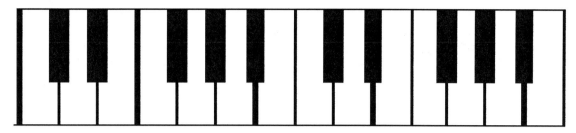

2. Shade an F#min9 Chord

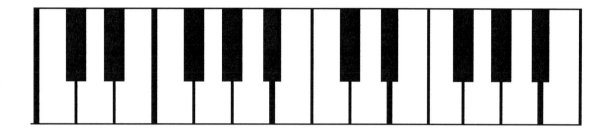

3. Shade an Emin9 Chord

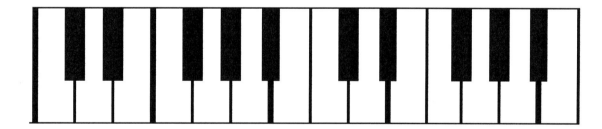

4. Shade a E♭min9 Chord

"Dominant Ninth Chords"

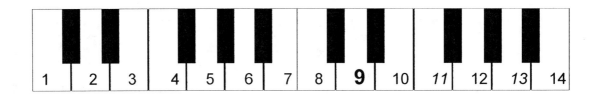

A dominant ninth chord is simply a **dominant seventh chord** with an added **nine.**

Or it can be remembered by this:

$$\boxed{\textbf{Keynote + III}^{\varnothing}}$$

For example, in C major, the III tone is **E.** So by simply playing an **E**$^{\varnothing}$ **chord** (or Emin7♭5) on top of a **C** (bass), a **C9** chord is formed:

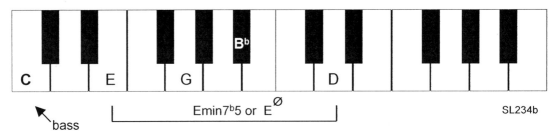

I personally prefer playing ninth chords with the 9th tone embedded in the middle of the chord:

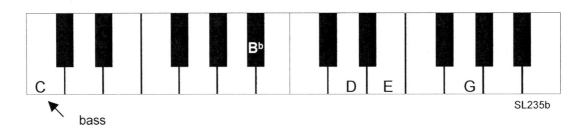

200

Exercises 14.5

1. Shade an E9 Chord

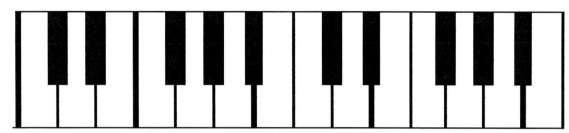

2. Shade an G♭9 Chord

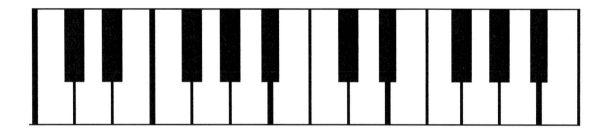

3. Shade an A♭9 Chord

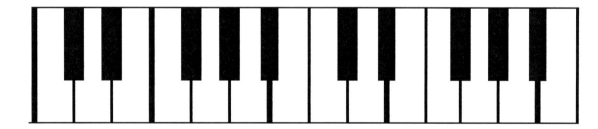

4. Shade a G9 Chord

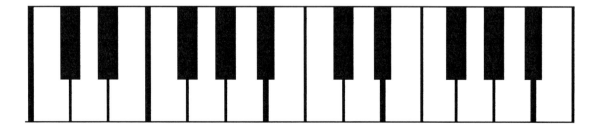

EXERCISE 14.6
Label the following chords

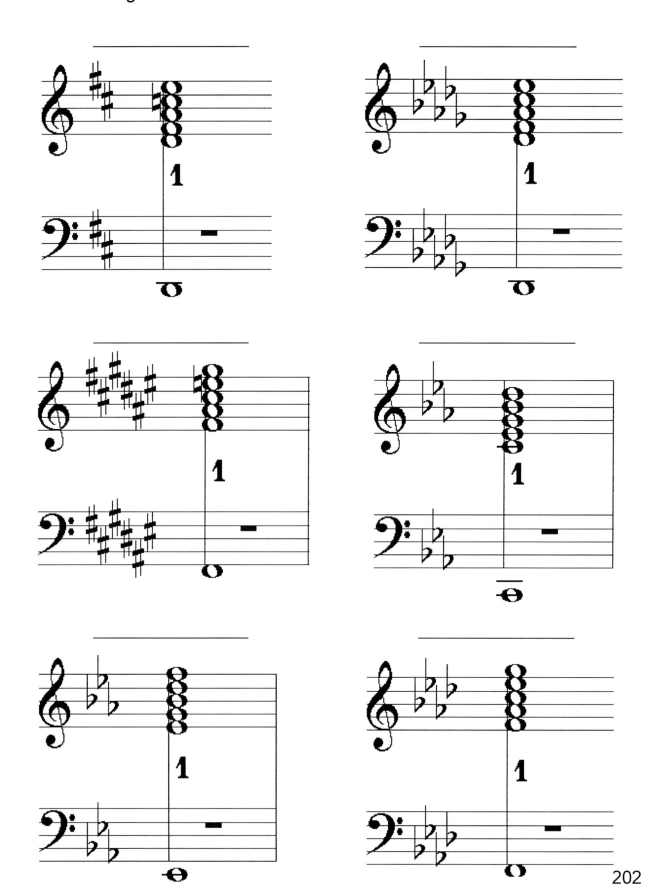

"Dominant Ninth Chords with added Sixth Note"

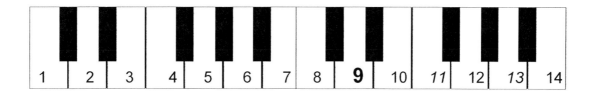

By adding the sixth tone of the scale to the Dom9 chord, a D9/6 chord is formed:

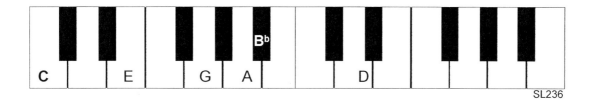

It can also be inverted to look like this:

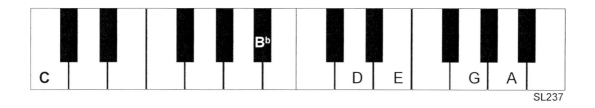

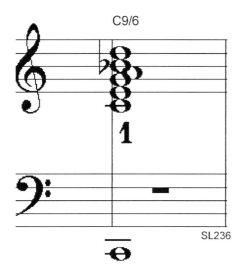

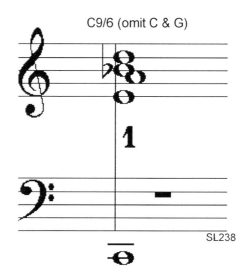

203

"The Circle of Fifths with Min9 & Dom9 / 6"

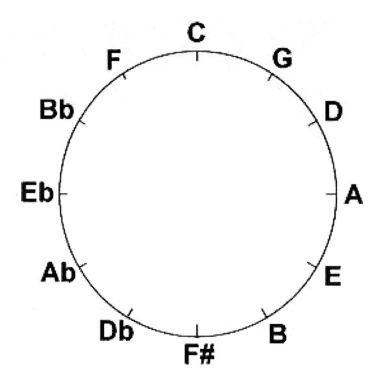

By simply switching from a min9 chord to the IV9 / 6 chord, the entire circle of fifths chart can be played.

Cmin9

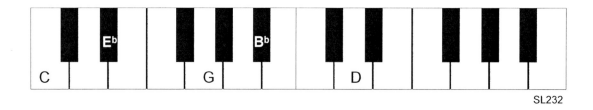

F9 / 6

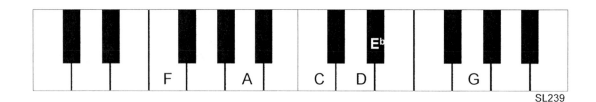

"The Circle of Fifths with Min9 & Dom9 / 6" (cont.)

Here is the inverted inversion of the F9 / 6 which is easiest to play after the Cmin9:

Note: **F** is played on the bass

Notice, that the **ONLY** difference between the Cmin9 and F9 / 6 is one note (the seventh is lowered in the same manner that it is when transforming from a Cmaj scale to an Fmaj scale).

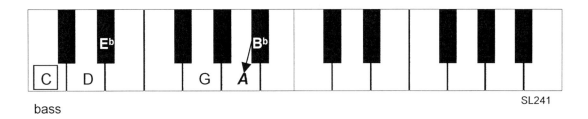

bass

This same pattern will follow until the circle returns back to the Cmin9 chord. That is, alternating between Min9 & Dom9 / 6 chords.

Cmin9 -- F9 / 6 -- B♭min9 -- E♭9 / 6 -- ...

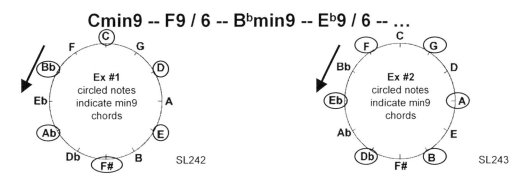

Remember: After playing the min9 chord, simply lower the 7th note to play the next dom9 / 6 chord. In actuality, all you really need to know are the min9 chords because the next chord on the circle is formed by lowering the seventh tone ½ step. Also, starting this exercise on C min will only include half of the min9 chords because the other half will be dom9 / 6 chords. To play the other half of the min9 chords, start the exercise on *Fmin9 --B♭9 / 6*

Tip: You should only have to use four of your right fingers. The keynote should be played on the bass.

"The Circle of Fifths with Min9 & Dom9 / 6" (cont.)

I personally recommend using the third inversion of the min9 chord. I use this inversion all the time and it is much easier to play and remember than the root inversion of the min9 chord. It also produces a "full" sound by playing the seventh note on the bottom. In addition, since the seventh note is the tone which is lowered, it is easier to remember to *lower* the *lowest* tone of the chord than a tone embedded in the middle of the chord.

Cmin9 (third inv.)

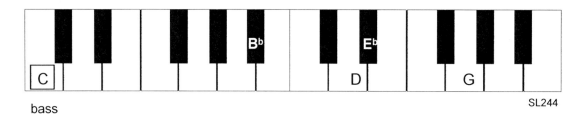

Notice that the Cmin9 (third inv) chord is also an Ebmaj7 chord (2nd Inv) without the "C" bass.

MIN9 = Relative Major Seventh Chord

By simply lowering the seventh note (the lowest note in a third inversion), the *next* dom9 / 6 chord is formed:

F9 / 6

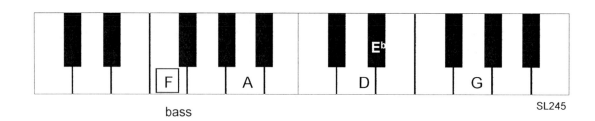

"The Circle of Fifths with Min9 & Dom9 / 6" (cont.)

The diagrams below show both exercises…

SL242

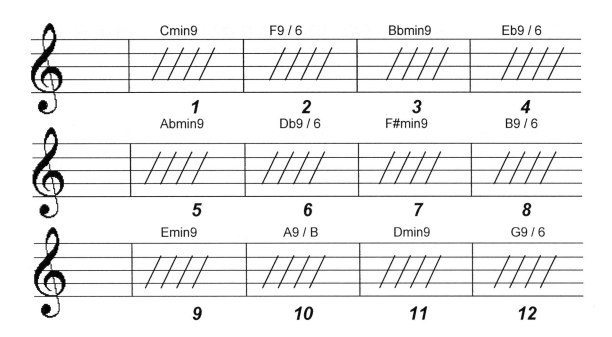

SL243

Note: Both of these exercises cover all 12 min9 & dom9 / 6 chords. Practice these exercises often as I guarantee that you'll use them in several songs.

"Using min9 -- 9 / 6 chords to resolve to the IV 9"

In blues and gospel music, the I, IV, and V chords are most likely to be dominant seventh, ninth or thirteenth (haven't studied those yet) chords. In previous chapters, you've studied the I -- IV progression.

This example will show you how to plug the "min9 -- 9 / 6" into a I -- IV chord progression.

ii – V – I with the IV chord ...

The IV chord is not the tonic chord (I) because there can only be one tonic in any given key. However, it can act as the "I" chord in various situations. That is, it can become the I chord for a very short period of time and the I chord can become the dominant chord. The best way to describe this progression is by simply playing a "2 – 5 – 1" chord progression in terms of the IV chord.

Here is an example of this in C major:

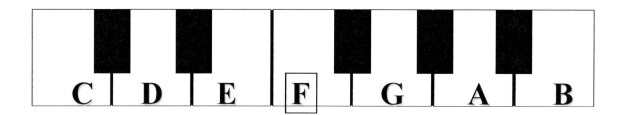

F is the IV tone in a C major scale

Here is a "ii – V – I" chord progression in terms of **F:**

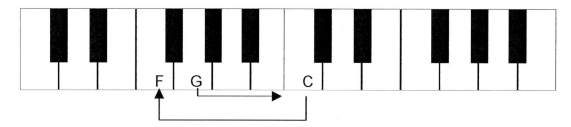

Now, substitute the corresponding min9 -- 9 / 6 chords:

$$\text{G}_{min9} -- \text{C}_{9 / 6} -- \text{F}_9 \quad \text{\small SL246}$$

"Using min9 -- 9 / 6 chords to resolve to the IV 9" _(cont.)

Here are examples of how this progression may be used:

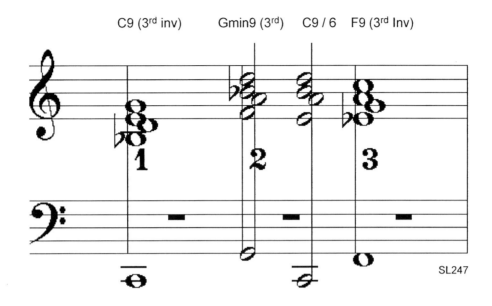

C9 (3rd inv)   Gmin9 (3rd)   C9 / 6   F9 (3rd Inv)

SL247

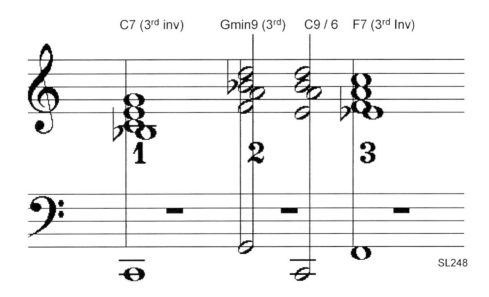

C7 (3rd inv)   Gmin9 (3rd)   C9 / 6   F7 (3rd Inv)

SL248

"Using min9 -- 9 / 6 chords to resolve to the IV 9" (cont.)

iii – vi – ii – V – I with the IV chord ...

The previous chord progression can be expanded by including the iii -- vi chords:

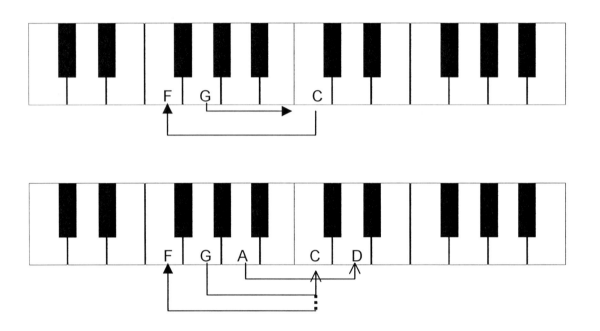

Now, substitute the corresponding min9 -- 9 / 6 chords:

Amin9 -- D9 / 6 -- Gmin9 -- C9 / 6 -- F9

Note: Keep in mind that we are still in the key of **C major.** The IV chord is just acting as a I chord for this progression. In most songs, the chords will eventually resolve back to the " I " tonic chord.

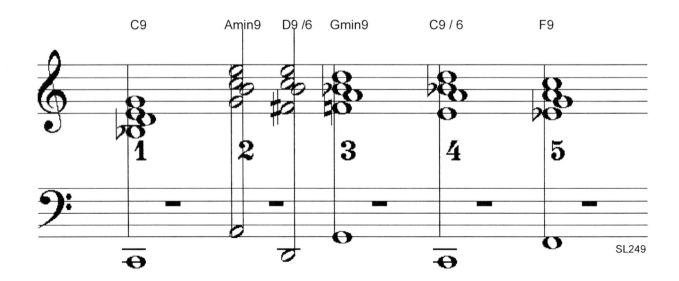

EXERCISE 14.7

Complete the following chart …

KEY	1st Chord	2nd Chord	3rd Chord	4th Chord	5th Chord	6th Chord
C	C9	Amin9	D9 / 6	Gmin9	C9 / 6	F9
F						B♭9
B♭			C9 / 6			E♭9
E♭						A♭9
A♭						D♭9
D♭						G♭9
F#				C#min9		B9
B						E9
E						A9
A		F#min9				D9
D						G9
G						C9

EXERCISE 14.8

Write the following chord changes to the progression above in the key of **A major**

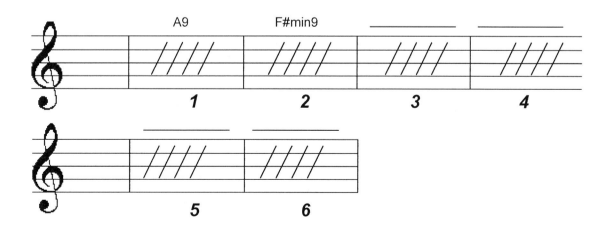

"Substituting Min9 chords for Min7 Chords"

I personally enjoy playing min9 chords in a 2 – 5 – 1 progression. Min9 chords not only sound more full, but they also produce a prettier sound. From previous chapters, you've studied how the **ii min7** chord is a dominant preparation to the **V7** chord which leads back to the **tonic (I) maj7 chord**.

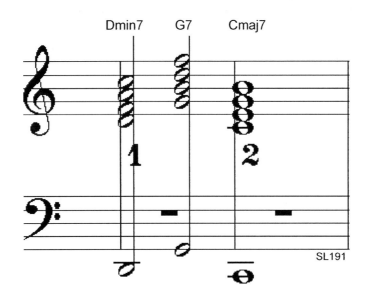

This same progression can be played with **iimin9, V9, and I maj9** chords:

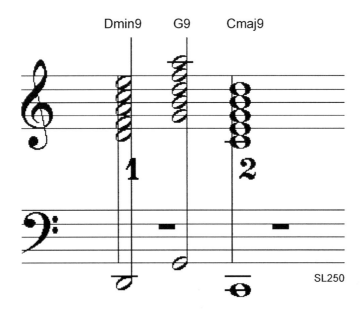

"I 9 -- IV 9 Turn – around!"

This chord progressions is commonly played in blues & gospel music. It is often used at the end of "up-tempo" gospel praise songs.

In C major, the I 9 chord is C9 and the IV 9 chord is F9. I prefer using the 3rd inversion for the C9 chord and the 2nd inversion for the F9 chord. This combination produces the smoothest transition:

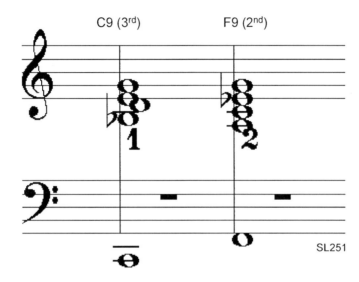

It is also common for the bass to *lead* up to each chord. This is done by playing a chromatic scale starting from the **ii** tone (to lead up to the IV 9 chord) and from the **vi** tone (to lead back to the I 9 chord)

CHROMATIC SCALE: A scale made up entirely of half steps in consecutive order. On the keyboard, it uses every key, black or white.

So, when transitioning to the IV9 chord, simply play every key from the ii tone to the IV tone on the bass. When transitioning from the IV 9 chord back to the I chord, play every key from the vi tone to the I tone.

Here's an example of this in C major:

Bass: C -- D – Eb – E – F – A – Bb – B - C ... and so on ... -- C9 -- F9 ...
Chromatic Scale   Chromatic Scale   SL252

C9   F9   C9

Note: This progression can be cycled however long you want (depending on the nature of the song). This technique is often called "**walking the bass.**" 213

"I 9 -- IV 9 Turn – around!" (cont.)

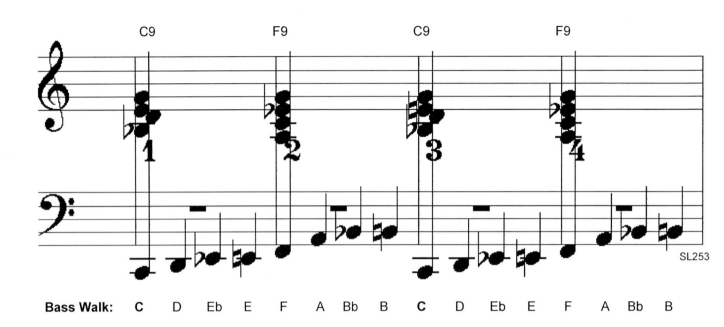

Bass Walk: C   D   Eb   E   F   A   Bb   B   C   D   Eb   E   F   A   Bb   B

LESSON 14 REVIEW
LIST THE SEVERAL WAYS IN WHICH NINTH CHORDS CAN BE USED:

_____

_____

_____

_____

_____

_____

_____

_____

_____

_____

_____

_____

_____

_____

_____

_____

Lesson Fifteen

"Eleventh & Thirteenth Chord Progressions"

In this lesson, we will study **eleventh & thirteenth chords.** In previous lessons, you've already learned several three, four, and five-toned chords (triad, seventh & ninth chords). In this lesson, we will study six & seven-toned chords called *elevenths & thirteenths.*

# of notes	Type of Chord
Three	Triad
Four	Seventh
Five	Ninth
Six	*Eleventh*
Seven	*Thirteenth*

"Major Eleventh & Thirteenth Chords"

As you've learned, when a chord extends beyond the octave tone (**viii**), any notes that are added above the viii tone are labeled with a number < 8 (greater than).

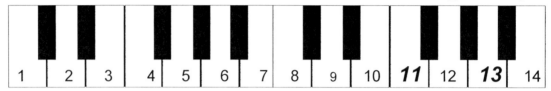

Thus, a major eleventh chord is simply a major ninth chord with an added 11th tone. For example, in C major, the eleventh tone is **F:**

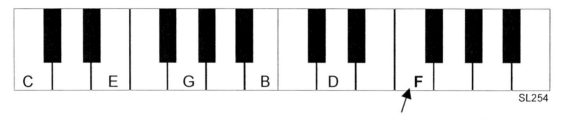

Added eleventh tone

A major thirteenth chord is a major eleventh chord with an added 13th tone. For example, in C major, the thirteenth tone is **A:**

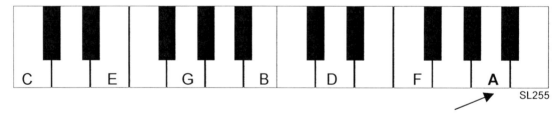

Added thirteenth tone

Note: For one to play all the notes shown above, this chord must be played with both hands. Another option is to not play the 3rd and 5th tones of the chord. Experiment with the different sounds and pick the one which best suits your need.

Remember: a *Maj9* chord includes the major seventh interval; a *Maj11* chord includes the major ninth interval; and a *Maj13* includes the major eleventh interval.

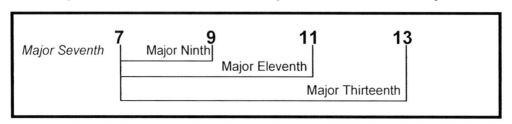

216

EXERCISE 15.1
Complete the following chart …

Maj11 Chord	1	3	5	7	9	11
C	C	E	G	B	D	F
F						
B♭						
E♭						
A♭						
D♭						Gb
F#						
B						
E			B			
A						
D						
G						

EXERCISE 15.2
Complete the following chart …

Maj13 Chord	1	3	5	7	9	11	13
C	C	E	G	B	D	F	A
F							
B♭							
E♭	E♭						
A♭							
D♭						Gb	
F#							
B							
E			B				
A							
D							
G							E

Exercises 15.3

1. Shade a D♭maj11 Chord

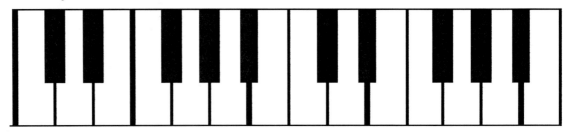

2. Shade an F#maj11 Chord

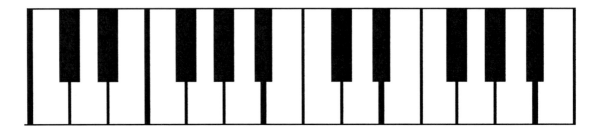

3. Shade an Dmaj11 Chord

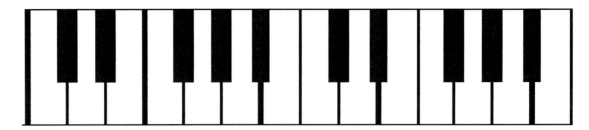

4. Shade a Emaj11 Chord

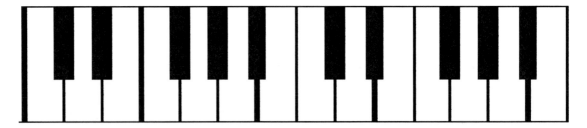

Exercises 15.4

1. Shade a D♭maj13 Chord

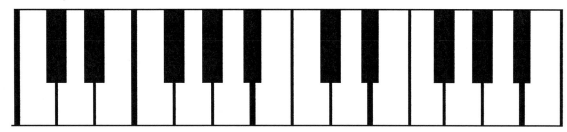

2. Shade a Cmaj13 Chord

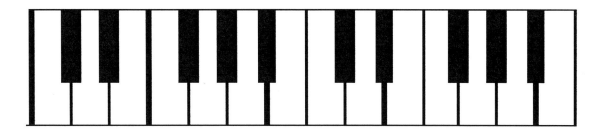

3. Shade an D maj13 Chord

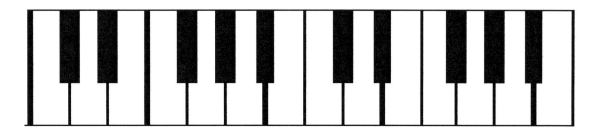

4. Shade an E♭maj13 Chord (hint: Invert the chord if necessary)

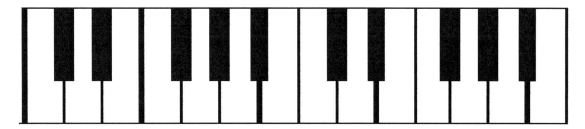

"Minor Eleventh & Thirteenth Chords"

A minor eleventh chord is simply a **minor ninth chord** with an added **eleventh tone**; *Or* it can be remembered by this:

i Minor Triad + ᵇvii Maj Triad

For example, in the key of C, the *i minor chord* is **C min** and the *flatted seventh major chord* is **Bᵇ maj.**

Cmin + Bᵇmaj = Cmin11

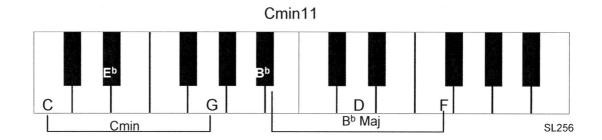

The example above is also known as a **POLYCHORD** (when two different chords are played at the same time). Both Eleventh and Thirteenth chords are classified as Polychords because two different chords are played simultaneously.

Min13 Chords

A minor thirteenth chord is simply a **minor eleventh chord** with an added **thirteenth tone**; *Or* it can be remembered by this:

i Minor7 + ii min Triad

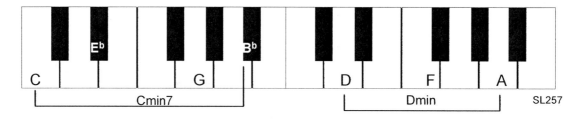

Exercises 15.5 (hint: Invert the chords if necessary)

1. Shade a Cmin11 Chord

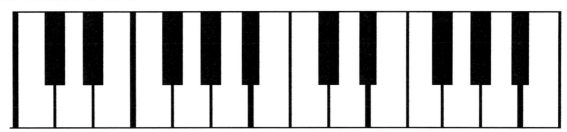

2. Shade a Dmin11 Chord

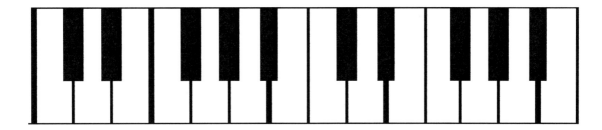

3. Shade an Emin11 Chord

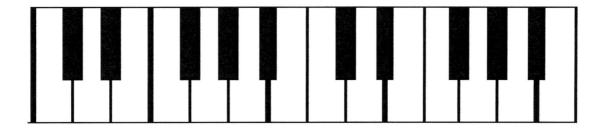

4. Shade an Amin11 Chord

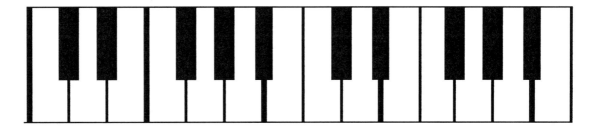

Exercises 15.6 (hint: Invert the chords if necessary)

1. Shade a E♭min13 Chord

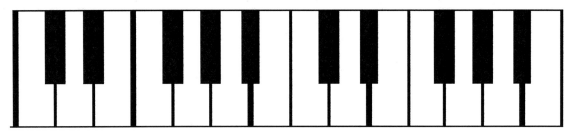

2. Shade an F#min13 Chord

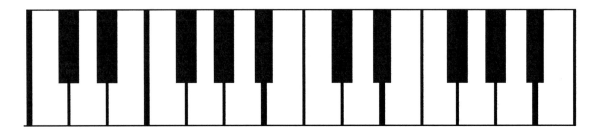

3. Shade an A♭min13 Chord

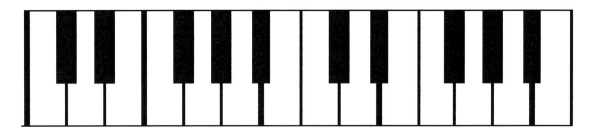

4. Shade an B♭min13 Chord

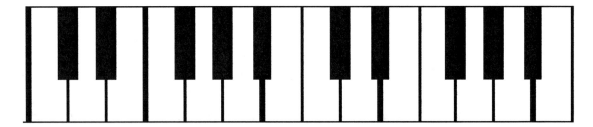

"Dominant Eleventh & Thirteenth Chords"

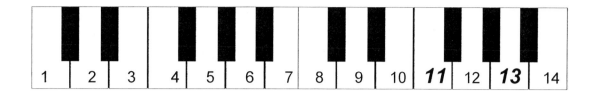

A dominant eleventh chord is simply a **dominant ninth chord** with an added **eleven.** Or, it can be remembered by this:

i Major Triad + ᵇvii Maj Triad

For example, in the key of C, the *i major chord* is **C maj** and the *flatted seventh major chord* is **Bᵇ maj·**

Cmaj + Bᵇmaj = C11

C11

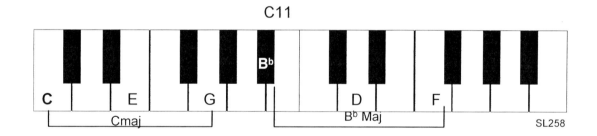

Dom13 Chords

A dominant thirteenth chord is simply a **dominant eleventh chord** with an added **thirteenth tone;** *Or,* it can be remembered by this:

i dom7 + ii min Triad

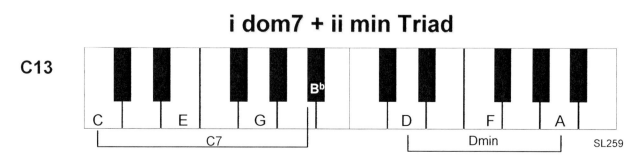

"Dominant Eleventh & Thirteenth Chords" (cont.)

The dom13 is often used in the place of seventh chords in several gospel and blues chord progressions. Because of it's distinctiveness, it can be used for just about any purpose in the **iii -- vi -- ii -- V -- I** chord progression:

I prefer cutting this chord to three simple tones. That is, the seventh, third, and thirteenth (or sixth) tone.

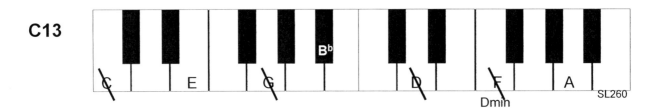

After omitting various notes, I then invert this chord to the third inversion (with the seventh note as the lowest tone ... this creates the best sound in my opinion).

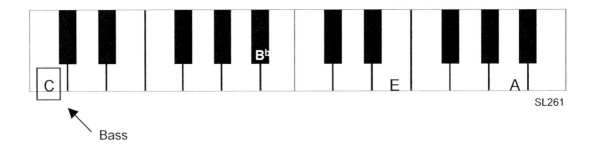

If you learn and practice ALL 12 OF THESE CHORDS, you won't regret it! I can't tell you enough how important it is to know these chords. As time progresses, you will use dom13 chords as *dominant preparations, secondary dominants, dominants, and tonic chords.* In other words, *dom13* chords work all around the piano!

Exercises 15.6

Complete the following chart (this will help you to learn all **twelve** dom13 chords) …

Dom13, Third Inversion *(with only the Seventh – Third – and Thirteenth tones)*

Dom13 Chord	1st Tone	2nd Tone	3rd Tone
C	Bb	E	A
F			
B♭			
E♭			
A♭		C	
D♭			
F#			
B			
E			C#
A			
D		F#	
G			

Exercises 15.7

Complete the following chart …

Dom13 Chord	1st Tone	2nd Tone	3rd Tone
C	Bb	E	A
		G	
			B♭
	D		
		B♭	
	E♭		
			E

"Using Dominant Thirteen Chords in Blues Chord Progressions"

In previous chapters, you've studied the **"12-bar blues progression"** with Seventh Chords. In this lesson, we will simply replace the *Seventh* chords with *Thirteenth Chords* and add a "walking bass."

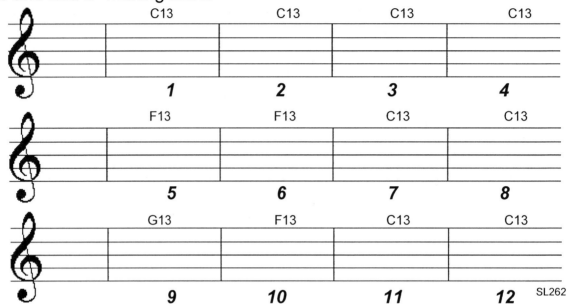

4 bars of C13, followed by 2 bars of F13; back to C13 for 2 bars followed by 1 bar each of G13 & F13; followed by 2 bars of C13 [ending]
(You may also access an audio example of this progression on **Piano Player Plus v1.0**)

BROKEN CHORDS & ARPEGGIATED ACCOMPANIMENTS

When the notes of a chord are played together, it is called a **BLOCK CHORD** (as shown above)

When they are not played together, it is called a **BROKEN CHORD**

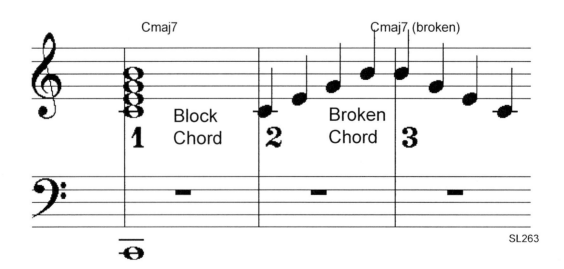

226

"Using Dominant Thirteen Chords in Blues Chord Progressions" (cont.)

When the notes of a chord are played sequentially, one after the other, it is called an **ARPEGGIO.** The word arpeggio comes from the Italian *arpeggiare,* which means "to play upon a harp." Notice that the arpeggios below outline each note of the indicated chords in root position. When a chord is repeated in the following measures, it is not necessary to repeat the chord symbol.

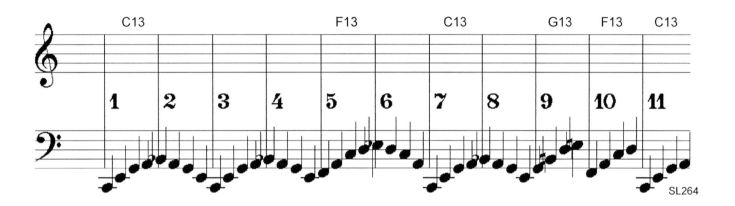

Notice how each chord is arpeggiated with the 1 – 3 – 5 – 6 (or 13) – & ♭7 tones. This is very common in blues music.

Here's an example of a C13 arpeggio:

C – E – G – A – B♭ – A – G – E – C

"walking up"   "walking back down"

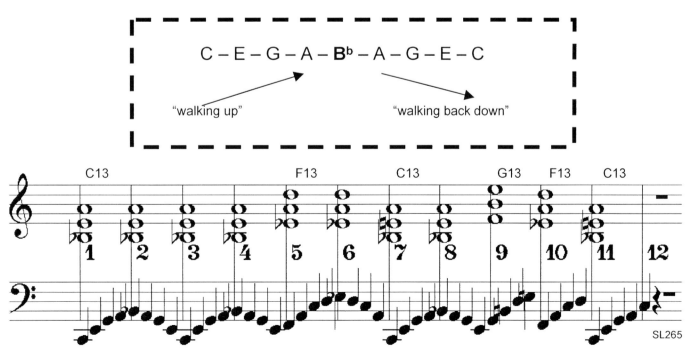

Lesson Sixteen

"Altering Chords"

Congratulations on completing your study on triads, sevenths, ninths, elevenths, and thirteenth chords. We will now study how to alter these chords in various situations.

# of notes	Type of Chord	Status
Three	Triad	Complete
Four	Seventh	Complete
Five	Ninth	Complete
Six	Eleventh	Complete
Seven	Thirteenth	Complete

"Introduction to Altering Chords"

Any chord, whether major, minor, augmented or seventh, can be 'modified' or 'altered' thereby changing its character or 'color'. In particular, with the dominant seventh which is mainly characterized by three notes: the **root**, **major third** and **minor seventh**; the fifth, ninth, eleventh and thirteenth *may be altered.*

Raising or lowering the notes of a chord and its extensions by a *half step* may change its dissonance. This increases the 'tension' of the chord and increases the sense of release as one moves to a *less dissonant* chord (for example, the tonic). Care must be taken that these **altered chords** are correctly numbered.

We will look at a few examples to see how this is done:

> 1.) The standard way of writing altered seventh chords is to identify the quality of the chord (whether major, minor or dominant)

> 2.) Then add the modified note in brackets. (If more than one note is altered, both are shown, one above the other in one pair of brackets, with the widest interval at the top).

> > **LOWERED** (flat) = *b or −*
> >
> > **RAISED** (sharp) = # or +

PianoPlayerPlus.com

"Introduction to Altering Chords" (cont.)

Examples: **C9 (+11)** represents a **C** ninth chord with the root, a major 3rd, a perfect 5th, a flattened 7th, a major ninth and a sharpened 11th;

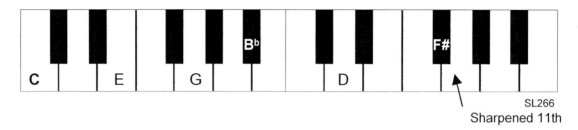

SL266
Sharpened 11th

… while **C#9 (#11)** represents a **C#** ninth chord with the root, a major 3rd, a perfect 5th, a flattened 7th, a major ninth and a sharpened 11th.

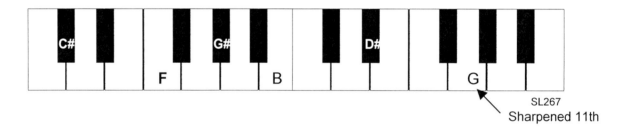

SL267
Sharpened 11th

C7(♭9 ♭5) represents a **C** seventh chord with the root, major 3rd, diminished 5th, minor 7th and minor 9th.

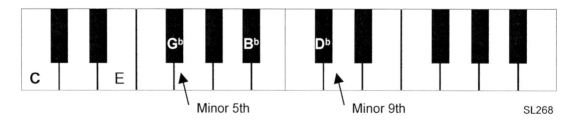

Minor 5th   Minor 9th   SL268

The main purpose of **altering** chords is to increase the effectiveness in a progression. In previous lessons, we've already learned how a dominant seventh is more effective than a dominant triad in "2 – 5 – 1" and other chord progressions.

"Altering Chords" (cont.)

The following chart shows various combinations of altered chords...

SL269	Maj7 (+5)	A major seventh chord with an added raised fifth tone
SL270	7 (-9)	A dominant seventh chord with an added lowered ninth tone
SL271	7 (+9)	A dominant seventh chord with an added raised ninth tone
SL272	7 (-5)	A dominant seventh chord with an added lowered fifth tone
SL273	7 (+5)	A dominant seventh chord with an added raised fifth tone
SL274	9 (-5)	A dominant ninth chord with the fifth tone lowered one-half step
SL275	9 (+5)	A dominant ninth chord with the fifth tone raised one-half step
SL276	9 (+11)	A dominant ninth chord with an added raised eleventh tone
SL277	11 (-9)	A dominant eleventh chord with an added lowered ninth tone
SL278	13 (-9)	A dominant thirteenth chord with the ninth tone lowered one-half step
SL279	13 (-9 -5)	A dominant thirteen chord with both the ninth and fifth tones lowered one-half step
SL280	13 (-9 +11)	A dominant thirteenth chord with the ninth lowered one-half step and the eleventh tone raised one-half step
SL281	13 (+11)	A dominant thirteenth chord with the eleventh tone raised one-half step
SL282	(-9)	Add lowered ninth tone
SL283	(-9+5)	Add lowered ninth and raised fifth tones
SL284	(-9 -5)	Add lowered ninth and fifth tones
SL285	+5	Add raised fifth tone
SL286	+9	Add raised ninth tone
SL287	+11	Add raised eleventh tone

Exercises 16.1 (hint: Invert the chords if necessary)

1. Shade an E7 (#9) Chord

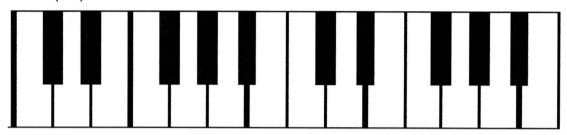

2. Shade a C#min13 (♭9) Chord

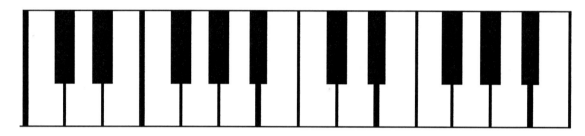

3. Shade an A♭7 (#9) Chord

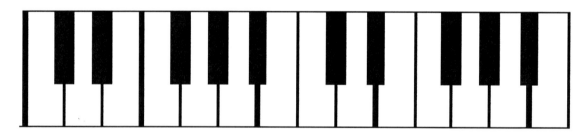

4. Shade a Dmin9 (#11) Chord

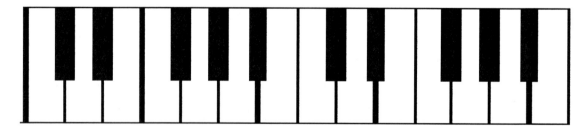

Exercises 16.2 (hint: Invert the chords if necessary)

1. Shade an F7 (♭9) Chord

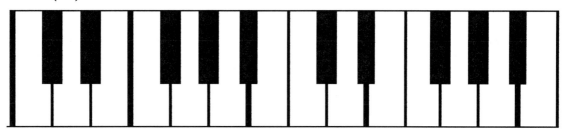

2. Shade a Cmin11 (#5) Chord

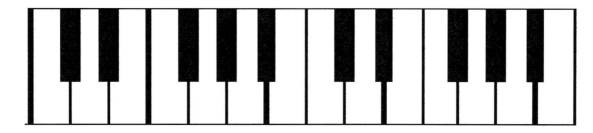

3. Shade a G9 (♭5) Chord

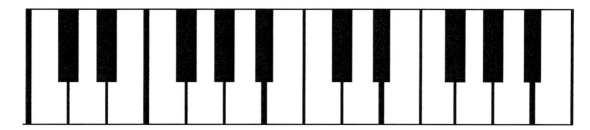

4. Shade an E♭7 (♭5) Chord

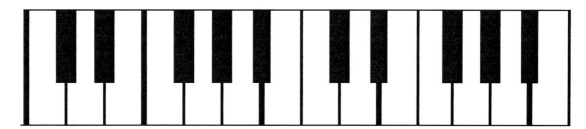

"Using Altered Chords in the 2 – 5 – 1 Progression"

It is common to use altered chords to change the "feel" of a chord progression. As you've learned, the "2 – 5 – 1" progression can be played with minor and major triads, seventh, ninth, eleventh and thirteenth chords. The "2-5-1" progression can also be played with **altered** seventh chords.

Here is the "2-5-1" chord progression with major, minor, and dominant seventh Chords:

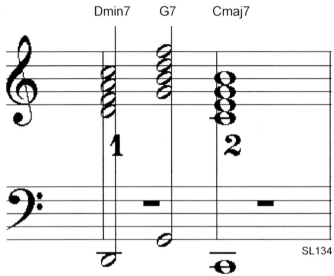

Here is the "2-5-1" chord progression with *just* dominant and major seventh Chords:

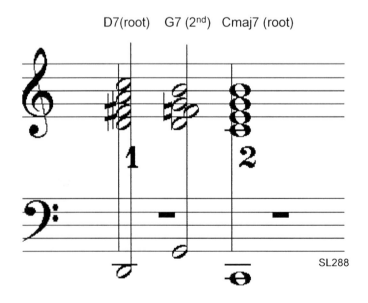

"Using Altered Chords in the 2 – 5 – 1 Progression" (cont.)

We will now use the dom7 (#9) , dom7 (#9 #5), and the min9 to play a "2 – 5 – 1" chord progression.

D7 (#9)

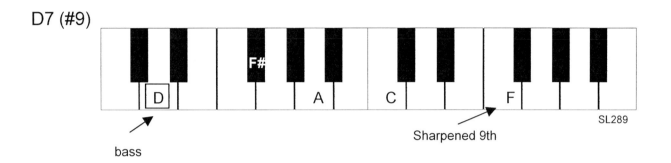

I prefer leaving out the 5th tone ...

D7 (#9) omit 5

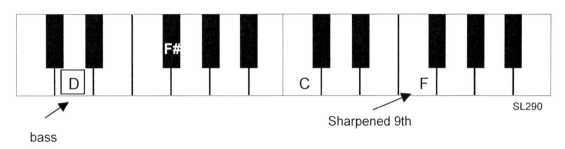

G7 (#9 #5)

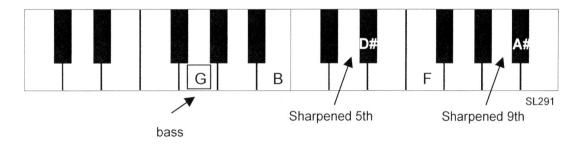

I prefer playing the 7th tone at the bottom ...

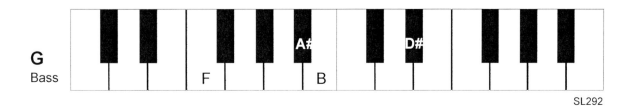

235

"Using Altered Chords in the 2 – 5 – 1 Progression" (cont.)

Cmin9

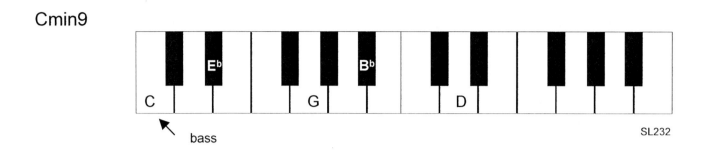

D7 (#9) -- G7 (#9 #5) -- Cmin9

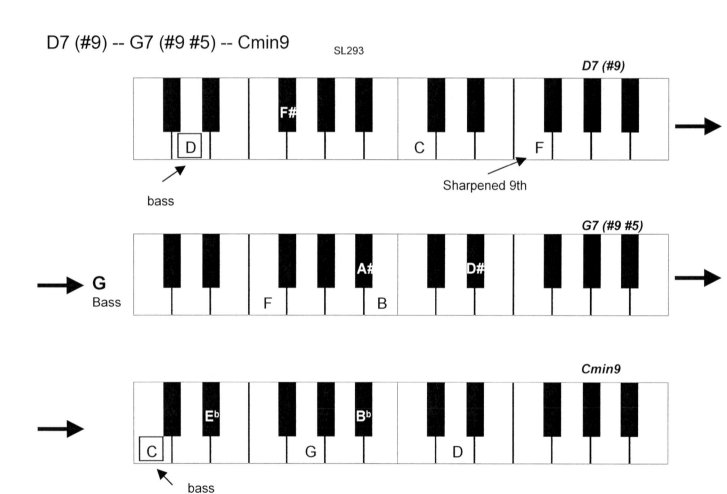

I strongly recommend using the **"Piano Player Plus 1.0"** Software to test yourself on ninth, eleventh, and thirteenth chords. With this program, you will be able to select random Polychords while using your ear to depict which chord it is. It will also help you to recognize altered chords. These types of exercises will be very helpful to your success in playing piano by ear.

PianoPlayerPlus.com

"Using Altered Chords in the 3 – 6 – 2 – 5 – 1 Progression"

We have already studied this progression with seventh chords:

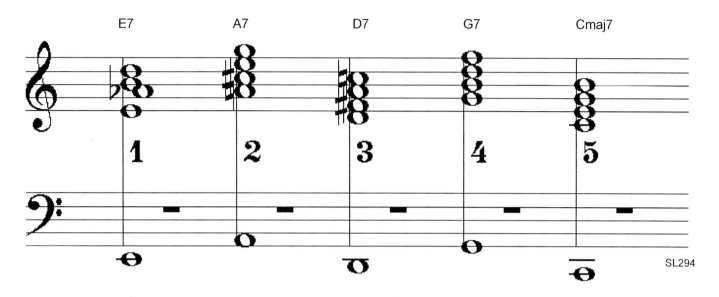

Try using the following alterations:

- Change E7 to **Emin7♭5 (or E $^{\varnothing}$)**
- Change A7 to **A7 (♭9)** -- [To create this chord, simply lower the D from the previous chord to C#]
- Change D7 to **Dmin9**
- Change G7 to **G13** -- [To create this chord, simply lower the C from the previous chord to B]
- Change Cmaj7 to **Cmaj9**

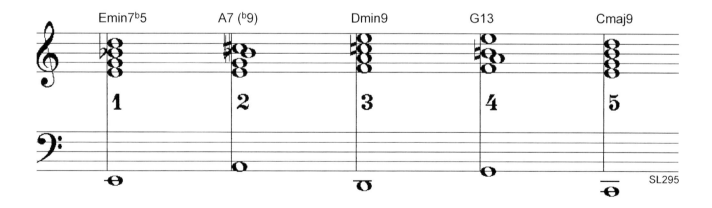

EXERCISE 16.3

Complete the chart below by filling in the missing chords for the following progression …

KEY	"iii"	"vi"	"ii"	"V"	"I"
C	Emin7 (♭9)	A7 (♭9)	Dmin9	G13	Cmaj9
D		B7 (♭9)			
E					Emaj9
F			Gmin9		
G				D13	
A					
B					
C# / D♭					C#maj9
D# / E♭					
F# / G♭					
G# / A♭					
A# / B♭					

EXERCISE 16.4

What is the purpose of *altering* chords?

_____

_____

What type of chords do you prefer to play a "ii – V – I" chord progression with? Please explain your answer.

_____

_____

_____

_____

"Using Altered Chords in the 7 - 3 – 6 – 2 – 5 – 1 Progression"

We have already studied this progression with triads & seventh chords:

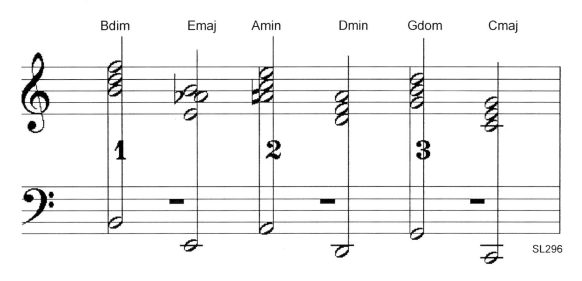

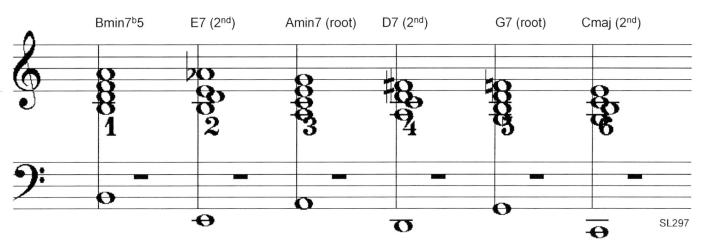

Try using the following alterations:
- Change Bmin7 ♭5 to **Bmin11**
- Change E7 to **E13 (♭9)**
- Change A7 to **Amin9**
- Change D7 to **Dmin7♭5**
- Change G7 to **Cmaj / G** -- [C maj triad over G bass]
- Add **Cmaj♭5 / G**
- Add **G13**
- Add **G9** (add 13) – *[Not necessary to play 11ᵗʰ tone]*
- Cmaj

239

"Using Altered Chords in the 7 - 3 – 6 – 2 – 5 – 1 Progression" (cont.)

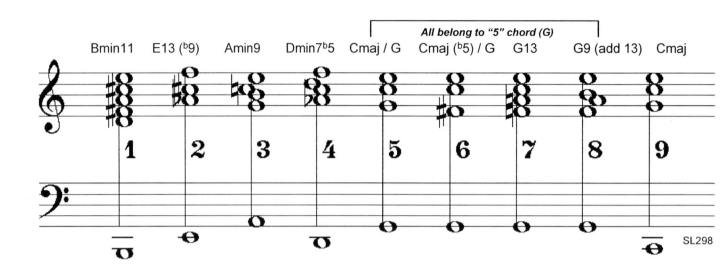

Exercises 16.5 (hint: Invert the chords if necessary)

1. Shade an E13 (#9) Chord

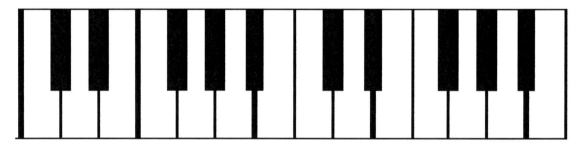

2. Shade a Gmin13 (♭9) Chord

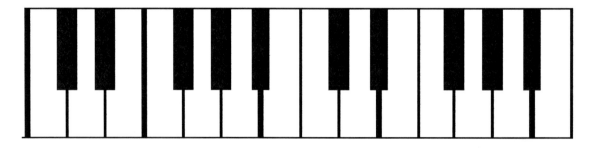

Lesson Seventeen

"Harmonizing Melodies"

In this lesson, we will learn how to take a melody and form various chords to accompany it. This is a common technique used especially by musicians who work with choirs. For example, if one composed a melody which included the i, iii, iv, vi, vii, and viii tone of a scale (as shown below), harmonizing this melody would mean playing a chord to accompany every note of the melody.

SL299

"Harmonizing a Melody in a Major Key"

To **HARMONIZE** a melody means to create a chord accompaniment for it. Since the **I, IV & V** (or V7) chords contain all the notes of the major scale, many melodies in a major key can be harmonized with just these three chords.

To determine the chords to be used, analyze the melody notes. Refer to the following chart to see which chord is generally used with each melody note of a major scale. When more than one chord can be chosen, your **ear** should always be the final guide.

SCALE DEGREE	CHORD
1, 3 , 5	I Chord
2, 4, 5, 7	V (or V7) Chord
1,4,6	IV Chord

There is also one scale degree which can be accompanied by a minor chord

SCALE DEGREE	CHORD
2	ii min Chord

From personal experience, here are the most common chords that I play with the following scale tones:

SCALE DEGREE	CHORD
1, 3 , 5	I Maj Chord
2	ii Min Chord
4,6	IV Maj Chord
7	V Chord

"Harmonizing a Melody in a Major Key" (cont.)

Here is a **C major scale** that is harmonized using only the **I, IV & V chords**:

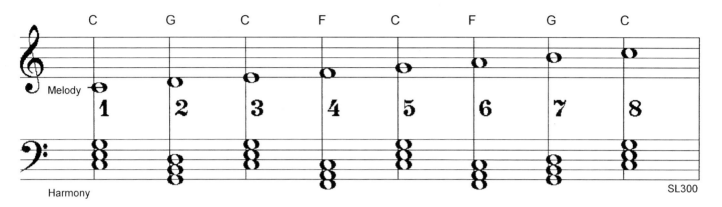

Here is a **C major scale** that is harmonized using the **I, ii, IV & V chords**:

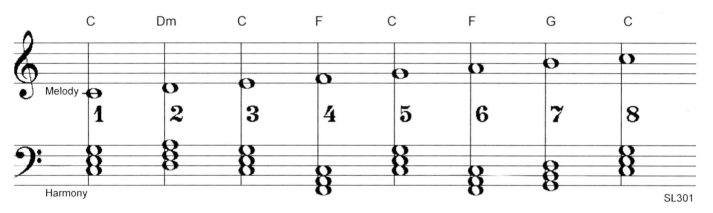

Note: Sometimes, the 2nd scale degree will require a V chord and sometimes it will require a ii chord. When not sure of which one to choose, play both chords with the melody and use your ear to pick the best combination.

When harmonizing a melody, I personally prefer that the chord be in the **inversion** which places the melody tone as the highest note. Here's an example of a C major scale that is harmonized with inverted **I, ii, IV & V chords**:

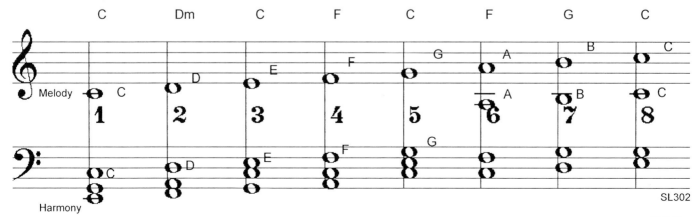

Note: Notice that the melody note is the highest tone of each chord

243

"Harmonizing a Melody in a Major Key" (cont.)

In some chord progressions, when the IV chord is played in it's root position, the I scale degree is the highest tone. That is also why a IV chord can be played both on the 1st degree, and the 4th / 6th.

For example, in C major, the IV chord is **Fmaj:**

The above diagram shows the Fmaj chord in it's first Inversion. That is, the **F tone** is the highest note. This chord usually accompanies the IV tone. However, sometimes, the chord is played in it's root position where **C** is the highest tone:

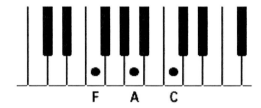

In this case, the IVmaj (F maj) is accompanying the 1st scale degree (C).

Keep in mind that most of the time, the I chord will accompany the 1st scale degree. However, when in doubt, try playing the IV chord (root position) and listen for which chord produces the best desired sound (in some instances, it **will** be the IV chord ... but let your **ear** be the judge).

Here is a **C major scale** that is harmonized using the **I, ii, IV & V chords** (The IV chord is substituted for the I chord):

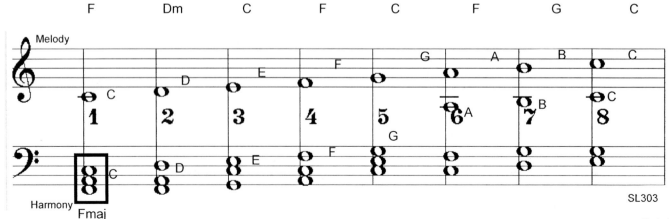

"Harmonizing a Melody in a Major Key" (cont.)

The **V** or **V7** chord can also be used to accompany the 2, 4, 5 & 7 scale degree.

For example, in C major, the V chord is **Gmaj:**

SL051

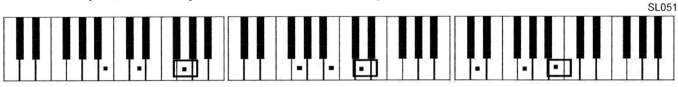

G is on top (V scale degree)   D is on top (ii scale degree)   B is on top (vii scale degree)

When played in the above progressions, the **V chord** can be used to accompany both the ii, V & vii scale degrees. Because the ii scale degree is usually accompanied by the **ii min chord,** and the **V** degree by the **I maj chord,** you must use your ear to determine which chord fits best.

The **G7** can be used to accompany the 4th scale degree:

F is on top (IV scale degree)

In most cases, the *I maj chord* will be used to accompany the I, III & V scale degrees because those are the tones that make up the **I maj** chord.

I maj (1st Inversion): Accompanies the 1st scale degree because this inversion puts the I tone on top.

I maj (2nd Inversion): Accompanies the 3rd scale degree because this inversion puts the III tone on top *(and the I tone in the middle).*

I maj (root position): Accompanies the 5th scale degree because this inversion puts the V tone on top *(and the I tone on the bottom).*

"Harmonizing a Melody in a Major Key" (cont.)

The following diagrams represent all eight accompanying chords of a major scale
(Using only the I, ii, IV & V chords)

> ### Important
> From this point on, when asked to harmonize a melody, please refer to this chart as it gives you all eight chords which correspond to each scale degree. It also provides you with the chord inversions that produce the smoothest transition while keeping the scale degree on top. As stated earlier, sometimes a chord substitution will occur. Otherwise, harmonize all melodies with these chords.

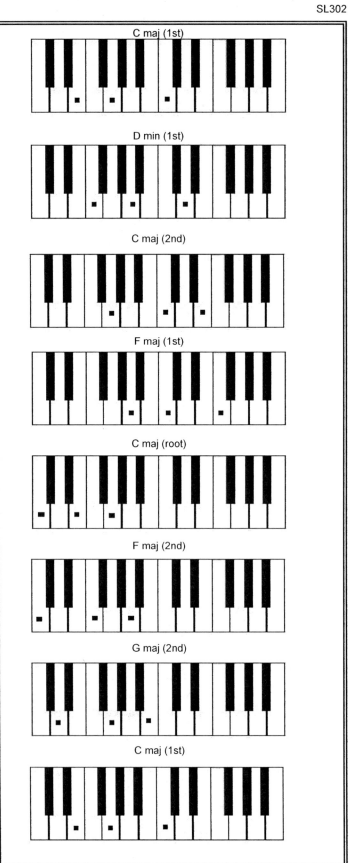

EXERCISE 17.1

Harmonize the following melodies (each display represents a melodic tone). **Normally, these notes would** *all* **be on one grand staff** (discussed in the beginning of this course).

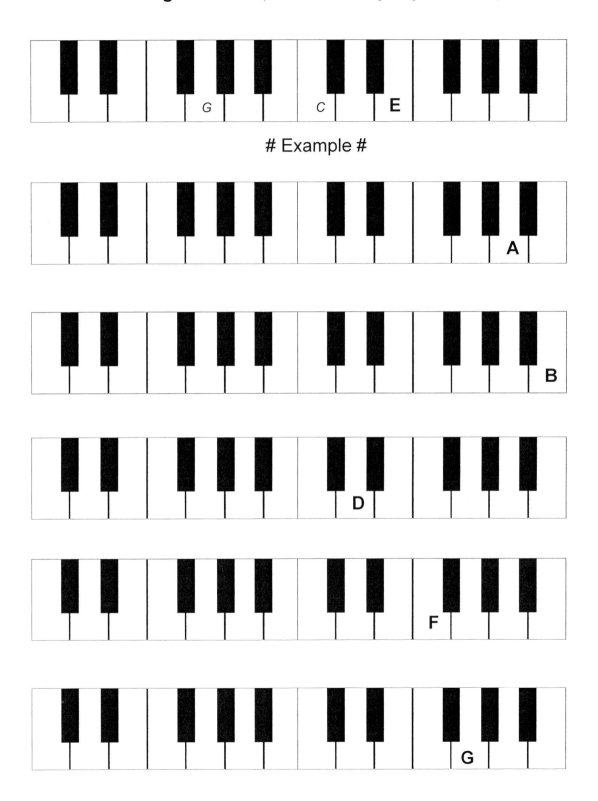

Example

EXERCISE 17.2

Harmonize the following melodies ...

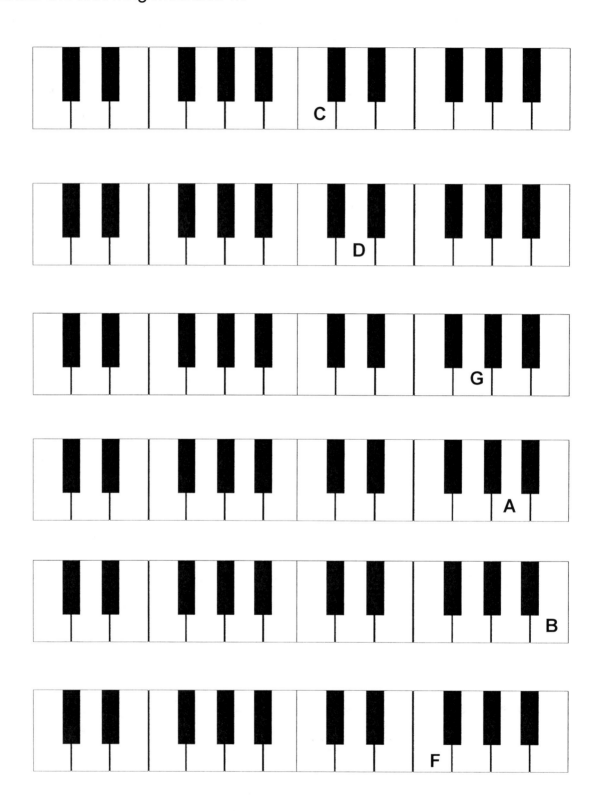

EXERCISE 17.3

Harmonize the following melodies …

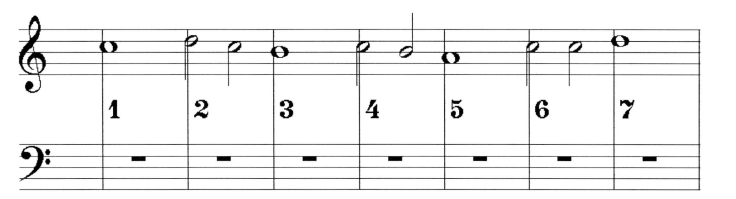

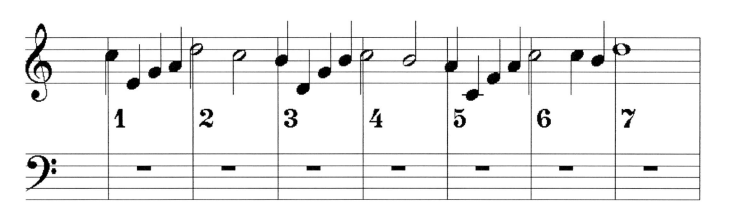

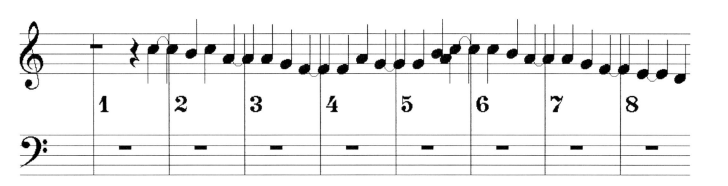

EXERCISE 17.4

Harmonize the following melodies ...

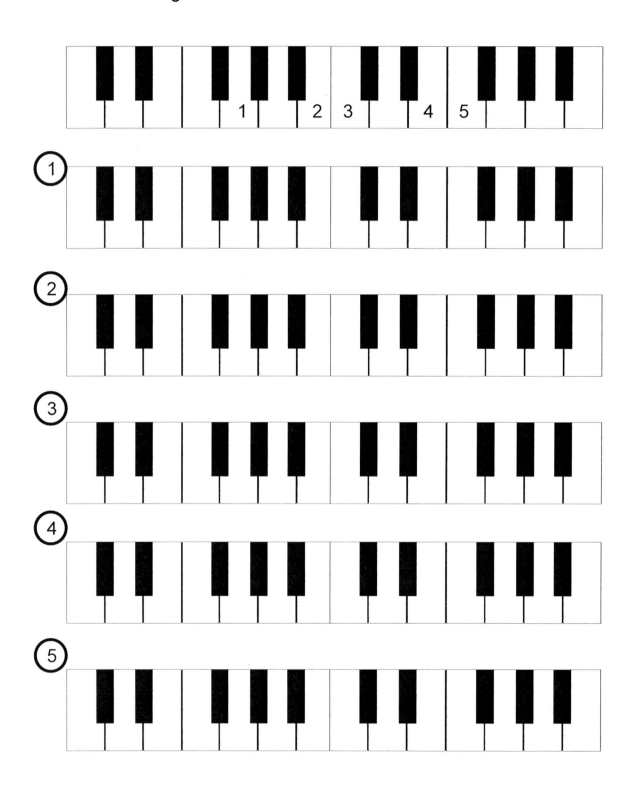

EXERCISE 17.5

Harmonize the following melodies …

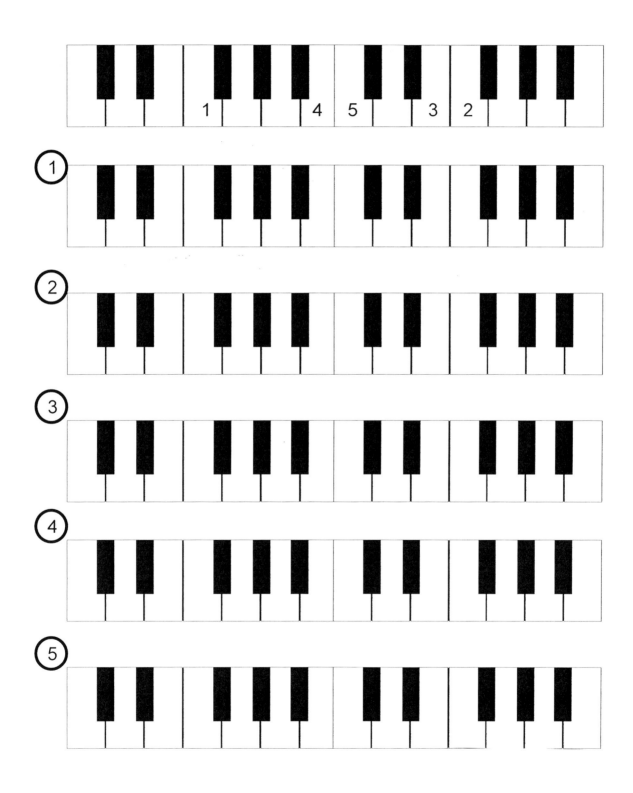

TWO STEPS TO HARMONIZING A MELODY...

1.) Figure out the Melody

a. Choose a **key center** (what major key your melody will be played in)

b. The notes of the melody should **only** use the notes of the major scale
(for most situations)
  -Thus, you have eight notes to figure out most melodies.
  -Use your ear to eliminate notes that don't fit

c. Apply the appropriate rhythm to your melody

2.) Use the I, ii, IV & V chords to harmonize the melody according to the *highest note*

a. Determine which corresponding chords will be used in situations where there can be more than one choice.

b. Look for chord inversions which are the easiest to transition from the previous chord

c. Apply the appropriate rhythm to your harmony

d. Look for Passing and Neighboring tones as these tones don't always require an accompanying chord

Passing Tones
Most melodies include tones that are not apart of the chord used for the harmony. These non-chord tones are called **NON-HARMONIC TONES.** When a melody passes from one chord tone to a *different* chord tone with a non-harmonic tone (a half or whole step) between, the non-harmonic tone is called a **PASSING TONE.**

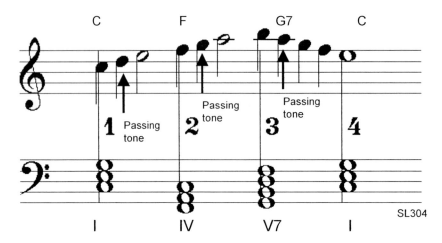

Passing and Neighboring Tones (Melody) ...

Neighboring Tones

When a melody passes from one chord tone back to the *same* chord tone with a non-harmonic tone (a half or whole step) between, the non-harmonic tone is called a **NEIGHBORING TONE**. It is an **UPPER NEIGHBORING TONE** when it is *above* the chord tone, and a **LOWER NEIGHBORING TONE** when it is *below* the chord tone.

Passing and neighboring tones are non-harmonic and usually occur on a weak beat. These tones should not be a factor in your choice of a chord to harmonize a melody.

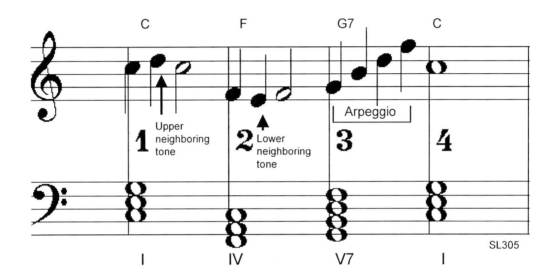

Determining which tones to harmonize

Since neighboring and passing tones lead to chord tones, they don't necessarily need to be harmonized. That is, they can be played in between chords. Below, you will find the melody to "Mary Had a Little Lamb." Notice, that some of the notes are chord tones and others are neighboring and passing tones:

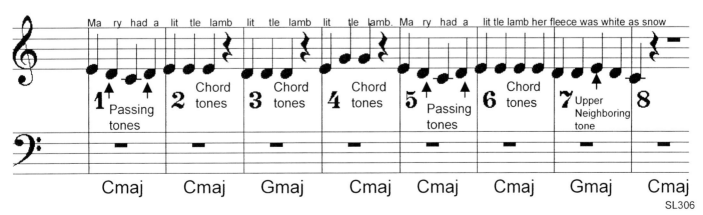

SL306

Passing and Neighboring Tones (cont.) ...

Recognizing Passing and Neighboring Tones

Ok … let's say you've figured out the melody to a song. In order to harmonize this melody, you must now separate the chord tones (which you wouldn't know yet if you've only figured out the melody) from the neighboring and passing tones.

Here are some tips for distinguishing chord tones in a melody

- **If a chord is being arpeggiated, it can be used to harmonize the melody**

  For example, if I created a melody like this: C – E – G – A – C. Notice that I actually arpeggiated a C major chord (played the notes of the chord separately). Thus, any other notes would be either passing or neighboring tones depending on their function. The "**A**" tone in this example is considered a **passing tone** because it is used to pass from one chord tone to another (from G -- C). I would then play this melody over a Cmaj chord.

- **If a note is played more than once in one measure, it is most likely a *chord* tone**

  Notice in the 2nd bar of "Mary had a Little Lamb" how the "E" tone is repeated three times in one bar. "E" is a chord tone of Cmaj. Thus, this bar is played over a Cmaj chord. This also occurs in bar three with three "D" tones. Since D is a chord tone of Gmaj, this bar is played over a Gmaj Chord.

- **If two different chord tones of the same chord are in one measure, that chord is most likely to be the accompaniment.**

  This is shown in the 1st measure of "Mary had a Little Lamb." The melody is "E – D – C – D." Since E & C are chord tones of Cmaj, this bar is played over a Cmaj chord. But also notice that there are two "**D**" tones and the previous rule says that if a "note is played more than once in one measure, it is most likely a chord tone." While this is still true, if there are two different tones of the **same** chord in one measure, this rule dominates the other rule because the chances are greater of this chord being the accompaniment (because **2** of 3 notes are being played in the melody instead of just **1** of 3). Thus, the "D" becomes a **passing tone** because it is used to pass from one chord tone to another (from E -- C).

- **Remember that most songs end with the V resolving to the I chord.**

  This is shown in the 7th measure of "Mary had a little lamb." Whenever there are tones from a V chord right before the ending of the song, those tones are most likely associated with the V7 chord which will eventually lead to the tonic chord (I). Notice, how there are 3 "**D**" tones. Since D is played three times in one measure and is also a chord tone of the Gmaj (or G7) chord, it is most likely to be played over a Gmaj or G7 chord. Thus, the "**E**" becomes an **upper neighboring tone** because it is used to pass from one chord tone back to the *same* chord tone.

Lesson Eighteen

"Techniques to Learning Songs by Ear"

In previous lessons, we've learned how to take a melody and form various chords to accompany it. In this lesson, we will take the melodies of various hymns and turn them into chords! These same techniques can be used not only to learn hymns, but virtually, all types of songs.

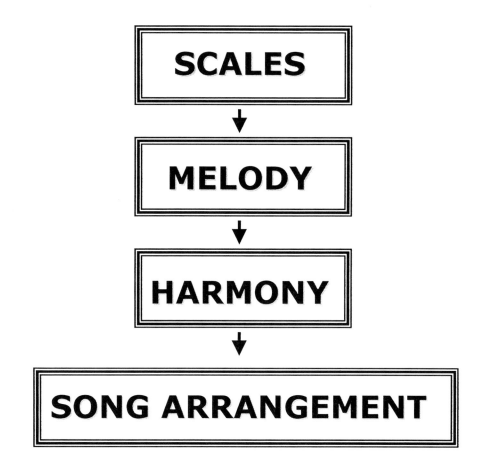

"Learning Songs by Ear"

In the next two chapters, we will study various hymns. Each hymn will be aimed at teaching a different technique. Keep in mind that by learning these hymns, you are not only learning **5 songs** but a countless number of techniques that can be used in *just about every song!* When studying a song, try to think of other songs that might share the same chord changes or melody.

Playing piano by ear involves the ability to hear the **same** chords and melodies in different songs. You will notice that a number of these hymns share various chord progressions. This is common in all types of music. For example, I've played chord progressions that were used both for love songs and gospel worship hymns. Of course, rhythms may be altered, but chords are universal! That is, they can be recycled and used in several songs over and over again!

So, it's not *just* a matter of memorizing each chord progression in every song, but simply recognizing them and being able to predict what chords occur next based on what chord has or is currently being played.

Here are the hymns that we will study in this lesson:

1. *Amazing Grace*
2. *Pass Me Not*
3. *O Come, Let Us Adore Him*

"AMAZING GRACE"

Amazing Grace is a gospel hymn written by John Newton, 1725 – 1807. Because of the popularity of this song, we've decided to lead you through the steps of playing this hymn by ear. Half of this technique depends on your ear and the other half depends on the techniques learned in previous chapters.

STEP ONE: Determine the Melody
Use your ear to determine and write down the melody of the hymn. Usually, the melody of gospel hymns include only the notes of the major scale but it is also common to see notes in the melody that are not apart of the major scale (Example: Notes of the blues or minor scale).

Note: **All songs will be learned in C major**

STEP TWO: Harmonize the Melody
You've practiced this technique in the last chapter with "Mary Had a Little Lamb." Simply, take the melody and determine the chords which best fit the melody. Remember, the **1, 3 & 5 tones** correspond to the I major chord; the **2** corresponds to the minor chord or V7 chord; the **4,6 & 1 tones** correspond to the IV major chord; and the **7 tone** corresponds with the V chord.

STEP THREE: Alter Chords (optional)
In previous chapters, you've learned several alterations to seventh, ninth, eleventh and thirteenth chords. After determining the chords of the melody in step two, you will notice various chord progressions that have been formed. For example, a *melody* may produce the following chords: amin -- dmin -- gmaj -- cmaj. From previous exercises, you should easily be able to observe that this is a "6 – 2 – 5 – 1" progression. Thus, you can substitute different chord progressions that you've learned earlier on in this course. Keep in mind that some chord substitutions may not sound correct. If this happens, simply move on to another alteration or chord substitution. Also, be creative when looking for chords to substitute. Keep your mind open to ninth, eleventh, and thirteenth chords. Explore sharpened ninths, and flatted fifths, etc.!

STEP FOUR: Listen (required!)
This is the most important step. After determining the melody, harmony, and altering various chords and progression, the last step is to listen. Listen for tones that sound out of place or progressions that can be made more "full" with chord substitutions. If you are playing along with a cassette, rewind the song several times and listen for parts in the song where you can enhance chords that you've already chosen. I can't express to you enough how important **listening** is to your musical performance. It is also the simplest of the four steps.

"AMAZING GRACE"

STEP ONE
"Determining the Melody"

Listen to **SL307** ("Amazing Grace Melody") with the Sound Library Program. Keep in mind that all melodies will be derived from the **C major scale**.

After listening to **SL307** ("Amazing Grace Melody"), attempt to play the melody on your piano. Re-play the sound file if you have to. Remember, there are **only** eight notes used for this melody. With that in mind, you should be able to use your ear and some of the techniques learned in this course to figure out the melody.

Also remember how **passing** and **neighboring tones** work. Many melodies will utilize neighboring tones. Use your ear to figure out if the neighboring tones are upper or lower. That is, whether the neighboring tone is higher or lower in pitch than the previous tone.

$\frac{3}{4}$ is the time signature for this song. Unlike $\frac{4}{4}$, there are **three** beats per measure. Listen to **SL308** for an example of a $\frac{3}{4}$ beat.

After playing the melody, *draw* the notes on the treble clef below. The words of the song are written underneath the area you should write each note. A few tones have already been given to you…

EXERCISE 18.1

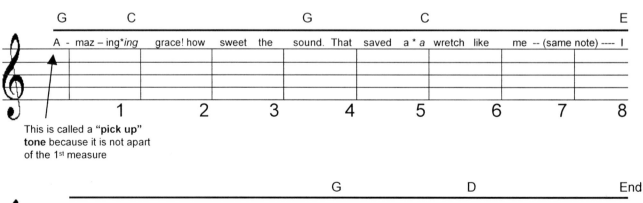

"AMAZING GRACE"

STEP ONE (cont.)

Here is the melody to "Amazing Grace." Compare this melody to yours on the previous page

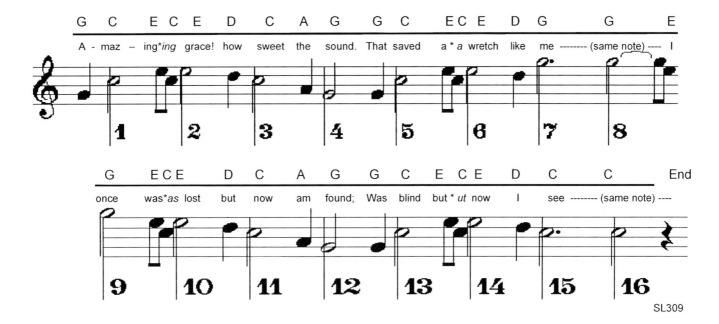

SL309

EXERCISE 18.2

1.**Circle** the notes on the diagram above which appear to be **chord tones.** Remember to use the principles on *"distinguishing chord tones in a melody"* (found in the previous chapter).

2.Draw a **square** around the notes on the diagram above which appear to be **passing tones.**

3.Draw a **triangle** around the notes on the diagram above which appear to be upper or lower neighboring tones.

STEP TWO

"Harmonizing the Melody"

Now that we've distinguished the chord tones from the passing and neighboring tones, we are ready to choose the *best sounding* accompanying chords.

"AMAZING GRACE"

STEP TWO (cont.)

"Harmonizing the Melody"

EXERCISE 18.3

Using the information from the previous exercise, **choose** the *best sounding* **accompanying chord (s) for each measure below:**

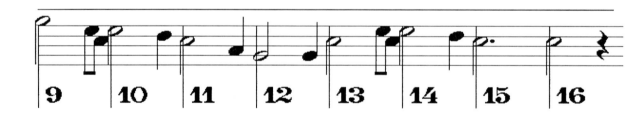

PianoPlayerPlus.com

"AMAZING GRACE"

STEP TWO (cont.)

"Harmonizing the Melody"

Here are the accompanying chords to the melody of this song. You will notice a few unexpected chords below. Try to figure out why these *"unexpected"* chords were used instead of the traditional chords learned in the last chapter. **Hint:** It has something to do with *certain* chord progressions.

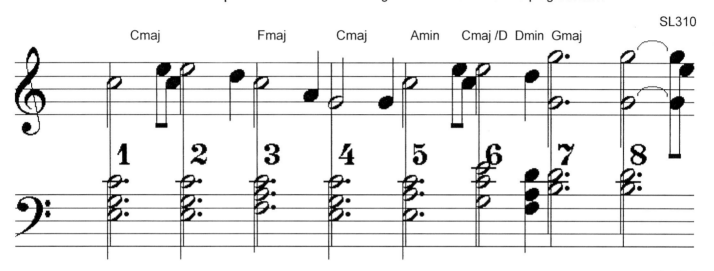

SL310

M = Maj
m = min

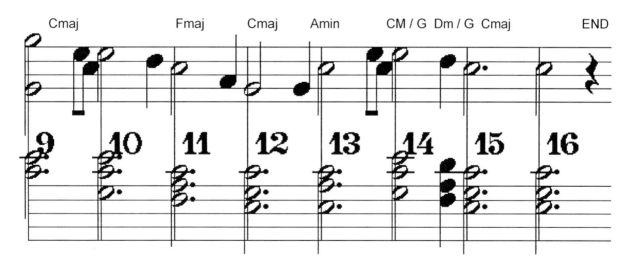

STEP THREE

"Altering Chords"

In my opinion, this is the best part of learning a song! This is the point where you have fun and make choices as to how you want the song to sound.

261

STEP THREE (cont.)

"Altering Chords"

Keep in mind that there are several ways to alter chords. As you become more experienced, you will find yourself doing a little bit of everything!

In this example, I decided that I wanted the song to sound **"bluesy – gospel*ish*"**. **Notice some of the chord replacements I use:**

Fmaj to **F9:** I changed the Fmaj chord in measure 3 to an F9 chord

Add **E7 (b9 +5)** after Cmaj: Since the Cmaj chord in measure 4 leads to an Amin chord in measure 5, I simply added an **E7 (b9+5)** right before the Amin chord. If you predicted the beginning of a "6-2-5-1" progression, you're right! This E7 chord will lead to an Amin9 chord which will lead to the ii… and finally to the V chord.

Amin to **Amin9:** I changed the Amin chord in measure 5 to an Amin9 to add a little "flavor."

Cmaj / D to **D9:** I changed the Cmaj / D (which can be considered a D11 because of the "G" and "E" tones) in measure 6 to **D9**. This will pull more to the Gmaj chord in the 7th & 8th measures.

Gmaj to **G13:** I've found that V13 chords are great chord substitutions for V7 chords. Actually, any extension can work along with a dominant chord (G7, G9, G11, G13). I prefer using dom11 or dom13 chords. Try substituting chords with these polychords and hear how full your piano playing will sound!

Note: Use the same substitutions / alterations for measures 9 – 14.

"AMAZING GRACE"

STEP THREE (cont.)

"Altering Chords"

Here is my altered version of "Amazing Grace." Let this serve as an example for you as you can use these alterations or come up with your own. Try raising a ninth, or lowering an eleventh. You never know what type of sound a chord makes until you try it. You will soon start playing alterations and stumble across chords that you'll use for the rest of your life. I'm **still** discovering new alterations and inversions that enhance my playing and I encourage you to do the same!

SL311

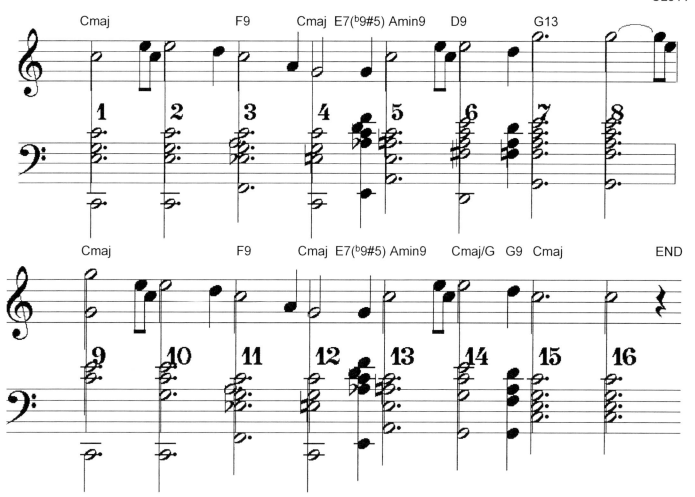

Note: It is not necessary to re-write a chord if it continues on to the next measure. As you can see, in measures 2, 8, 10 & 16, the chords are missing because the previous chord is being played again.

STEP FOUR

"Listening"

Listen to your version of "Amazing Grace." Then, listen to my version (SL311). Yours should sound similar (if not better!). If you hear any chords or tones that sound out of place, slow down and try to fix your mistakes. It is very important to use your ear during this step.

"AMAZING GRACE"

CONGRATULATIONS on completing
your first song in this course!

EVALUATION
Please answer the following questions on a scale of 1 – 5.

I understand how to determine the melody in a song.

1   2   3   4   5

I understand how to distinguish chord tones from passing and neighboring tones.

1   2   3   4   5

I understand how to take chord tones and form accompanying chords based on techniques that I've learned.

1   2   3   4   5

I understand how to alter chords to produce a desired sound.

1   2   3   4   5

I am able to listen to my piano playing and point out mistakes, if any.

1   2   3   4   5

If your score is:

23 + Excellent
20 – 22 Good
15 – 19 Average
8 – 14 Need Improvement
7 & below Repeat Course

"PASS ME NOT"

STEP ONE
"Determining the Melody"

Listen to **SL312** ("Pass Me Not Melody") with the Sound Library Program.

After listening to **SL312** ("Pass Me Not"), attempt to play the melody on your piano. Re-play the sound file if you have to. Remember, there are **only** eight notes used for this melody. With that in mind, you should be able to use your ear and some of the techniques learned in this course to figure out the melody.

After playing the melody, *draw* the notes on the treble clef below. The words of the song are written underneath the area you should write each note. A few tones have already been given to you…

EXERCISE 18.4

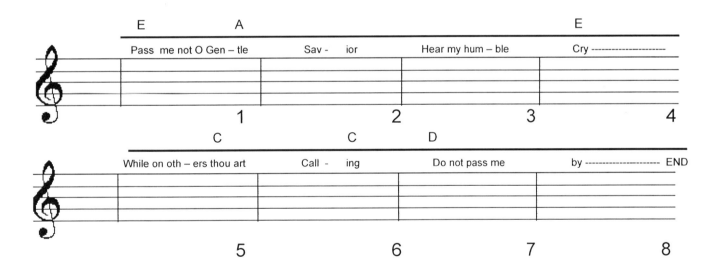

"PASS ME NOT"

STEP ONE (cont.)

Here is the melody to "Pass Me Not." Compare this melody to yours on the previous page

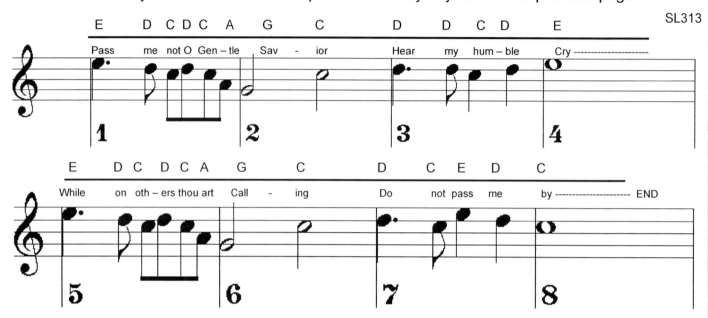

EXERCISE 18.5

1.Circle the notes on the diagram above which appear to be **chord tones.** Remember to use the principles on *"distinguishing chord tones in a melody"* (found in the previous chapter).

2.Draw a **square** around the notes on the diagram above which appear to be **passing tones.**

3.Draw a **triangle** around the notes on the diagram above which appear to be upper or lower neighboring tones.

STEP TWO

"Harmonizing the Melody"

Now that we've distinguished the chord tones from the passing and neighboring tones, we are ready to choose the *best sounding* accompanying chords.

"PASS ME NOT"

STEP TWO (cont.)
"Harmonizing the Melody"

EXERCISE 18.6

Using the information from the previous exercise, **choose** the *best sounding* **accompanying chord (s) for each measure below:**

"PASS ME NOT"

STEP TWO (cont.)
"Harmonizing the Melody"

Here are the accompanying chords to the melody above. Again, you will notice a few unexpected chords below. Try to figure out why these *"unexpected"* chords were used instead of the traditional chords learned in the last chapter.

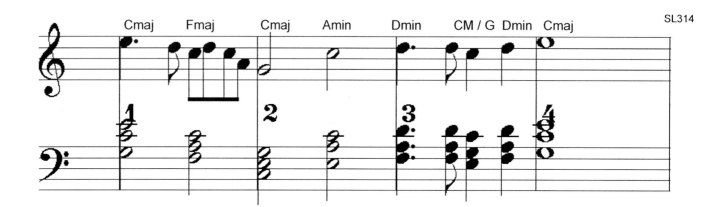

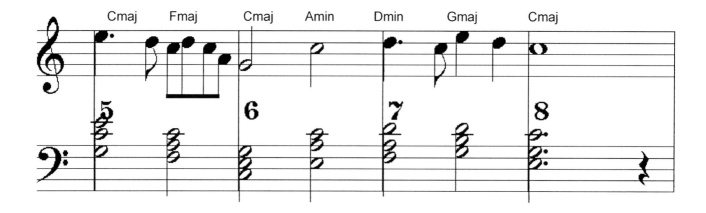

STEP THREE
"Altering Chords"

As you've probably noticed from the last song, altering and substituting chords can make a huge difference in how a song is played. Alterations literally turn a song into whatever *"mood"* the musician desires.

"PASS ME NOT"

STEP THREE (cont.)

"Altering Chords"

Remember ... there are a countless number of ways to alter chords. Use the *"Altered Chords"* chapter to help guide you through the process (if needed).

Fmaj to F9: I changed the Fmaj chord in measure 1 to an F9 chord

Cmaj to Bmin7 (^{b}5^{b}9) **& Add E7 (^{b}9 +5)** before Amin9: Since the Cmaj chord leads to an Amin chord in measure 2, I chose to go another route and substitute the Cmaj for a Bmin7 (^{b}5^{b}9). My reason for doing this was to create a "7 – 3 – 6 – 2 – 5 -1". By simply adding an **E7 (b9+5)** right before the Amin chord, the "7-3-6-2-5-1" chord progression is complete.

Amin to Amin9: I changed the Amin chord in measure 5 to an Amin9 to add a little "flavor."

Cmaj / D to D9: I changed the Cmaj / D (which can be considered a D11 because of the "G" and "E" tones) in measure 3 to **D9.** This will pull more to the G9 chord.

Gmaj to G9: I've chosen to use a G9 chord (this chord allows me to keep the melody on top). Actually, any extension can work along with a dominant chord (G7, G9, G11, 13). I normally prefer using dom11 and dom13 chords but in this case, I want to preserve the melody by playing a chord that puts "C" on top.

Add "6-2-5-1": When a "2-5-1" chord progression occurs (as in measures 3 & 4), it is common to play another "6-2-5-1" progression starting from the resolving I chord (this is basically a *"fill in"* progression). In playing this chord progression, I chose to use an A7 (^{b}9) – D7 (^{b}9) – and G7 (^{b}9) chord.

Note: Use the same substitutions / alterations for measures 5 – 6.

"PASS ME NOT"

STEP THREE (cont.)

"Altering Chords"

Here is my altered version of "Pass Me Not." Let this hymn *also* serve as an example to you as you can use these alterations or come up with your own. Try raising a ninth, or lowering an eleventh. Where you see the potential for a *nice* chord progression, don't be afraid to add it in! A prime example is my "7-3-6-2-5-1" progression starting at measure two. Use your imagination!

SL315

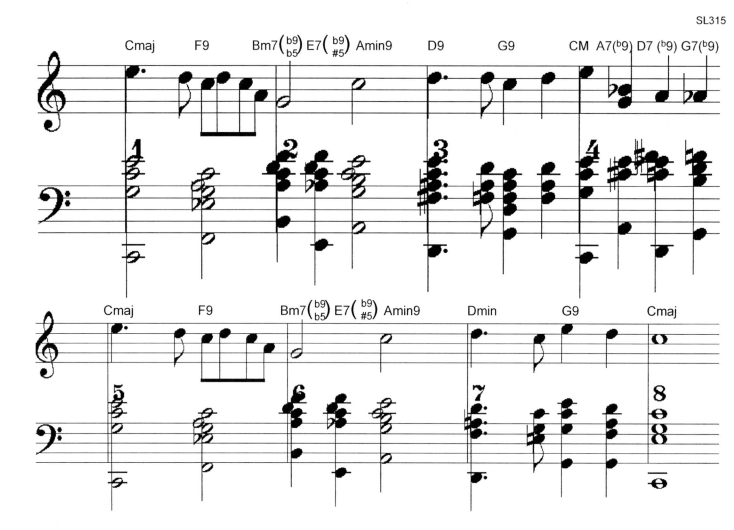

STEP FOUR

"Listening"

Listen to your version of "Pass Me Not." Then, listen to my version (SL315). Yours should sound similar (if not better!). If you hear any chords or tones that sound out of place, slow down and try to fix your mistakes. It is very important to use your ear during this step.

270

"O Come, Let Us Adore Him"

STEP ONE
"Determining the Melody"

Listen to **SL316** ("O Come, Let Us Adore Him") with the Sound Library Program.

After listening to **SL316** ("O Come, Let Us Adore Him"), attempt to play the melody on your piano. Replay the sound file if you have to. Remember, there are **only** eight notes used for this melody. With that in mind, you should be able to use your ear and some of the techniques learned in this course to figure out the melody.

After playing the melody, *draw* the notes on the treble clef below. The words of the song are written underneath the area you should write each note. A few tones have already been given to you...

EXERCISE 18.7

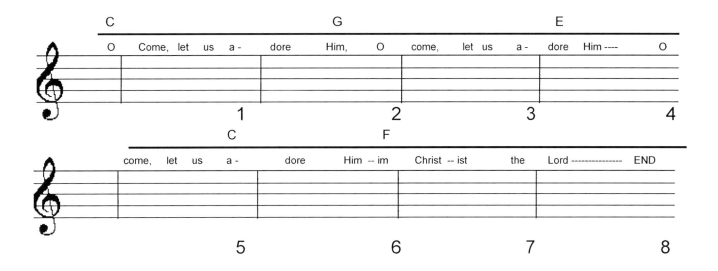

"O Come, Let Us Adore Him"

STEP ONE (cont.)

Here is the melody to "O Come, Let Us Adore Him." Compare this melody to yours on the previous page

SL317

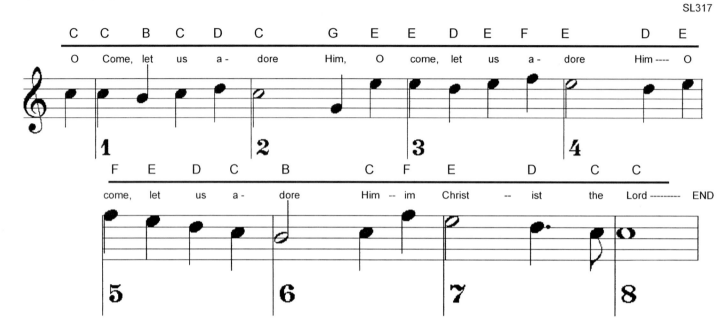

EXERCISE 18.8

1.Circle the notes on the diagram above which appear to be **chord tones.** Remember to use the principles on *"distinguishing chord tones in a melody"* (found in the previous chapter).

2.Draw a **square** around the notes on the diagram above which appear to be **passing tones.**

3.Draw a **triangle** around the notes on the diagram above which appear to be upper or lower neighboring tones.

STEP TWO

"Harmonizing the Melody"

Now that we've distinguished the chord tones from the passing and neighboring tones, we are ready to choose the *best sounding* accompanying chords.

"O Come, Let Us Adore Him"

STEP TWO (cont.)

"Harmonizing the Melody"

EXERCISE 18.9

Using the information from the previous exercise, **choose** the *best sounding* **accompanying chord (s) for each measure below:**

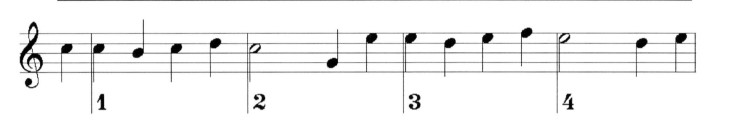

"O Come, Let Us Adore Him"

STEP TWO (cont.)
"Harmonizing the Melody"

Here are the accompanying chords to the melody above.

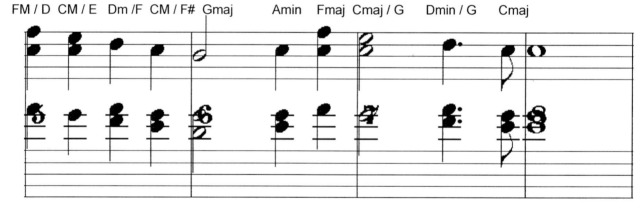

M = Major
m = Minor

Note: These symbols can also be used when there is not enough room.

STEP THREE

"Altering Chords"

As you've probably noticed from the last two songs, altering and substituting chords can make a huge difference in how a song is played. Remember ... alterations can literally turn a song into whatever *"mood"* the musician desires.

"O Come, Let Us Adore Him"

STEP THREE (cont.)

"Altering Chords"

Remember … there are a countless number of ways to alter chords. Once again, you can use the *"Altered Chords"* chapter to help guide you through the process (if needed).

Fmaj to **Dmin7 (^{b}5):** I changed the Fmaj chord in measures 3 & 6 to a Dmin7 (^{b}5). When seeing a IV -- I progression, it is common to replace the IV (F) with a ii min chord. This is actually the beginning of a "ii – V – I" chord progression.

Add **D9** after Cmaj / G: Since the Cmaj chord in measure 4 leads to Dmin / G (also a G9 chord), I chose to add a D9 chord to set up a "ii – V –I" progression.

Dmin / G to **G9** (measures 1, 4&7)**:** In actuality, this chord is already a G9 because of the F & A tones in the Dmin chord (A is the 9th tone of a G9 chord). We are simply notating it differently to show an obvious "2 – 5" relationship between the D9 and G9 chords (in measures 4 &7).

Add **A7 (^{b}9)** after **G9** (measure 4)**:** Since the next chord is Fmaj / D (also a Dmin7 chord), I chose to add an A7 (^{b}5) chord. This creates a " 6 -- 2" relationship which is the beginning of a "6-2-5-1" chord progression.

FM / D to **Dmin7** (measure 5)**:** In actuality, this chord is already a Dmin7 because of the F & C tones in the Fmaj chord (C is the 7th tone of a Dmin7 chord). We are simply notating it differently to show an obvious "6 – 2" relationship between the A7 (^{b}9) and Dmin7 chords.

Dm / F to **F6** (measure 5)**:** In actuality, this chord is already an F6 because of the D tone in the Dmin chord (D is the 6th tone of an F6 chord).

CM / F# to **D7 / F#** (measure 5)**:** Since the CM / F# chord leads to Gmaj, I decided to change this chord to a D7 over F# bass. (F# is one-half step below G so it pulls to G *greatly*)

Add **E7 (^{b}9 +5)** after Gmaj: Since the Gmaj chord leads to an Amin chord in measure 6, I chose to add an E7 (^{b}9+5). My reason for doing this was to create a " 3 – 6 – 2 – 5 -1". By simply adding an **E7 (b9+5)** right before the Amin chord, the "3-6-2-5-1" chord progression is complete.

Amin to **Amin9:** I changed the Amin chord in measure 6 to an Amin9 to add a little "flavor."

"O Come, Let Us Adore Him"

STEP THREE (cont.)

"Altering Chords"

Here is my altered version of "O Come, Let Us Adore Him." Once again, let this hymn along with the previously learned hymns serve as examples to you as you can use these alterations or come up with your own. Try raising a ninth, or lowering an eleventh. Be Creative!

SL319

STEP FOUR

"Listening"

Listen to your version of "O Come, Let us Adore Him." Then, listen to my version (SL319). Yours should sound similar (if not better!). If you hear any chords or tones that sound out of place, slow down and try to fix your mistakes. As like the previous songs, it is very important to use your ear during this step.

276

Lesson Nineteen

"More Hymns ..."

In the previous lesson, we've learned four steps to learning virtually any song:

1.) Determining the Melody

2.) Harmonizing the Melody

3.) Altering Chords

4.) Listening

In this lesson, we will *continue* to use these **four steps** to play two more hymns:

"Jesus Loves Me"

"Joyful, Joyful, We Adore Thee"

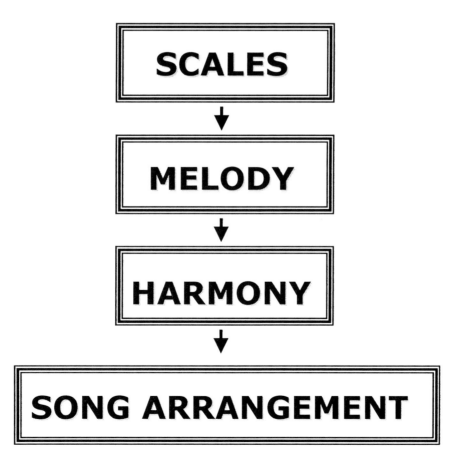

"Jesus Loves Me"

STEP ONE
"Determining the Melody"

Listen to **SL320** ("Jesus Loves Me") with the Sound Library Program.

After listening to **SL320** ("Jesus Loves Me"), attempt to play the melody on your piano. Re-play the sound file if you have to. Remember, there are **only** eight notes used for this melody. With that in mind, you should be able to use your ear and some of the techniques learned in this course to figure out the melody.

After playing the melody, *draw* the notes on the treble clef below. The words of the song are written underneath the area you should write each note. A few tones have already been given to you…

EXERCISE 19.1

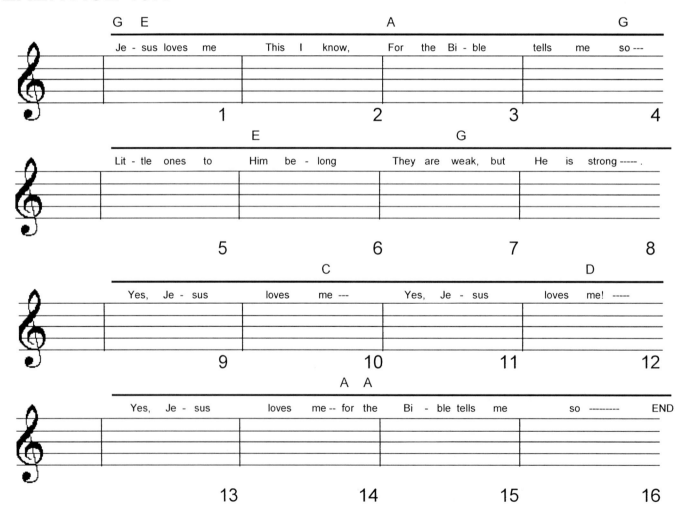

"Jesus Loves Me"

STEP ONE (cont.)

Here is the melody to "Jesus Loves Me." Compare this melody to yours on the previous page

EXERCISE 19.2

1. Circle the notes on the diagram above which appear to be **chord tones.** Remember to use the principles on *"distinguishing chord tones in a melody"* (found in chapter 17).

2. Draw a **square** around the notes on the diagram above which appear to be **passing tones.**

3. Draw a **triangle** around the notes on the diagram above which appear to be upper or lower neighboring tones.

STEP TWO

"Harmonizing the Melody"

Now that we've distinguished the chord tones from the passing and neighboring tones, we are ready to choose the *best sounding* accompanying chords.

"Jesus Loves Me"

STEP TWO (cont.)
"Harmonizing the Melody"

EXERCISE 19.3

Using the information from the previous exercise, **choose** the *best sounding* **accompanying chord (s) for each measure below:**

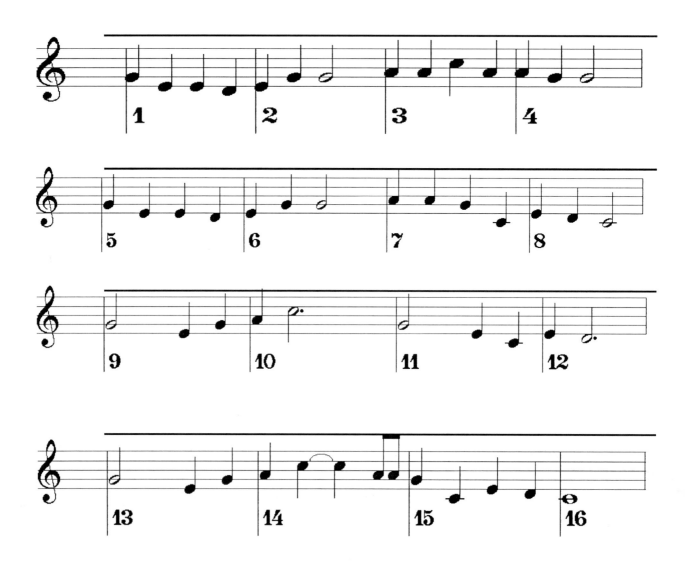

"Jesus Loves Me"

STEP TWO (cont.)

"Harmonizing the Melody"

SL321

Here are the accompanying chords to the melody above.

STEP THREE

"Altering Chords"

It's that time again … since you've played three songs already, I assume that you've got a pretty good understanding of why we alter chords and the difference altered chords can make in a song. You've probably noticed that we add chords frequently to create various chord progressions. This is common in all types of songs. Using your ear, you should be able to add, replace, or alter chords depending on the desired sound.

281

STEP THREE (cont.)

"Altering Chords"

Remember … there are a countless number of ways to alter chords. Don't forget to use the *"Altered Chords"* chapter to help guide you through the process (if needed).

Add **Gmin9 -- C9 / 6 before Fmaj:** Remember the min9 --dom9 / 6 progression that leads to the IV chord? I chose to use this progression in measures two, six, nine & thirteen to lead to the IV chord (Fmaj in measures 3, 7 , 10 & 14). This chord progression falls on the 3rd and 4th beat of the 2nd measure.

Add **F#dim** after Fmaj (measure 3): It is common to play the IV# diminished chord right after a IV chord (especially when the IV chord resolves back to the I chord).

Add **dmin7 --G9** after Cmaj (measure 4): As you learned in one of the previous songs, it is common to add a "2-5-1" progression after a "I" chord (it functions as a "fill in"). In this case, we're simply adding a dmin7 -- G9 (ii – V) progression that will lead back to Cmaj.

Dmin / G to **G9** (measures 8 & 15): In actuality, this chord is already a G9 because of the F & A tones in the Dmin chord (A is the 9th tone of a G9 chord).

Add **Dmin7 (^{b}5)** after Fmaj: I added a Dmin7 (^{b}5) in measures 7, 10 &14. When seeing a IV -- I progression, it is common to replace the IV (F) or add a ii min chord (measures 10 & 14). This will also set up a "vi – ii – V – I" progression in the next measure. (Also, try playing a B^{b} on the bass. When a Bb is used on the bass, the chord is then called a B^{b}9)

Add **"6-2-5-1":** Whenever the "I" chord falls to the "V" chord (as in measures 11 & 12), a "6-2-5-1" progression can be played starting from the I chord (since the progression will eventually lead to the V chord also). In playing this chord progression, I chose to use an A7 (^{b}9) – D9 – and G9 chord.

STEP THREE (cont.)

"Altering Chords"

Here is my altered version of "Jesus Loves Me." Once again, let this hymn along with the previously learned hymns serve as examples to you as you can use these alterations or come up with your own. Try raising a ninth, or lowering an eleventh. Be Creative!

SL322

STEP FOUR

"Listening"

Listen to your version of "Jesus Loves Me." Then, listen to my version (SL322). Yours should sound similar (if not better!). If you hear any chords or tones that sound out of place, slow down and try to fix your mistakes. As like the previous songs, it is very important to use your ear during this step.

"Joyful, Joyful, We Adore Thee"

STEP ONE
"Determining the Melody"

Listen to **SL323** ("Joyful, Joyful, We Adore Thee") with the Sound Library Program.

After listening to **SL323** ("Joyful, Joyful, We Adore Thee"), attempt to play the melody on your piano. Re-play the sound file if you have to. Remember, there are **only** eight notes used for this melody. With that in mind, you should be able to use your ear and some of the techniques learned in this course to figure out the melody.

After playing the melody, *draw* the notes on the treble clef below. The words of the song are written underneath the area you should write each note. A few tones have already been given to you…

EXERCISE 19.4

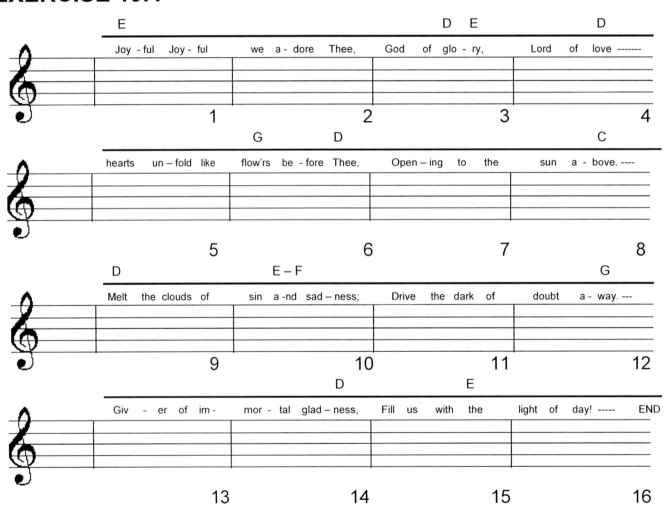

"Joyful, Joyful, We Adore Thee"

STEP ONE (cont.)

Here is the melody to "Joyful, Joyful, We Adore Thee." Compare this melody to yours on the previous page

SL324

EXERCISE 19.5

1.Circle the notes on the diagram above which appear to be **chord tones.** Remember to use the principles on *"distinguishing chord tones in a melody"* (found in chapter 17).

2.Draw a **square** around the notes on the diagram above which appear to be **passing tones.**

3.Draw a **triangle** around the notes on the diagram above which appear to be upper or lower neighboring tones.

STEP TWO

"Harmonizing the Melody"

Now that we've distinguished the chord tones from the passing and neighboring tones, we are ready to choose the *best sounding* accompanying chords.

285

"Joyful, Joyful, We Adore Thee"

STEP TWO (cont.)
"Harmonizing the Melody"

EXERCISE 19.6

Using the information from the previous exercise, **choose** the *best sounding* **accompanying chord (s) for each measure below:**

"Joyful, Joyful, We Adore Thee"

STEP TWO (cont.)

"Harmonizing the Melody"

SL325

Here are the accompanying chords to the melody above.

STEP THREE

"Altering Chords"

Let's *now* move on to altering these chords ...

"Joyful, Joyful, We Adore Thee"

STEP THREE (cont.)
"Altering Chords"

Remember … there are a countless number of ways to alter chords. Don't forget to use the *"Altered Chords"* chapter to help guide you through the process (if needed).

Gmaj to **Fmaj9** (measures 2 & 6): I decided to change the Gmaj chord to an Fmaj9 (adds more "flavor" to the progression).

Add **B♭9** after Fmaj9 (measure 2, 6 & 14): After we altered the Gmaj chord (to an Fmaj9), the relationship then becomes a "IV -- I chord progression (measure 2 -- 3). As you've learned in previous songs, it is common to replace the IV (F) chord or add a ii min chord. However, in this case, we're going to play the iimin7 (♭5) over B♭. Since B♭ is the bass note, we've used **B♭9** instead of Dmin7 (♭5) / B♭.

Cmaj / G to **D9** (measure 4): Since the Cmaj / G chord leads to a Dmin / G (or G9) chord, we've decided to set up a "2 – 5 – 1" progression. The **D9** will lead to the **G9**, which will lead back to the **Cmaj** chord in measure 5.

Dmin / G to **G9** (measures 4, 8 & 16): In actuality, this chord is already a G9 because of the F & A tones in the Dmin chord (A is the 9th tone of a G9 chord).

Emaj / G# to **G#maj (♭5)** $^{add\ 13}$ (measure 11): Since the Emaj / G# leads to Amin, I decided to add an altered chord to add more "flavor." This chord is a G#maj with a lowered 5th. The only reason the "13th" tone is added instead of being the title of the chord is because I **don't** want the 9th and 11th tones included (if the chord was G#maj13 (♭5), this would include the 9th and 11th tones). Sometimes, you will notice these types of alterations where you only want certain tones played.

Amin to **Amin9:** You've seen this enough … you should know why I did this!

Replace Dmaj -- Gmaj with **D9 -- G9** (measure 12): I simply replaced a "2-5" chord progression with triads to a "2-5" progression with ninth chords.

STEP THREE (cont.)

"Altering Chords"

Here is my altered version of "Joyful, Joyful, We Adore Thee." Once again, let this hymn along with the previously learned hymns serve as examples to you as you can use these alterations or come up with your own. Try raising a ninth, or lowering an eleventh. Be Creative!

STEP FOUR

"Listening"

Listen to your version of "Joyful, Joyful, We Adore Thee." Then, listen to my version (SL326). Yours should sound similar (if not better!). If you hear any chords or tones that sound out of place, slow down and try to fix your mistakes. As like the previous songs, it is very important to use your ear during this step.

CHAPTER SUMMARY

These **five** hymns should have served as examples to how you can easily determine the melody of a song, harmonize the melody, alter a few chords, and listen to the finished product.

This course has allowed you to study the theory behind major, minor, diminished, seventh, ninth, eleventh, and thirteenth chords. It is now your job to practice and be able to both memorize these chords on paper and by ear. The sound library is available for you to hear each chord and progression. Utilize it and become familiar with common progressions like the "2 – 5 – 1" or "6 – 2 – 5 – 1."

As you noticed, several chords were used *over and over again*. I chose to alter these chords the same way to show you how many different roles **one** chord can play. As you learned, some chords can serve as "3" chords to the "6th" chord. Other chords "set up" "2 – 5 – 1" chord progressions. Remember, there are unlimited options when improvising. You can do whatever your mind imagines when playing music. If you want to be very creative and throw a "7 – 3 – 6 – 2 – 5 – 1" chord progression in the middle of a I -- 5 progression, go ahead and do so! The main importance is that your altered progression pulls toward the same chord as the original progression.

Before you show off your piano skills to your family and friends, we have just one *more* lesson to complete …

Lesson Twenty

"Improvising"

In the last two lessons, you had the opportunity to learn five hymns **step – by – step!** In this *last* chapter, we will study a few improvisational techniques.

What is Improvising?

To devise or provide from whatever material is given; to compose and perform certain operations without previous preparation

In Jazz, Blues & Gospel music, being able to **improvise** is a requirement! There may be situations where the key of a song must be transposed or a verse repeated. In other words, you never know when you must change the way a song or chord progression is played.

"Improvising"

As you noticed in **Step Three** of the last chapters, many progressions were added to enhance the sound of the songs.

HERE ARE SOME IMPROVISATIONS YOU MIGHT WANT TO THINK ABOUT WHEN THE...

"I" Chord resolves to the "IV" chord

SL327 — Add a **Vmin9 -- I 9 / 6 Chord Progression**: This progression can **always** lead to the IV chord. I play it all the time! In C major, this progression is: Gmin9 -- C9 / 6 -- F9 (or any other type of F chord)

SL328 — Add a **vimin9 -- ii 9 / 6 -- Vmin9 -- I 9 / 6 Chord Progression**: This is simply an expansion of the previous progression. It plays the same pattern on the vi and ii tones as well as the V and I tones. Since the V -- I **pulls** toward the IV chord, this progression can be used whenever you have "time" to sneak it in! In C major, this progression is: Amin9 -- D9 / 6 -- Gmin9 -- C9 / 6 -- F9

SL329 — Add a **IV#9 chord** right before the IV chord: If the IV chord is a dom9 chord, simply add the dom9 chord a half step higher to create a IV# 9 -- IV 9 progression. This sounds great in blues & gospel music. For example, in C major, this is: C9 -- F#9 -- F9 (try it!)

"I" Chord resolves to the "V" chord

SL330 — Add a **ii 9 chord**: The ii 9 chord can always lead to **Gmaj, G7 or G9 chords.** In C major, simply sneak a D9 chord right before the G9 (or maj, 7, etc.)

SL331 — Add a **ii min (^{b}5)**: I use this chord right before I notice a I chord over a V bass. For example, if I see a Cmaj / G, I would play a **Dmin (^{b}5)** right before the Cmaj / G chord. You probably noticed this progression in many of my altered versions of the hymns.

SL332 — Add a **ii 7 (^{b}9)**: This chord functions similar to the **ii 9 chord.** It can be used right before Gmaj, G7 or G9 chords. In C major, this progression is: D7 (b9) -- G9 -- Cmaj (also a 2 – 5 – 1 chord progression).

"Improvising" (cont.)

HERE ARE SOME <u>MORE</u> IMPROVISATIONS YOU MIGHT WANT TO THINK ABOUT WHEN THE...

"I" Chord resolves to the "VI" chord

SL333 — Add a **iii7($^b9^\#5$)**: Usually when the I chord resolves to the vi chord, this is a beginning of a "6 – 2 – 5 – 1" chord progression. By simply adding a iii7 with alterations, a "3 – 6 – 2 – 5 – 1" chord progression can be formed. In C major, this is: Cmaj -- E7 ($^b9^\#5$) -- Amin9 -- D7 ($^b9$) -- Cmaj / G

SL334 — Add a **iii7**: Functions the same as the previous chord.

SL335 — Add a **viimin7 ($^b9^b5$) -- iii7 ($^b9^\#5$) Progression:** This is simply adding the vii chord to the "3 – 6 – 2 – 5 – 1" chord progression above to create a "7 – 3 – 6 – 2 – 5 – 1" chord progression. Notice that the vii -- iii progression is leading to the vi chord so if you wanted remain at the vi chord, simply disregard the "2 – 5 – 1."

EXERCISE 20.1

List a way you could improvise in a song that has a I chord that resolves to a V chord:

_____
_____
_____
_____
_____

"Improvising" (cont.)

"Transposing a Key"

SOLFÈGE & TRANSPOSITION

SOLFÈGE is a system of reading notes by assigning a different syllable to each note. The following syllables are used for all major scales as they relate to the scale degrees:

F major

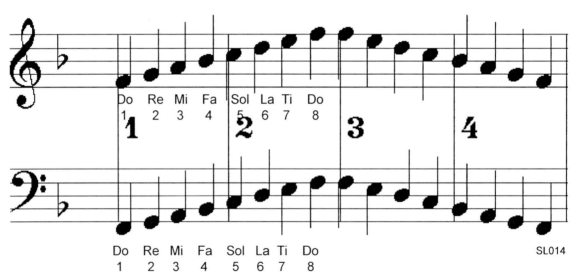

MOVEABLE DO means that the syllables apply to the same scale degrees, regardless of what key you are in. For example, in the key of F, the keynote **F** is called "Do." In the key of C, the keynote **C** is also called "Do."

"Improvising" (cont.)

"Transposing a Key"

When a melody is rewritten with the exact same sequence of notes and intervals into another key, it is called **TRANSPOSITION.** This raises or lowers the notes to make a melody easier to sing or play, or so it can be played by an instrument in another key.

The easiest way to transpose is by interval. For example, if a melody is in the key of C and you want to transpose it to the key of D, then you would rewrite all notes a major 2nd higher:

Melody in C

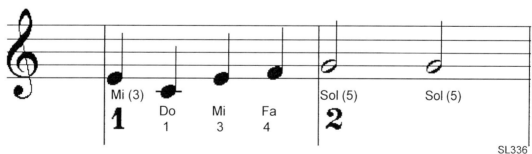

Melody in D

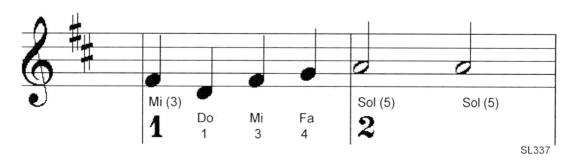

EXERCISE 20.2

Transpose the following **hymn** melody into the key of **G:**

"Joyful, Joyful, We Adore Thee" (Key of C)

Key of G

EXERCISE 20.3

Transpose the following **hymn** melody into the key of **F**:

"Jesus Loves Me" (Key of C)

Key of F

EXERCISE 20.4

Transpose the following **accompanying chords** into the key of **A:**

C Major

SL338

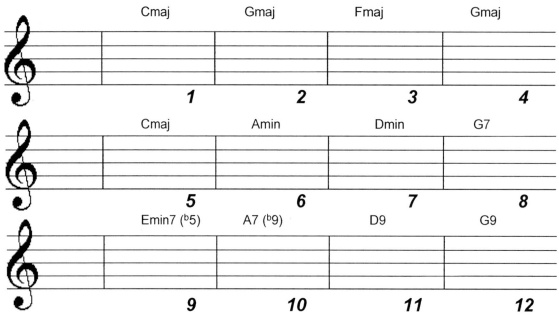

A Major

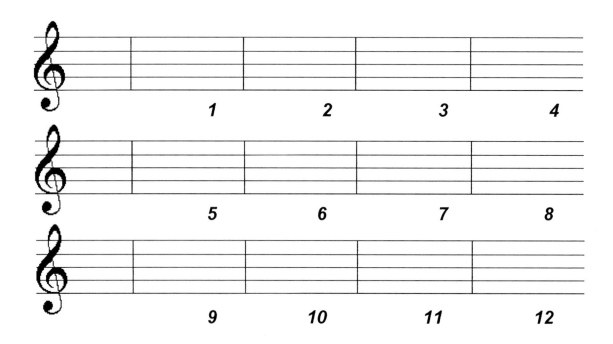

CONCLUSION

Dear Musician,

It has been an honor and a privilege to offer you this course and I hope that it has been a blessing to you in your piano playing. I encourage you to take the techniques, principles, and exercises in this course and practice them weekly, if not daily. As you progress in your piano playing, you will find that many of the chord progressions that you play are shared in several songs. I cannot express how important it is to be able to recognize these "overused" progressions.

I also recommend that you try our **full version** of the "Piano Player Plus v1.0 Software." A trial copy has been included with this course. You can use this software to test yourself on various scales, melodies, chords, progressions, key transpositions, and more.

You will also get e-mails from us periodically sharing with you special offers and new products. If you feel this product has helped you tremendously, don't hesitate to buy one of our advanced courses.

Lastly, it will be greatly appreciated if you visit our website and fill out our course evaluation so that we may better serve you and other customers in the future. You may do this by visiting http://www.hearandplay.com/customers.html

Thank you again for choosing Hear & Play Music!

Jermaine A. Griggs

President & CEO of Hear & Play Music, Online!
http://www.HearandPlay.com
1-877-856-4187
webmaster@hearandplay.com

CERTIFICATE OF COMPLETION

CONGRATULATIONS
On completing HearandPlay.com's

"Secrets to Playing Piano By Ear"

Piano Course v1.0

Piano Player Plus v1.0 Certificate of Completion:

Complete the code below for a free gift! (Valued at $59) Visit: http://www.hearandplay.com/customers.html to confirm the code.

___ ___ ___ ___ ___ ___ ___ ___ ___ ___ ___ ___

You are given a single digit code after completing each chapter test. Write each chapter's code above and enter them in at the website to redeem your free prize!